The Natural Classical Guitar

Lee Ryan has been playing the guitar since the age of seven and has studied in master classes of Andrés Segovia, Michael Lorimer, and others. He received an M.A. in music from San Diego State University, where he taught for seven years. His experiences with Transcendental Meditation gave him the inspiration for the natural approach to the guitar described in this book.

The Natural Classical Guitar

The principles of effortless playing

Lee F. Ryan

Prentice-Hall, Inc., *Englewood Cliffs, New Jersey 07632*

Library of Congress Cataloging in Publication Data

RYAN, LEE F.
   The natural classical guitar.

   Bibliography: p.
   Includes index.
   1. Guitar—Instruction and study. I. Title.
MT580.R9   1984   787.6'1'0712   83-21234
ISBN 0-13-610071-6
ISBN 0-13-610063-5 (pbk.)

Editorial/production supervision and interior design by Fred Bernardi
Cover design by Hal Siegel
Manufacturing buyer: Pat Mahoney

Printed in the United States of America

10 9 8 7 6 5 4 3 2 1

ISBN 0-13-610071-6
ISBN 0-13-610063-5 {pbk.}

PRENTICE-HALL INTERNATIONAL, INC., *London*
PRENTICE-HALL OF AUSTRALIA PTY. LIMITED, *Sydney*
EDITORA PRENTICE-HALL DO BRASIL, LTDA., *Rio de Janeiro*
PRENTICE-HALL CANADA INC., *Toronto*
PRENTICE-HALL OF INDIA PRIVATE LIMITED, *New Delhi*
PRENTICE-HALL OF JAPAN, INC., *Tokyo*
PRENTICE-HALL OF SOUTHEAST ASIA PTE. LTD., *Singapore*
WHITEHALL BOOKS LIMITED, *Wellington, New Zealand*

Contents

Preface   *ix*

Acknowledgments   *xi*

Chapter 1
THE TEN PRINCIPLES OF EFFORTLESS PLAYING   *1*

Chapter 2
INCREASE MIND–BODY AWARENESS
Tune in to the Present   *15*

Chapter 3
NATURAL CONCENTRATION
Focus the Mind Effortlessly   *35*

Chapter 4
DYNAMIC RELAXATION
Balance the Opposites in Sitting and Hand Positions   *53*

Chapter 5
THE PLAY–RELAX TECHNIQUE
Use the Spaces Between the Notes *79*

Chapter 6
REFINING YOUR GUITAR SKILLS
Pay Attention to the Details *117*

Chapter 7
LEARNING FROM THE MASTERS
Use Natural Study Methods *153*

Chapter 8
MIND OVER FINGERS (I)
Visualization for Guitarists *175*

Chapter 9
MIND OVER FINGERS (II)
Visualizing and Realizing
the Musical Meaning of a Piece *191*

Chapter 10
SHARING YOUR ENJOYMENT OF MUSIC
The Delight of Playing Recitals *229*

Chapter 11
ENSEMBLE PLAYING AND OTHER TOPICS
Enjoy Playing with Others *255*

Chapter 12
FROM THE GUITAR TO THE SELF *265*

Bibliography *277*

Index *289*

Preface

Classical guitar playing can be easy and natural. It can be dynamic and yet relaxing at the same time. These ideas may seem surprising to guitarists who have heard that the guitar is a "difficult" instrument that requires a struggle to master. Certainly good playing requires intelligent work, but not struggling or "trying hard." In fact, the "try hard" approach actually slows down the learning process. What is needed is a more natural, less strained approach.

The Natural Classical Guitar offers an approach to classical guitar playing that is enjoyable and fruitful right from the start. This approach emphasizes quiet, thoughtful methods of study that bring results without struggling. You already have within you the ability to be an excellent player. All you need to do is patiently develop that ability.

This is not a book of progressive lessons for the complete beginner. It covers advanced topics and assumes at least some knowledge of basic note reading and music theory. However, although this book is oriented toward classical players with some experience, the beginner will find many useful ideas on basic techniques such as sitting, hand positions, making strokes, and study methods. Most students, whatever their level, will find that *The Natural Classical Guitar* will be a helpful supplement to what they learn from other sources.

The Natural Classical Guitar is a practical handbook of ideas, information, and inspiration for guitarists. Because the book is meant to be a reference and the chapters are more or less independent units, it is not necessary to read the material in order. Just go to whatever topic you find interesting. However, it is helpful to look at Chapter 1 first because it gives a good overview of the book. The book is organized around a set of ten principles that constitute a total approach to the internal *player* as well as the external *playing*. It is vitally important for successful playing that the guitarist develop himself personally as well as technically. Thus, you will find ideas here to help unfold both the inner and outer areas of guitar playing.

Some of the inner areas covered are:

increasing your personal and musical awareness by settling your mind and relaxing your body
learning to concentrate for more effective practice and performance
preparing for recitals and reducing stage fright
applying what you learn on the guitar to your personal development

Some of the outer areas covered are:

learning to let nature take the excess effort out of your right- and left-hand technique
advanced techniques such as special right-hand strokes, tonal shading, effortless shifting, damping, hinge bars, tremolo, and vibrato
playing fast scales and arpeggios securely
applying a twelve-step plan for studying a piece

The principles and techniques in *The Natural Classical Guitar* are not new. They have been derived from various sources: from master guitarists, particularly from Andrés Segovia and his students, from other fine musicians, and from philosophers of East and West. These ideas have been tried and proven many times over. If intelligently adapted to your own unique characteristics, the ideas here will produce excellent results for your playing.

Keep in mind that the majority of ideas and techniques presented here have arisen from practical guitar-playing experience and are meant to be used, not just read. Some are meant to be worked out mentally without the guitar, but most require that you have your guitar in hand. So, consider each idea carefully and then experiment with it on the spot. If you get good results immediately, fine. If not, work on it and change the approach if necessary so that you obtain good results. Always ask yourself the all-important questions: "Does this *work*?" and "Is this natural *for me*?"

I wish the readers of this book an enjoyable odyssey with the guitar. It is my hope that the natural approach will help aspiring guitarists to realize their great musical and personal potential as easily and quickly as possible.

$\mathcal{A}$cknowledgments

I would like to express my indebtedness to the many people who have contributed to this book directly and indirectly. I am especially grateful to Maharishi Mahesh Yogi for the practical and inspirational ideas in his teaching that apply both to the guitar and everyday living. I also owe much to Michael Lorimer from whom I learned how to play and teach the guitar in a natural, spiritually uplifting way. John Saveliff deserves special thanks for his excellent drawings, careful music copywork, and patient modeling for the photographs in the book. His moral support for the book was also a blessing.

To Robert and Catherine Strizich I wish to express my gratitude for taking time from their busy schedule to read and make valuable comments on the manuscript. To Gregg Nestor, Craig Carter, and David Jones I extend my appreciation for many useful ideas. And I must not forget to thank my guitar students who read over and tried out many of the techniques in the book.

Maurice Roy, Jr. made an excellent contribution to the book with his fine photographs. Brian Mears also deserves thanks for his help in producing the drawings. When I started with the book, Paul Sutherland was very encouraging and steered me toward the right literary agent. J. Kent Nilsson, an old and valued friend, has been a marvelous devil's advocate and has helped to bring this book into focus. Now that I am at the end of this long list, I arrive at my greatest helper, my wife Joann. She has given me a great deal of constructive editorial assistance. But, most important of all, she has been patient and supportive throughout this project.

CREDITS

Music copywork by John Saveliff; Illustrations by John Saveliff and Brian Mears; All photographs not otherwise credited by Maurice Roy, Jr.

CHAPTER OPENING PHOTOGRAPH CREDITS: *Chapter 1:* Falls in Anderson Creek canyon by Philip Hyde, ©1965, Philip Hyde; *Chapter 2:* Still Pond by Maurice Roy, Jr.; *Chapter 3:* Guitar soundhole, by Maurice Roy, Jr.; *Chapter 4:* Guitarist relaxing and playing simultaneously, by Maurice Roy, Jr.; *Chapter 5:* Play–Relax stroke, by Maurice Roy, Jr.; *Chapter 6:* Hinge bar, by Maurice Roy, Jr.; *Chapter 7:* Andrés Segovia teaching at USC, by Fred Benedetti, 1981; *Chapter 8:* Guitarist visualizing his hands, by Maurice Roy, Jr.; *Chapter 9:* Portrait of Fernando Sor by Goubaud, engraved by M. N. Bate, photo by Roger-Viollet, Paris; *Chapter 10:* Andrés Segovia in concert, by Bruce Parker; *Chapter 11:* Chamber music group (Mark Attebery, Gregg Nestor, Karen Victor) by Burton Nestor, Professional Photographic Services, San Diego; *Chapter 12:* Guitar at La Jolla Beach by Dick Faust, 1981.

CHAPTER OPENING QUOTATION CREDITS: *Chapter 1:* From Fernando Sor, *Method for the Spanish Guitar*, translated from the original by A. Merrick, reprint of the London edition (New York: Da Capo Press, 1971); *Chapters 2, 3, 6:* Copyright ©1965 by Denise Restout, ed., trans., assisted by Robert Hawkins, from the book *Landowska on Music* (Briarcliff Manor, N.Y.: Stein and Day, 1965). Reprinted with permission of Stein and Day Publishers; *Chapter 4:* From Aldous Huxley, *The Art of Seeing* (New York: Harper & Row Publishers, 1942); *Chapters 4 and 5:* From Lao Tzu, *Tao Te Ching*, translated by Gia Fu-Feng and Jane English (New York: Alfred A. Knopf, Inc., 1972); *Chapters 5 and 6:* From *Joys and Sorrows* as told to Albert E. Kahn by Pablo Casals (New York: Simon and Schuster, Inc., 1970); *Chapter 8:* From "A Cellist's Guide to the New Approach," by Claude Kenneson. ©1974 Claude Kenneson. Reprinted by permission of Exposition Press, Inc., Smithtown, New York; *Chapter 10:* From the "Introduction" to *Early Music* (October 1979) by Gustav Leonhardt (London: Oxford University Press); *Chapter 12:* From "Spiritual Dimensions," an interview with Karl-Heinz Stockhausen by Peter Heyworth, *Music and Musicians* (May 1971); From Yehudi Menuhin and William Primrose, *Violin and Viola* (New York: Macmillan Publishing Co., 1976). Copyright ©1976 by Yehudi Menuhin (Part One), William Primrose (Part Two), and Denis Stevens (Part Three). Reprinted by permission of Macmillan Publishing Co.

The Natural Classical Guitar

1.

The Ten Principles of Effortless Playing

I have always preferred hearing it said of a performance, "He appears to be doing nothing, that appears so easy!"

Fernando Sor, *Method*

The mind that is parallel with the laws of nature will be in the current of events and strong with their strength.

Ralph Waldo Emerson, *Power*

The best guitarists make playing look easy. In fact, it *is* easy for them. Such effortlessness may seem to be a distant goal for the average player. However, with a natural, unhurried approach and the ten principles discussed here, you can experience that ease in a relatively short time. For greatest success with this approach, keep in mind that it is meant to be a holistic one, that is, it encompasses all the elements of guitar playing. The premise is that the various elements are so closely interconnected that a truly effective way of studying the guitar must ultimately include them all. Thus, although it can be helpful to use only one or two of the ten principles discussed here, the effect will be much greater if you use all ten together.

This chapter will give you an overview of the natural approach to the guitar and the ten principles of effortless playing. It includes short descriptions of each principle with emphasis on the first one. The first principle is the most important, but it is so elegant and simple that it can be described here in brief form. It does not require a chapter of its own. Besides, the other nine principles and their respective chapters flow from that first principle and provide abundant elaborations on it. Such is the method of nature: start from a basis of utter simplicity and from it create complex and beautiful forms.

Now follows a list of the ten principles.

1. Let Nature Support Your Playing
2. Increase Mind/Body Awareness
3. Develop Natural Concentration
4. Cultivate Dynamic Relaxation
5. Apply the Play–Relax Technique
6. Refine Your Guitar Skills
7. Learn from the Masters
8. Use the Mind Over Fingers Approach

9. Share Your Enjoyment of Music
10. Evolve from the Guitar to the Self

Short descriptions of these principles are presented on the following pages.

1. LET NATURE SUPPORT YOUR PLAYING: DO LESS, ACCOMPLISH MORE

One of the root ideas of successful guitar playing is *minimum effort* or "do less and accomplish more." This implies that you should use no more personal effort than is necessary to produce good musical results. You let nature do the rest. This approach of aligning yourself with the power of nature is the basic theme of this book. In this approach to the guitar, it is especially important to avoid forcing and straining because it is not enjoyable and does not produce good playing. It is better to conserve your energy and find ways of playing in which nature will support you most.

The conscious seeking of nature's help for our actions is an ancient idea found in many cultures and advocated by many men. As the American writer Emerson put it, "All powerful action is performed by bringing the forces of nature to bear upon our objects . . . ." The philosophies of the East such as Yoga, Taoism, and Zen also expound this idea. Gaining the support of nature is nothing mystical or obscure. It is a practical, down-to-earth way of solving everyday problems with the least effort. Thus the intelligent woodsman finds it easier to split a log if he allows the natural force of gravity to help him bring down the axe. Similarly, the intelligent guitarist finds it easier to press down the strings with the left-hand fingers if he lets the natural weight of his arm provide much of the pressure. Using the power of nature in such ways is typical of successful guitarists and of successful people in general.

The Chinese Taoists use the particularly vivid image of water flowing effortlessly downstream to show how little energy is required for successful action when we allow nature to support us.[1] The water, unlike many of us, does not struggle or strain to reach its goal. Instead, it overcomes all obstacles by simply flowing around them. It takes the path of least resistance and lets gravity help it to go downhill. Thus the water uses the minimum energy required to get where it is going. The action of the water is a clear example of how nature "does less and accomplishes more." This tendency toward economy in nature is so pervasive that modern physics describes it with an important principle, the *principle of least action.*

---

[1]David R. Brower, ed., *Of All Things Most Yielding* (New York: Friends of the Earth/ Ballantine Books), pp. 14, 16.

Nature loves economy and least action so much that she makes you feel a bit frustrated with the guitar until you learn to play it according to these rules. To avoid frustration, you can take the principle of least action in general and the effortless flow of water in particular as nature's models for your playing. This economical approach does not imply that you should become lazy or indecisive in your playing habits. Far from it. It means work, but work that consists of finding more efficient ways of playing. It means taking every possible advantage of the natural principles of balance, gravity, and leverage to conserve energy. And finally, it means stripping away all excess tension and movement so that you do just what is necessary to play beautifully.

The underlying idea of least action is to play in accordance with the natural tendencies of the music, the guitar, and your fingers and not force yourself against them. Thus, for example, if one left-hand fingering for a passage does not sound right and seems to take too much effort, even after a reasonable amount of practice, then it is best not to cling to it stubbornly. Like the water, you can get around obstacles easily by seeking an alternate path. Just look for a more musical, more flowing fingering that requires less effort. There are many examples throughout this book of how to use less effort and play more effectively, but Chapters 4, 5, and 6 are specially devoted to this idea.

When you play the guitar in tune with least action—and thus with nature's support—you will know it because it will be a positive, enjoyable experience. It will be smooth and easy because you will have cut out all unnecessary effort. On the other hand, when you are not playing with least action, the guitar will seem difficult because you are trying too hard and are not letting nature support you. In the latter case, remember to be gentle with yourself and listen to what the quiet voice of nature is telling you. Set goals for yourself, but do not try to force the results. Simply be persistent and let guitar study become a natural part of your daily life. "Make haste slowly," as the proverb goes. This is the path of fastest progress.

2. INCREASE MIND/BODY AWARENESS: TUNE IN TO THE PRESENT

The guitarist may have a fine teacher, excellent instruction books, and a good collection of guitar records, but of what value are these things if the player is only marginally aware of what is going on in his mind, body, and music? If the player is not aware of an unproductive attitude, excess tension in the fingers, or scratchy tone quality, then how can he correct these problems? A teacher may point out such difficulties in lessons, but it is important that the student be aware of them when he is practicing at home. For that reason, everything the guitarist can do to increase his awareness of himself and his playing is helpful.

Most successful people say that a considerable degree of *self-awareness* is important for high achievement. When your awareness is sharp, it is easy to see the best way to accomplish a given task. For that reason, it is good to develop the habit of focusing your attention in an unbiased, unforced way on the present moment. The Chinese Taoists recommend to "wash and cleanse your vision," be "open to all things," and "move with the present."[2] Thus, if you want to get the most out of life, you need to *see, hear,* and *feel* what is going on *now.* To get the full value from eating an apple, your full attention needs to be on the apple; to get the most enjoyment from playing the guitar, your full attention needs to be on the guitar. When you are focused on what is happening *now,* you are able to respond most effectively to a situation. On the other hand, if you are distracted by past regrets or future concerns, you will not enjoy what you are doing and you will not do it well. Being focused on the present is obviously important for guitar study and performance. In playing, for example, when your mind is on the music, your performance will go well. But if your mind is off on negative feelings about a past performance or concern about a passage at the end of the piece, then you will lose the flow of the music and make mistakes.

Putting your attention on what is happening now is a direct way of increasing your awareness. Two powerful, indirect ways are to *settle your mind* and *relax your body.* These approaches will help your guitar playing, especially if you do them on a regular basis. Settling the mind means reducing your mental activity in a natural way to its simplest, quietest level. Then your awareness will become clearer and sharper. For that reason, the Taoists say, "Empty yourself of everything./Let the mind rest at peace."[3] When your mind is not stirred up with excess thought waves, then it can clearly reflect its surroundings like a calm lake. In such a state you can perceive things as they really are and thus deal with them most effectively.

Relaxing your body is another way to heighten awareness. When your body is not tense and fatigued, you will sense more easily how it feels and how to use it best. In guitar playing such increased body awareness means that you can avoid such common problems as the tension created by unconsciously hunching up your shoulders. There are many ways to relax your body. For one thing, physical relaxation comes as a natural by-product of the process of settling your mind. There are numerous other approaches to body relaxation, such as walking and hatha yoga. In any case, when your mind and body are quiet, you will become acutely aware of the entire guitar-playing

[2]Lao Tzu, *Tao Te Ching,* trans. Gia-Fu Feng and Jane English (New York: Vintage Books, 1972), chapters 10, 14.
[3]Ibid., chapter 16.

process. You will find it easy to notice problems and correct them. But, more important, you will become keenly aware of the delightful subtleties of the music you play. And, once you are aware of those subtleties, you will be able to express them in your playing. Everything will improve when your awareness is heightened.

Chapter 2 describes practical ways to increase awareness of your mind, body, and guitar playing. Ways to keep your mind on the present, to become aware of the roles guitarists play, to settle your mind, and to relax your body are included.

3. DEVELOP NATURAL CONCENTRATION: FOCUS THE MIND EFFORTLESSLY

Natural concentration is just the logical extension of the previous principle of increasing awareness. It requires that you have the ability to focus your awareness on one thing at a time. Everyone knows the value of such concentration in guitar study and performance, but few guitarists do anything to improve it, which is an unfortunate situation because good concentration is central to fine guitar playing. When your mind is focused perfectly on the music you are performing, you do not make mistakes or forget where you are. In the same way, when you concentrate well during your study sessions, you get the most out of them and do not waste time and energy.

Most guitarists do not attempt to improve their concentration because it seems to be too difficult. However, concentration is not difficult when approached properly. It can be improved in a natural and unforced way. The basic approach is to reduce the activity in your mind and then focus it sharply on one thing. The mind-settling techniques presented in Chapter 2 can be used to quiet and order the mind and thus make the focusing process easier.

The most effective way of focusing your mind is the *natural concentration technique.* This is a technique that has been derived from the practical teachings of Yoga.[4] There has unfortunately been some misunderstanding about the correct procedure. It is often thought that you must force your mind to concentrate. However, forcing simply does not work. With the natural approach to concentration, you can effortlessly keep your mind on whatever aspect of your playing you desire, such as the melodic line, your right-hand strokes, or your left-hand movements. Chapter 3 describes this natural, psychological approach to concentration as well as a complementary physiological approach.

[4]*Bhagavad Gita,* trans. Maharishi Mahesh Yogi (Baltimore: Penguin Books, Inc., 1969), chapter VI, 12, p. 406; and *How to Know God: the Yoga Sutras of Patanjali,* trans. Swami Prabhavananda and Christopher Isherwood (New York: New American Library, 1969), section I, 17 and section III, 1.

4. CULTIVATE DYNAMIC RELAXATION: BALANCE THE OPPOSITES

When you play the guitar in complete accord with nature's principle of least action—that is, with just the right amount of effort—a balanced state of mind and body is created. This state can occur in many different activities besides playing the guitar. The writer Aldous Huxley has called it *dynamic relaxation.*[5] Its chief characteristic is a balance of the opposite tendencies of tension and relaxation in both mind and body; in other words, paradoxical as it may seem, activity is combined with relaxation. One might say that dynamic relaxation is the state in which tension and relaxation are used in exactly the right places at the right times. Everyone who achieves a high level of skill in a psychophysical activity of any kind has experienced this state to some degree. The guitarist in this state feels perfectly relaxed even when playing demanding pieces in concert. Playing becomes effortless and the music flows out beautifully with few or no mistakes.

To gain a deeper understanding of dynamic relaxation as it relates to the guitar, it is illuminating to see how this idea is expressed in such philosophies as Yoga and Taoism. According to these teachings, all of the diversity of nature is just a dynamic, ever-changing manifestation of a single underlying reality.[6] Even the complete opposites of life are just the extreme parts of the same basic substance. The Taoists call these opposites *yang* and *yin. Yang* and *yin* originally meant the sunny and shady sides of a mountain, but eventually came to stand for all the polar opposites of life—light and dark, masculine and feminine, good and bad, firm and yielding, activity and rest, tension and relaxation, sound and silence, rational and intuitive, work and play, mind and body. These opposite tendencies are present in the individual as well as in music and all nature. According to the ancient wisdom, if one wants to have the greatest success and fulfillment in life, he needs to bring all of his opposite tendencies into dynamic balance. This balance is achieved by avoiding extremes and pursuing the "middle way" or "golden mean." The Taoists say that "the sage avoids extremes, excesses and complacency."[7] Similarly, the Yogic idea is that the realization of full human potential is for those who are moderate in eating, sleeping, and activity.[8] In Aldous Huxley's terms, we can say that one's life becomes fulfilling when the individual properly combines activity and relaxation in the state of "dynamic relaxation."

The idea of *balancing opposites,* or *dynamic relaxation,* has very practical implications for guitar playing. Dynamic relaxation is not just a fuzzy idea. It is a supremely efficient approach to playing the guitar because it implies that

---

[5]Aldous Huxley, *The Art of Seeing* (New York: Harper and Brothers, 1942), p. 37.
[6]Lao Tzu, *Tao Te Ching,* chapters 1, 42, 51; and Patanjali, *How to Know God,* section I, 45.
[7]Lao Tzu, *Tao Te Ching,* chapter 29.
[8]*Bhagavad Gita,* chapter II, 48, p. 135 and chapter V, 3, p. 333.

it is best to do exactly what is necessary to achieve a desired musical result—no more, no less. Thus no effort is wasted. Balancing the opposites of tension and relaxation is of special significance for guitar technique. For example, when your sitting position has just the right balance of tension and relaxation in the muscles, you will not experience much fatigue because little energy will be required to maintain the position. Chapters 4 and 5 deal with such matters of balance in detail. Chapter 4 discusses how you can cultivate natural, dynamically relaxed sitting and hand positions. Chapter 5 introduces a technique to develop dynamic relaxation in the actual playing movements. This technique is discussed under the next heading.

5. APPLY THE PLAY–RELAX TECHNIQUE: USE THE SPACES BETWEEN THE NOTES

The master guitarists all have somewhat different approaches to technique. However, they all have one thing in common. They all have learned, more or less consciously, to make playing easy and natural for themselves. They play the guitar as naturally as we speak our own language. Every guitarist should aim for that easy, natural touch and avoid anything that feels cramped or strained. One way to achieve that touch is through the *Play–Relax technique.*

The Play–Relax technique leads to effortless, dynamically relaxed right- and left-hand movements. The technique is based on the ancient idea that if you want to achieve a given result, you must first master its opposite. The Taoists say, for example, "yield and overcome; bend and be straight; empty and be full."[9] The contemporary Cuban guitarist Leo Brouwer recommends this same approach to his students. This means that if you want to play properly, you must learn to relax properly. In this Play–Relax approach, you learn to balance the activity of playing by taking full advantage of the opportunity to relax your hands and fingers *between the notes and playing movements.* When a balanced alternation between playing and not playing has been achieved, that is, when dynamic relaxation is established, guitar playing becomes almost effortless.

Some guitarists do experience dynamic relaxation in their playing, but infrequently and unpredictably; others have not yet experienced it. Whatever the case, it is a natural state and all that is needed is a good method of cultivating it. The Play–Relax technique is a systematic, *conscious* method that helps make dynamic relaxation a regular occurrence. Thus the experience of dynamic relaxation is not left to chance.

Chapter 5 gives many practical applications of the Play–Relax technique for the guitar. The technique is applied to right-hand rest and free strokes,

[9]Lao Tzu, *Tao Te Ching*, chapter 22.

left-hand slurs and stretches, synchronization of the two hands, development of fast scales and tremolo, reduction of fatigue, and the practice of entire pieces.

6. REFINE YOUR GUITAR SKILLS: PAY ATTENTION TO THE DETAILS

One of the more important principles of artistic guitar playing is to pay attention to musical and technical detail. Only when the tone is uniformly beautiful, when the fingering flows effortlessly, when unwanted notes are damped, when the melodic line is elegantly shaped—only then will it be possible for the music to exhilarate you and elevate you to a higher plane. Only then will it be possible for you to experience the joy of dynamic relaxation. Every great musician knows this and thus spends a lot of time on details. It should also be pointed out here that much of the charm of music comes from the performer's handling of the subtle matters of accent, articulation, phrasing, and fingering.

Without attention to the fine points, playing the guitar will not be completely satisfying. An awkward left-hand change here, an unwanted bass note there, a missed note, an accent in the wrong place—all these neglected details detract from the music and from the satisfaction of the player. It is like the guitar maker who did not quite put the bridge in the right place or who forgot to clean off the excess glue from the joints. It is plain that more craftsmanship is required from both the guitarist and the guitar maker.

Thus, to get the most out of the music, it is essential to spend time on the fine points of your playing—on the "unfinished business," so to speak. In so doing, you are attuning yourself to the way of nature. A look at the colorful structure of a butterfly wing, the exquisite spiral of a chambered nautilus, or the fine veins of an oak leaf will make it clear that nature loves subtle details. So, in Chapter 6 we will imitate nature and deal with fine points such as tone quality, nail care, tone color, articulation, damping unwanted notes, natural fingering, making left-hand connections, and hinge bars.

7. LEARN FROM THE MASTERS: USE NATURAL STUDY METHODS

One of the easiest and most natural ways of learning the guitar is by *imitation* of fine players. Imitation is the traditional master–student learning process that has produced many excellent musicians through the centuries. In fact, this learning method has produced good results in every area of endeavor, from bricklaying to spiritual development. In Yoga, for example, even today there is a strong tradition of the master handing down his knowledge directly to his disciples. It is a profound experience to learn directly from one who has deep knowledge. With respect to the guitar, this process cuts down considerably the time it takes to learn to play well. By using a master player or teacher as a model you avoid the common mistakes that students make. From a master teacher or player you also learn to be fully aware of the depth and beauty of the music you are playing so that you can make your performances artistic. But the most important thing that you can learn from a real master is how to make maximum use of your human potential.

Chapter 7 delves into the value of the imitative learning process and the master–student relationship. It includes a description of how Maestro Andrés Segovia teaches his classes. The chapter also deals with other natural study methods such as regular, goal-directed practice, breaking down problems, intelligent repetition, slow practice, memorization, the use of the metronome, and other techniques that will help you get the most from your guitar study time in an enjoyable way.

8. USE THE MIND OVER FINGERS APPROACH: VISUALIZE AND LET IT HAPPEN

As Fernando Sor has pointed out, playing the guitar is more a matter of *skill* than *strength*. Playing the guitar well definitely involves physical work with the fingers. However, the fingers have a much lighter task if you quietly use the power of your mind to seek out the most natural techniques. Many guitarists think that if they just get enough "finger action" through endless repetition of exercises and pieces, then they will play well. This is not necessarily so. They usually waste much time and energy grinding in bad habits and wonder why they are improving so slowly. The "brute force" approach may eventually produce some results, but it is very tiring and inefficient. Using the *mind over fingers* approach works much better.

Mind over fingers means, among other things, developing your inherent capacity for inner *visualization* or "mental picturing" so that you can achieve your guitar goals more readily. Most people visualize, but not clearly or systematically. Visualization, when practiced as a systematic technique, has been used with excellent results in many areas of life, including personal development, athletics, and music. Many successful people say that whatever you can picture in your mind, you can do. A number of famous musicians, including guitarists, use "mental picturing" and "mental hearing" to sharpen their musical skills and to help achieve their career goals.

In order for your conscious mind to fully utilize its visualizing power, it needs to work in an integrated way with your body and subconscious mind. And to do that you must *visualize and let it happen*. First, clearly visualize a desired musical result in your conscious mind. Then get the conscious mind into the background and allow the natural intelligence of your body and subconscious mind to help you carry out your musical intentions. For maximum success with visualization, it is essential to trust that your body and subconscious will do what you want. It is not necessary to force them to do your bidding. With only a mental picture and a minimum of prompting from the conscious mind, the body and subconscious can perform very complex movements on the guitar with little effort.

Once you have learned the basic classical guitar skills, you can use the visualization approach to work out many musical problems. Whatever you can conceive in your mind, you can eventually play with your fingers. If, for example, you have a clear concept of the sound of Bach's *Prelude, Fugue,* and *Allegro,* your fingers will be guided to the best technique for playing it— provided your conscious mind does not interfere too much with the natural process. This mental approach is a potent learning tool that can save a considerable amount of time and energy for the guitarist.

Chapters 8 and 9 elaborate on how visualization can greatly enhance the way you study, interpret, and perform with the guitar. Chapter 8 shows how to apply visualization to such things as phrasing, mental practice and memorization, left-hand shifts, counting problems, and increasing scale speed. Chapter 9 describes a twelve-step visualization approach to learning a piece of music for the guitar. To illustrate how the steps work, they are applied in detail to a sample piece. In Chapter 10 there is a discussion of how visualization can help you prepare for a recital.

9. SHARE YOUR ENJOYMENT OF MUSIC: HELP TO HARMONIZE SOCIETY

It is natural to share your enjoyment of the guitar with others. It is unnatural to be afraid and keep your talent to yourself. Of course it is just common sense not to play when you are ill-prepared. But, when you are playing well in the practice room—even just a simple piece—and it makes you feel good, the natural desire is to want everyone to share that feeling with you. So why not play for other people? When you do, you find out that, although it is a joy to play for yourself, it can be many times more enjoyable to play for others. This extra enjoyment comes from a special kind of energy exchange between you and the audience. This happens in a very strong and noticeable way when the audience is receptive and when you achieve the natural state of dynamic relaxation in your playing. At such times, you and the audience become perfectly synchronized with the rhythm and feeling of the music. When this occurs, everyone gains energy and goes away from the performance uplifted. Even you, the performer, rather than feeling drained by the effort, feel stronger and happier than before the performance. This experience can happen in a living room with a small group of friends or in a large hall filled with people. Thus the guitarist can perform an important social function by his playing: that of making people feel happier, more harmonious, and more peaceful.

It does take some time and patience to reach a level where you feel calm and confident about playing for others, but it is all worthwhile. Playing recitals, besides performing a social function, is a great challenge and opportunity for you to surpass what you think are your mental and physical limits. In Chapter 10, which deals with recitals, ways are discussed to help you achieve higher levels of performing. Some of the topics are: planning a program, recital visualization, "dry runs," yoga for stage fright, warming cold hands, dealing with mistakes, relaxing during concerts, and evaluating your performance.

Just as it is natural to share your delight in the guitar by playing solos for others, it is also natural to share musical enjoyment by playing in ensembles with other musicians. That can also be an energizing, uplifting experience. One of the many values of ensemble playing is that it teaches you to harmonize your playing with others and yet maintain the unique character of your part. It also helps your solo playing a great deal, because you learn the meaning of rhythmic discipline and how to balance the various elements in a piece of music. Chapter 11 deals with ensemble playing as well as other topics of interest such as sight reading, repertoire, and improvisation.

10.   EVOLVE FROM THE GUITAR TO THE SELF: EXPERIENCE THE TRANSFORMING POWER OF MUSIC

When my students begin taking lessons, I suggest to them that the guitar is more than just a musical instrument. I tell them that it is an excellent means of self-development. When you study it intelligently, it can help you learn to concentrate better, to memorize more easily, to improve mind–body coordination, to perform well while remaining relaxed, to get along well with others, and to harmonize yourself with your environment.

In essence, classical guitar playing is a refined discipline that can help you realize your full potential and become a happier individual. If it is studied in a natural way without stress and strain, it will put you more at peace with yourself and your surroundings. Both your life and your music will become more effortless and fulfilling. Keep in mind that just as your guitar studies can improve your personal life, what you do to improve your personal life will also be reflected in your guitar playing. Thus your study of music and the guitar is really a way of self-development, which will ultimately lead you to a state of complete attunement with yourself and your environment. When you have achieved that state, you will have developed your full mental, physical, and spiritual potential and will be able to actualize it in daily life. Chapter 12 expands on the transforming power of music and how it can help you transcend the limits of your ordinary self.

Now you have a vision of the natural approach to the classical guitar and its basic principles. This approach is really nothing new. Rather it is a revival of the wisdom of the past. This wisdom has always suggested that you harmonize yourself with the laws of nature if you want to be successful in anything—including music. The ancient Chinese called these laws of nature the Tao (the "Way") and taught that one must be in tune with the Tao in order to lead a fruitful life. Thus the sage Lao Tzu says:

> *The wise student hears of the Tao and practices*
> *it diligently . . .The Tao alone nourishes and*
> *brings everything to fulfillment.*[10]

---

[10]Ibid., chapter 41.

2.

Increase Mind-Body Awareness

tune in to the present

To be aware, to be conscious at all times is what appears to me the worthiest in my thoughts and in my work.

Wanda Landowska, *Landowska on Music*

Fine guitar playing is only possible when you are keenly aware of yourself and the entire playing process. Becoming aware of yourself and your playing is an interesting and enjoyable game of self-discovery. There are, of course, many things to discover. Is your mind wandering? What are you telling yourself when you are playing? Do your finger movements feel flowing and natural or do they feel tense and awkward much of the time? Is it comfortable to hold the guitar? Is the guitar too big or too small for you? Are your shoulders hunched up or relaxed? Is your tone golden and round or tinny and rough? Are you aware of the relative tension and relaxation in the phrasing of the music you are playing? What is the emotional feeling you have about the music? Do you feel the music in your head, your heart, or your insides? What do you want from the guitar and what is your attitude toward it?

Increasing awareness is the most basic requirement for improving your playing. It is not just a question of discovering and changing something mechanical in technique, but also of finding ways to make your perceptions sharper, particularly the senses of hearing, seeing, feeling, and intuition. Thus you need to fine-tune the awareness of the *internal* player as well as the skills of *external* playing.

It is necessary to be more than just vaguely aware of your playing and any problems you might have with it. It is important to have a very clear awareness of what you are doing and specific ways of dealing with difficulties. You may know, for example, that you need to relax, but exactly what part of your body needs to relax and how can you do it? The techniques in this chapter will help cultivate heightened awareness and the ability to relax the various parts of the body. We begin with a discussion of the value of putting your attention on what is happening *now* in your playing; following that are some thoughts on the roles guitarists play; then we describe ways to quiet your mind for greater awareness; next are some practical techniques for relaxing your body; finally we talk about getting to know your guitar better.

16

SEEING, HEARING, AND FEELING IN THE PRESENT

Noncritical Awareness

The natural approach to the guitar places strong emphasis on being fully aware of what you are doing at each moment when you are practicing or performing. For that reason, it is good to develop a calm, unbiased *noncritical* awareness of yourself and your playing as it actually is. With this kind of awareness you step back from your playing, so to speak, and simply observe what is happening at the moment. This means, for example, really *seeing* your left-hand finger movements, really *hearing* the sounds that are produced and really *feeling* the sensations of making the right-hand strokes. When you have this kind of awareness in your practice sessions, problems can easily be seen and solved; in fact, many will be solved automatically. With this awareness in your performances, you will be able to play with spontaneity and few mistakes.

Not Worrying About Results

In guitar performance, the value of not being worried about results should be obvious. To get the most from your playing, it is essential to focus your awareness on what is happening *now* in your playing, not on a past or future result. For example, if you are worried about what people have said or will say about your playing, you will become distracted, exert yourself too much, and make mistakes. On the other hand, if you have a calm approach and are not concerned about results while you are playing, then your awareness will be clear. It will be free to focus on the only thing over which you really have any control—the immediate actions of playing and making music.

Excess Conscious Effort

Because guitarists often worry about results and try too hard, their thoughts are often in the past or future instead of being in the now. Like the tennis players that Timothy Gallwey describes in his book *The Inner Game of Tennis*, they are distracted from the present because they are praising or criticizing themselves under their breath according to how well or badly they think they are playing.[1] Many players are not fully aware that they are doing this. They need to see that talking to yourself only gets in the way; it prevents you from seeing, hearing, or feeling what is happening.

In practice sessions, the excess conscious effort and mental chatter make

[1]Timothy Gallwey, *The Inner Game of Tennis* (New York: Random House, 1974), p. 25.

it difficult to see and correct faulty habits. However, the most annoying result of excessive effort is that it causes guitarists to become tight and make mistakes when they are performing. During practice sessions and performances players often mutter distracting things to themselves such as: "Relax your right hand!" or "Don't press so hard!" or "Oh God, here's the rough part." or "You nitwit, why did you play that wrong note again?" Even positive thoughts can get in your way. For example, guitarists often say to themselves, "Hey, I'm playing really well and I'm almost finished," at which point concentration is lost and they stumble at the end of the piece.

Letting Go

A better approach to playing is to be quietly aware of it and *let go* of the undue mental effort and self-criticism. When you notice that you are talking to yourself too much, just let go of the talk in a gentle way and turn your attention back to your playing. Take your playing as it comes and avoid labeling it good or bad. If your playing is going well, leave it as it is; if it is not, then make the necessary changes without self-condemnation. With this calm approach, you will be able to perceive your playing more as it actually is and thus evaluate it better. Moreover, you will be letting your body and subconscious mind alone so they can function freely and naturally.

Dropping needless mental chatter helps to develop a calm, noncritical awareness of your playing. However, even though you become aware of the chatter, it is not always so easy to get rid of it. The mind-settling techniques described later in this chapter can be very helpful for reducing such "mental noise."

Develop Body Awareness

Now let's apply noncritical awareness to the physical part of your playing. At this point we will not discuss the development of more sensitive hearing; that will be taken up in the next chapter. Here we will be mainly concerned with sharpening the senses of sight and touch, that is, becoming acutely aware of how your body feels and looks when you play. This kind of body awareness is called the *kinesthetic* sense. It specifically refers to being sensitive to the degree of tension in the muscles. Usually guitarists have too much tension in various parts of the body, although sometimes there is not enough. With a good kinesthetic sense the guitarist will be able to use just the right amount of tension to achieve a given result. (For more on this, see Chapters 4 and 5.)

Many players have little awareness of their bodies. For example, guitar students frequently become so absorbed in reading the notes of a piece that they do not see or feel what is going on with their hands, fingers, and other parts of the body. As a result, some parts of the body become tense, causing the student to suffer physical discomfort or fatigue and make mistakes. Since the student usually has practiced this way many times, bad habits are acquired unconsciously.

During a lesson, the usual remedy is to tell the student everything that is wrong and how to correct it. "Try to relax, slow down, don't press so hard with the left hand, relax the little finger, change the fingering!" The student grimaces and tries to do everything he is told—often muttering under his breath in the process. The suggestions are all good, but the student often does worse than before. Why? Because there are too many corrections and the student becomes anxious about them and tries too hard to implement them. Result: excess tension and frustration.

Here the teacher can be very helpful. He can simply stop saying so much. Better not to give the student so many instructions at once; just give him one thing to think about at a time. Even better, the teacher can dispense with regular verbal instructions for a moment and simply direct the student's attention to one aspect of what he is actually doing with his fingers. This will have the effect of increasing the student's awareness without overburdening his mind. It is remarkable how often technical and musical difficulties resolve themselves automatically in the light of increased awareness.

Take the case of a beginning student. She was totally focused on the written notes she was trying to play and was unaware that the left-hand fingers were pressing too hard and making excessive movements and that the left hand was weak because the wrist was bent too much (see Chapter 4, "Balancing the Left Hand"). To get her attention away from the printed notes, she was asked to memorize a very short section from her piece.[2] Then she was asked to simply *watch and feel* what the left hand was doing as she played the phrase. No other instructions were given. It was fascinating to see her hand spontaneously relax and assume a more natural way of functioning. The excess pressure was reduced, the movements became smaller and the wrist seemed to decide that it was stronger when it was not bent so much. All these corrections came about with practically no instructions given. It was not even necessary to tell the girl about her mistakes. When she increased her awareness of the left hand by watching and feeling it with full attention, then her own intuition and inherent body wisdom helped her improve in a natural way. She was allowing nature to support her playing. With this natural teaching approach there may still be a need for some conventional teaching instructions, but they can be reduced considerably to the benefit of both teacher and student.

---

[2]Guitar teachers may find it is much easier to teach both younger and older beginners by rote rather than by using music. The famous pedagogue Shinichi Suzuki has amply proven how well this rote method works for children learning to play the violin. Beginners do much better if they can focus completely on learning basic technique and some easy pieces instead of trying to learn notes and technique at the same time. When the student knows the basics well and can play some easy pieces by heart, then note reading can be introduced.

Every guitarist can easily apply the body awareness approach to his own playing. With this approach you can learn how to play with minimum effort by simply watching and feeling your hands and fingers in a quiet, noncritical way and letting them make their adjustments without too many commands from the mind. Of course not every guitar problem can be solved by simply observing the fingers and letting them find their own way. Such an approach may just result in sloppy playing. Frequently it is necessary to analyze the problem first and then allow the fingers to work naturally. Both methods of problem solving are useful and can be combined fruitfully. Now let's consider another area where you can increase your awareness: guitar role playing.

ROLE-PLAYING AWARENESS

In the *Inner Game of Tennis* Timothy Gallwey sketches out the different roles that tennis players tend to play on and off the court.[3] Tennis role playing can give us interesting insights about guitar role playing. Each tennis role is acted out in a kind of game that the player plays with himself. Players choose roles for themselves more or less consciously and express these roles in their styles of playing. Thus some players have a careful, defensive style while others play offensively; some are interested only in form while others are fiercely competitive; and some are cool and detached.

To a great extent the roles and styles that Gallwey talks about are found in the guitar world. Guitar players also have their games. There is the shy, cautious player who tries to avoid mistakes at all costs and does not relish playing for other people; there is the aggressive type who plays every note to the back of the hall; there is the formal player who is less concerned with hitting all the notes than with how elegant his interpretation is and how fluid his fingers look; yet another style is the competitive one in which the player is out to play more notes more perfectly and in less time than anyone else; lastly, there is the detached type who plays beautifully without nervousness or strain and apparently is not concerned about the outcome. Of course most players exhibit a mixture of these roles, although one tends to dominate. Guitarists' motivations are similar to those of tennis players. Some play to prove themselves, some do it for fun and friendship, some play as a way of relaxing, and still others enjoy the guitar in a "disinterested" way. The styles are naturally related to the motivations of the player.

It is useful for guitarists to become aware of whatever role playing they are engaged in because they often do not realize that they are doing it and that it is affecting the way they play. When players become aware of their role playing, they may want to ask themselves why they are acting out a particular

---

[3]Gallwey, *The Inner Game of Tennis,* pp. 62, 107ff.

role and whether it is producing good results for their guitar performance. Every style of playing has its advantages and disadvantages. A highly competitive player, for example, on the positive side, often polishes his technique to a high degree and thus is able to play complex, challenging pieces. However, on the negative side, in his zeal to out-perform other players, he may try tempos that are too fast for him or try to play pieces that are beyond his present technical ability. In other words, his ego may be getting in his way.

If the guitarist is not satisfied with his role or type of playing, he might find it helpful to try an unfamiliar style in order to balance any extreme tendencies he may have. The aggressive guitarist might try out the style of the calm, detached type for a change—and vice versa. In fact, two such contrasting types of concert players actually tried out each other's roles and found it very helpful. The aggressive player was able to tone down his approach somewhat so that his playing was not overly rough and the detached player was able to put more energy into his approach so that it was not overly quiet. Neither player lost anything in this process. Both gained dimensions in their playing that had been missing. Both found more *balance* in their approaches.

The very shy and cautious player can also benefit from exchanging roles. Being cautious does have its good points because caution prevents many mistakes; however, the other side of the coin is that playing can be so cautious that it is inhibited. As an experiment, the shy guitarist might try out the role of the aggressive player to help overcome his shyness. For him, this may mean getting up to play without hesitation at every chance; it may mean deliberately playing loud; it may also mean mentally picturing himself as an extrovert.

This role playing can be enjoyable and profitable for guitarists who want to break out of rigid patterns. However, role playing should be viewed as a temporary aid since the best role to play is that of your simple, natural self. It is unprofitable to make a big effort to be someone you are not. This can actually create tension for you and others when your act is too transparent. This does not mean that it is useless to attempt to change your style of playing, but rather that it is a waste of time to *force* yourself to change. It certainly will not hurt you to drop the negative aspects of a role you are playing nor will it hurt to picture yourself as a successful guitarist and then take reasonable actions to realize that picture.

When you are playing roles, remember that your true, natural self is unlimited in potential and therefore much bigger than any particular role you may assume. So the ultimate goal in guitar playing is to let your natural self come out and express itself spontaneously in your music. You may find that your "role" will change naturally according to the music you play and the performance situation. With some experience you will find that being your natural self is by far most appealing to audiences. People generally appreciate sincerity and spontaneity in a performer and feel uncomfortable with pretentiousness and studied actions. The mind-settling and relaxation techniques in this chapter will help to develop naturalness and spontaneity.

Whatever the case, the game of playing the guitar should be an enjoyable one and should not be taken too seriously. It is very easy to be led by your ego into a stressful, overly competitive role where playing is a very serious business indeed. Putting yourself under such pressure is not particularly healthy. However, there is no reason why you should not aim at playing as well as possible or why you should not have a certain sense of competition. Just do not forget that it is healthy to retain a sense of distance from and humor about your playing. Simply because you played a piece poorly in a recital or cannot play as fast as the guitarist down the block does not mean that you are a bad person. You do not need to *identify* yourself with your shortcomings. Just regard these shortcomings as a sign that you can still grow and learn more about playing. This is what makes it all so interesting.

Now we will turn to some ways of relaxing the mind and body so that the natural self can come out more easily.

SETTLING YOUR MIND

As mentioned earlier in this chapter, when guitarists are practicing or playing a piece, they frequently are distracted because they talk to themselves about their playing—either mentally or out loud. It is also common that they are bothered by other distracting thoughts, experiences referred to as "mental chatter" or "mental noise." Guitarists may also be distracted by physical tensions while playing. Thus there may be a number of things going on in the mind and body that keep the player from seeing his playing as it actually is. So, what can be done about these obstacles to awareness? One remedy, which we have already discussed, is simply to let go of the mental chatter and cultivate a quiet, noncritical awareness of your playing. That remedy can be very helpful but it is often not enough.

Two more fundamental ways of increasing your awareness and getting rid of distractions are *settling your mind* and *relaxing your body*. These two approaches can be used together to good effect since mind and body are intimately interconnected: settle the mind and the body relaxes; relax the body and the mind settles. When the mind and body are quiet, then the stage is set for you to concentrate completely on your playing. That is when you obtain the best results.

Settling the mind is a way of clearing it of the "mental noise" that can disrupt your playing and distort your perception of it. It is particularly helpful to settle your mind just before studying or performing. When you go through this mental quieting process, noncritical awareness tends to come about very naturally. When the mind is relatively quiet and uncluttered, everything becomes clearer. You are able to hear your body telling you to correct a cramped sitting position, to find a more flowing fingering, or to slow down your practice tempos. With a quiet mind, you can also appreciate the more subtle aspects of the music you play. If the mind is not quiet, then it is difficult to be aware of these things.

The process of quieting the mind has an interesting scientific parallel in the third law of thermodynamics from physics. Basically this law says that, as temperature decreases, order increases. For example, if you cool down hot, disorderly steam sufficiently, then you get the orderly structure of ice crystals. There is an analogous law that works in the mind-settling process. What you do in that process is to reduce your "mental temperature," so to speak, with the result that the mind becomes more orderly. This orderliness manifests itself in a concrete way in the coherence and synchronization of the brain waves as measured in scientific studies.[4] Other studies show that various human abilities are improved by the mind-settling process. Thus there seem to be some solid reasons to practice some way of quieting the mind.

Mind-Settling Techniques

Most people realize the value of a quiet mind, at least intuitively. A person who approaches problems calmly is generally admired. However, the majority of people do not practice any systematic technique to develop mental calmness. There are many techniques available. They are not absolutely essential for playing but they can be very helpful to the guitarist who is interested. Many professional musicians, including guitarists, practice some method of settling the mind. Some of the methods are very simple and can be practiced immediately without special instruction. Others require some instruction and at least a small investment of time. Whatever method you choose, keep in mind that *making an effort to settle the mind does not work.* Attempts to do such things as "make the mind blank" actually tend to increase mental activity. The process must be effortless in order to be effective. Now let's look at a few of the ways to quiet the mind.

Sitting Quietly, Eyes Closed   This is a very simple technique that only the most impatient people cannot do. It involves finding a comfortable chair, closing the eyes, and relaxing all the muscles for five to ten minutes. When you are finished with this process, it is best to open the eyes slowly and not to jump up too quickly. This is because the mind and body settle down when you relax and close your eyes; thus opening your eyes too quickly or jumping up suddenly is a shock to the system. This technique can be done before practicing or playing in order to clear the mind and relax the body. Of course it

---

[4]H. Bloomfield, *TM: Discovering Inner Energy and Overcoming Stress* (New York: Delacorte Press, 1975), p. 73ff.

it can be done during practice sessions when a break is needed or at any other time for that matter.

"Watching the Breath"   Another way of quieting your mind is to focus your attention easily on your breathing for two ten-minute periods each day. In this process, you sit comfortably, close the eyes, and simply direct your awareness to the sensation of the breath as it passes in and out of the nostrils. Let the breathing flow naturally. If your mind wanders away from the breathing process, then very gently bring it back. Forcing your mind to focus on the breathing is not effective. Just give it a gentle nudge in that direction. If you have distracting thoughts, just be neutral to them and let them go. Do not try to force them out. Keep returning to your breathing. Watching the breath helps you to disengage your mind from excess thinking activity and prepares you for guitar study and performance. Even if you only do the technique before performances, it is still helpful. It produces relaxation, reduces nervousness, and improves concentration.

The TM Technique   Many people in all walks of life, including guitarists and other musicians, have found the practice of the Transcendental Meditation (TM) technique to be a systematic, simple, and effortless way to quiet the mind and relax the body for greater success in their activities. It is noteworthy that more scientific studies have been done on TM than on any other mind-settling technique. The studies have shown that it improves concentration, memory, hearing, and creativity in addition to reducing stress and nervousness.[5] It is particularly helpful for developing the good mind–body coordination that is so important for musicians. The technique does not make a person passive, but rather it gives him more energy for dynamic activity. The advantages of the TM technique are that it is easy to learn, has been shown to be scientifically valid, and is taught in a systematic, standardized way in most countries in the world.[6] In order to learn it properly one must find a qualified teacher and take the prescribed course.[7]

In sum, there are various ways of settling the mind. If you are interested in learning one of these techniques, it is best to look carefully at what is available and choose the one that seems right for you. If you decide to do a mind-settling technique, it is similar to guitar practice. It is best to do it regularly. When you are regular with the practice, the mind becomes habituated to the settling process and the inner quietness becomes more profound. When the quietness becomes deeper during the process, then your awareness will be sharper when you come out of it and start working with the guitar. Your entire approach to playing the guitar and solving musical problems will improve

[5]Ibid., p. 91ff.
[6]Ibid., p. 10ff.
[7]Ibid., pp. 26–30.

when your mind is quiet and alert. There is an experience common to all of us that will illustrate the value of a settled mind. There has probably been at least one time when you were very quiet and were not thinking specifically about the guitar and then suddenly a solution to a thorny guitar problem popped into your mind. But when you were *trying* to solve the problem directly, nothing came! From this example, it should not be difficult to see that the quietness gained from regular practice of a simple mind-settling technique would help you to discover solutions to guitar problems more easily.

RELAXING YOUR BODY

The mental approach to increased awareness and relaxation is through settling the mind. The physical approach is through relaxing the body. Remember that these two approaches are complementary; just as settling the mind relaxes the body, practicing a good body relaxation technique will help to quiet the mind.

As we discussed in the first part of this chapter, it is vital for the guitarist to become aware of his body so that he can learn to relax and play with less effort. The guitarist especially needs to become sensitive to the relative degree of tension and relaxation in the muscles. With the majority of players there seems to be a great deal of misplaced muscular tension. As intelligent musicians know, a certain amount of tension is required to play, but it should be just the right amount at the right time and place.

Excess Tensions of Guitarists

The following list presents the most common points of excess tension that guitarists experience. Check through this list to see if there are some tensions that you have not noticed or have not yet eliminated from your playing.

1. one or both shoulders hunched up
2. excess pressure of the right forearm on the guitar (from trying to control the right hand too much)
3. contortion of the facial and neck muscles (the muscles around the mouth, the jaws, and the neck often tighten in sympathy with the muscles of the arms and hands, particularly during difficult passages; guitarists make the most amazing faces when they try hard!)
4. excess tension in the legs (usually from improper sitting position or from getting angry with yourself; see Chapter 4, "Sitting Position")
5. back tension (comes mainly from sitting too long without breaks, not sitting up straight, twisting the spine too much and sitting with the right

leg too far out to the right; many players also have tension from back problems not related to the guitar; see Chapter 4, "Sitting Position")

6. excess neck tension (from turning the neck stiffly to the left and trying too hard to watch and control the left hand—even to the point of craning the neck over the fingerboard in order to watch every finger movement)

7. excess left-arm tension (usually from faulty hand position or holding the elbow too high in the air for too long)

There are other common tension problems related to hand position and sitting that are covered in the chapter on *dynamic relaxation,* so we will not deal with all of them here. However, the following general method can be used to release whatever undue physical tension you may discover.

The "Stop and Let Go" Technique

This simple technique is a conscious process for getting rid of such excess tensions as are mentioned in the previous list. It is practiced as follows: If you notice unwanted tension or pain anywhere in the body while playing or even just while sitting with the guitar, then *immediately stop* what you are doing and allow your attention to go to the tense part of your body. Now let go of the tension as much as possible. Massage or shake out the tense part or get up and move it around to help release the tightness. The tension will normally dissolve quickly and then you can resume playing from the relaxed state. For example, if you become aware that your neck is tense from turning it too hard to the left to watch the fingerboard, then stop playing right away and roll your neck around to release the tension. Massage it if necessary. When the tension is gone and you want to start playing again, be sure to avoid putting the neck back into a strained position.

Here is another example of how the technique works: If you become aware that your right hand has become tight while you are playing Villa-Lobos' *Etude No. 1* (which has a complex arpeggio) or a similar fast piece, stop playing immediately, let the entire shoulder, arm, and hand hang loosely at your side, and shake it out. Then go back to a relaxed position and continue playing. Every time you feel some tightness, do not wait. Stop right away and release the tension.

When you first use this body relaxation technique in your practice sessions, you may be stopping and letting go every thirty seconds—if you really are aware of your excess tensions. But that is just fine. If you apply the technique every time you feel some tightness in any part of the body, then greater body awareness and relaxation will become an automatic habit. You will gradually get rid of all superfluous tension in your playing. By all means, once you are aware of any needless tension or pain, be sure to relieve it because, if you let it accumulate, it may result in some chronic physical problems.

If you experience excess tension in spite of this technique, then the problem may be caused by something other than simple muscular tension. Consider changing such things as your way of sitting, your hand positions, the way you make the strokes, or the shape of your nails. In any case, it is good to continue to use the "stop and let go" technique. As you cut down the unnecessary tension, playing and practicing will become a joyful experience rather than drudgery. You will be following the natural principle of least action: "doing less and accomplishing more."

General Body Awareness and Relaxation

The "stop and let go" technique is very helpful for becoming aware of and relaxing specific muscles *after* they have become tight. However, it is even better to become aware of and prevent excess tension *before* it comes up by relaxing the entire body on a daily basis. Preventive relaxation is particularly good to help you get rid of the many smaller tensions that you do not usually notice. Remember that when part of the body is tight while you are playing, it will be a waste of your energy and at least a minor distraction. The methods described in this section are general ways of promoting body awareness and relaxation that help prevent energy-wasting tightness.

Rest   The most direct approach to body relaxation is sleep. While this may seem obvious, many musicians keep very irregular hours and, as a result, the muscles often are fatigued and tense. Your body will be much more relaxed and you will be more aware of its needs if you get a regular amount of sleep every night—not too much, not too little. It is good to pay attention to your body when it is begging for rest. When you are well-rested, everything about your guitar playing will go better. Plenty of rest is important for self-confidence, concentration, and relaxed body and hands. If you are unusually tired, you might try taking short naps during the day. It is amazing how rejuvenating even a brief nap can be. (See Chapter 10, "Relax on the Day of the Recital.")

Massage and Stretching   Either giving yourself a light body massage or having someone else do it for you is a very pleasant way of relaxing. Massage promotes circulation and helps keep the muscles and joints flexible. It is particularly beneficial for the guitarist to massage the hands and fingers where flexibility is all-important. The hands can be massaged in different ways, such as rubbing and squeezing all the joints (cracking them is not necessary), pulling and twisting each finger (gently!), and rubbing and pressing the palms and the backs of the hands.

Stretching exercises of various kinds can be beneficial for the whole body and particularly for the left-hand fingers.[8] There are some that can be

---

[8]*Stretching* by Bob Anderson (Bolinas, Ca.: Shelter Publications, 1980) describes many useful body-stretching exercises.

done without the guitar which can be quite useful. The most valuable type of stretching is the lateral type because it increases the player's ability to make the necessary left-hand reaches between frets. A lateral stretch exercise can be done by using the right-hand fingers to press the left-hand fingers apart as shown in Figure 2–1.

Figure 2–1 A finger-stretching exercise

A Total Relaxation Technique (Progressive Relaxation)[9]   There is one simple technique that you can do by yourself to relax the entire body in just a few minutes. Even if you do nothing else to relax, this technique will bring many benefits.

Begin the technique by lying down on the floor on a comfortable mat or blanket with eyes closed and arms at your sides. If it is not convenient to lie down, then sitting in a comfortable chair will do. Now go through the following procedure of tensing and relaxing the different muscle groups of the body. It helps to inhale and hold the breath on the tension phase and exhale on the release. First, tense up the toes and hold them that way for five seconds. Now release the tension completely and feel the contrast. Next, tense up the toes, feet, and calves, hold the tension for five seconds, and release. Now tighten up the toes, feet, calves, and thighs for the same amount of time and then let go. Feel the relaxation as deeply as possible.

Next, tighten up the buttocks for five seconds and let go. Now do the same tension-release procedure with the abdomen and lower back, making

---

[9]*Progressive Relaxation* by Edmund Jacobson (Chicago: University of Chicago Press, 1942) is the standard work on this relaxation method.

sure to exhale on the release phase. Proceed to tighten up your arms and clench your fists for another five seconds and then release. Do the same with your shoulders and upper back. Again clench your fists and contract the arm muscles and then let go thoroughly. Finally, inhale, tighten all your muscles for a few seconds, let go and feel a big wave of deep relaxation flow through your whole body. Exhale completely to help the process along. The entire exercise should not take longer than three or four minutes—unless you feel so relaxed you do not want to get up!

After the above exercise you will feel refreshed, relaxed, and mentally alert. When you have done it a few times you will be able to relax thoroughly in a very short time. The more regular you are with it, the more habituated your body will become to being relaxed. After some experience with the exercise, you may want to dispense with the tensing phase and simply let the muscles relax as much as possible. Just let the muscles unwind in the same order as in the above exercise—toes, feet, calves, and so on. This is one of the most valuable techniques for immediate relaxation. You can use it anywhere there is a chair or a floor. It is an excellent way to let go before a performance or study session.

Yogic Postures and Breathing *Hatha yoga* is a form of physical culture that has proven itself highly effective over a period of several thousand years. It consists of postures and breathing exercises that can be beneficial to a performing guitarist. These exercises will help you to increase your body awareness and will produce muscle relaxation, improved circulation, oxygenation of the brain cells, and flexibility of the whole body—including hands and fingers. *Hatha yoga* is an excellent form of physical culture because, unlike other types, it does not use up much energy. The postures simply involve *holding* the body in various positions—mainly bending and stretching positions—rather than doing the rapid, often tiring muscle contractions of the common forms of exercise.

When the yogic postures are done correctly, most people find that they actually gain energy. Doing ten to fifteen minutes of simple postures once or twice a day has a very powerful effect. The yoga approach is definitely in tune with the least action principle: You get the most from doing the least. It is good to understand that one does not have to be an "India rubber man" to do the simpler postures and benefit from them. The important things to keep in mind are:

1. Learn the postures correctly, preferably from a good teacher, although books can be helpful.[10]
2. Do the postures in loose clothing on a soft blanket or mat.
3. *Never* overstrain to do the postures.

[10]A good beginning yoga book is Richard Hittleman's *Be Young With Yoga* (New York: Warner Books, 1962).

Never overstraining means that if you are doing the bend-and-touch-the-toes pose, you bend only to a point slightly beyond where you start to feel a strain and then stop. That is enough for that session. Gradually you will be able to bend more easily. If you do overstrain, you may injure yourself. It is just like overstraining to do a left-hand stretch on the fingerboard. You may hurt your hand in the process. It is better to stretch just a tiny bit beyond the point of strain each time and make comfortable progress.

To sum up, yoga postures can be very relaxing and energizing for guitarists. Daily practice is best, but even if you only do it occasionally—such as on concert days—it is still beneficial. If you follow the postures with one of the breathing exercises in Chapter 3 and/or one of the mind-settling techniques, you should feel very good indeed.

Physical Exercise   Many guitarists find that some kind of physical exercise, either on a regular basis or on the day of a concert, helps them to unwind. The most common forms of relaxing exercise are walking, cycling, and swimming. These and other forms can be good, but it is very important not to wear yourself out doing them. Whatever exercise you do should relax and energize you so that your mind and body are in top shape. Avoid any exercises that cause tightness or fatigue in the arms and hands.

Diet   An integral part of mind/body awareness for guitarists is to pay attention to how the food you eat affects your studying and playing. If you are alert, you may make some very interesting discoveries about how you feel after eating a certain kind or certain quantity of food. The effects of food are often immediate, but may sometimes be delayed until several hours after you eat. You will naturally want to eat those foods that make your mind sharp and your body energetic and avoid those foods that dull the mind and drag down the body. A bit of experimentation with different types and quantities of food and a lot of listening to your body will produce intriguing results. See Chapters 3 and 10 for further discussions of diet.

Other Awareness/Relaxation Methods   There are many ways to increase body awareness and promote relaxation—so many, in fact, that it is not possible to discuss them all here. Some additional approaches are described in Chapter 10. Remember that the best techniques are those that are simple, take a limited amount of time or effort, and produce good results.

You always have the option to do nothing about body awareness and relaxation. However, if you are having difficulties with your playing or feel that it could be better in some way, experiment with one or more of the above techniques. If you do, you will be in good company. A number of the top concert guitarists—to say nothing of other musicians—use some technique to increase awareness and promote relaxation. This is not surprising because the condition of your body is an intimate part of your music making. It should be in good shape. When your body is relaxed and well-rested, when your circulation is good, your muscles are toned up, your hands and fingers are flexible and your nerves are strong, then playing will be relatively easy and enjoyable for you. On the other hand, when your body is not in good shape, playing may be more like a struggle.

GUITAR AWARENESS

Getting to Know Your Guitar

You will get much more from your guitar playing if you know the instrument well. Many players do not know much about their guitar except that it is a nice wood box on which to make sounds. It is very interesting to explore your guitar in different ways. Find out as much as you can about how it was made. Visit a guitar maker's shop. Look at a book on guitar construction. Then explore the guitar physically. *Touch* the instrument and its different parts: the texture of the various kinds of wood (what are they?); the shape of the neck and body; the weight of it; the contour of the fingerboard; the tension of the strings under your fingers; the way the machine heads work. *Look* at the instrument: the grain of the wood; the way the joints are put together; the design of the rosette (how was it made?); the label of the maker inside; the height of the strings above the fingerboard; the length of the strings from nut to saddle; the color of the woods (are they stained?). *Listen* to the instrument: the sound of a slur; the sound of your knuckle rapped on the soundboard; the quality of the overtones of the open strings; the duration of the treble notes; the relative mellowness or hardness of each note; the different tone colors that can be produced by the right hand; the intonation up and down the fingerboard; the balance of loudness between treble and bass; the volume of sound close up and at a distance; the depth or shallowness of the tone. *Smell* the instrument: the fragrance of the wood at the soundhole; the pungency of the finish; the metallic odor of the machine heads. Of course one question is always interesting. How does your guitar compare with others? You will no doubt find it intriguing to get together with other players to experience how different instruments look, feel, and sound.

Guitar Size

An important consideration in guitar awareness is the size of your guitar. The size of the instrument should be well-suited to your hands and body. Not everyone will be comfortable playing a big concert Ramirez (or similar instrument) which has a long string length and a wide neck. My 1966 Ramirez, for example, has a 66.5 cm. string length and the neck is 5.3 cm. at the nut and 6.4 cm. at the 12th fret. Keep in mind that a good deal of the guitar repertoire from the classical era of Sor, Aguado, and Giuliani was played on instruments with between 55 and 63 cm. string lengths—much shorter than the 64 to 66+ cm. of most present-day guitars. Shorter string lengths and narrower necks (5 cm. or less at the nut) greatly facilitate playing for those with small or average size hands. Such an arrangement makes large stretches much easier. (Five-fret stretches between the index and little fingers are not uncommon in the guitar literature.) In spite of the fact that most modern classical guitars have the longer string length, it is still possible to find good "short scale" guitars in various price ranges. Thus there is no need to strain and stretch your fingers unnaturally on a guitar that may sound good but is too large for you.

There are naturally many things to learn about your guitar. If you take some time to explore the character and resources of your instrument, you will find many fascinating details to help you play more easily and with greater subtlety and understanding. You will find, as the great concert artists have, that the guitar can become an intimate and perfectly natural part of yourself. You will become completely comfortable holding it, playing it, and expressing yourself through it.

SUMMARY

A natural way to make steady progress in your guitar studies is to cultivate a quiet, noncritical, but sharp awareness of what is happening *now* in your mind, your body, and your guitar. It takes some time and patience to develop this sharp awareness, but it is of such great importance that it is definitely worth your attention. To achieve this awareness it is necessary to learn how to drop excess mental effort and chatter. When your mind is clearer and less "noisy," it will start to cooperate with your body instead of fighting it. With a quiet mind it is much easier to recognize excess physical tension and let it go. When you have less mental and physical tension, the mind and body will work as an integrated unit and your playing will be more in harmony with the natural principle of least action. You will not have to "do" so much, and thus playing will become an easy, enjoyable experience. Another aspect of increasing your awareness of yourself and your playing is to see what kind of psychological role you are acting out with the guitar. Be sure that whatever role you are playing is having a good effect on your mind and your guitar performance. If you are not pleased with your role, you might try changing it. Remember that the best "role" is that of your natural, spontaneous self.

Two fundamental and complementary ways of increasing your awareness are settling your mind and relaxing your body. Some mind-settling techniques are: the "stop and let go" technique, rest, massage, progressive relaxation, yoga postures, and certain nonfatiguing forms of physical exercise, such as walking. In the process of becoming aware of the mind and body, diet is an important consideration because it can make the guitarist's mind either sharp or dull. The guitarist should also get to know his guitar. It is good to touch it, look at it, smell it, and above all, listen carefully to its many voices. If the guitarist knows his instrument like a good friend, it will respond to him better. He will be able to coax more music from it with less effort.

If you have experimented with some of the different ways of increasing your mind/body awareness, you have prepared the ground for good concentration. As every guitarist knows, good concentration is essential for excellent playing. However, contrary to what many believe, concentration need not be difficult. In fact, it can be a spontaneous, natural process. Discovering a natural approach to concentration is the subject of the next chapter.

3.

Natural Concentration

focus the mind effortlessly

> *Awkwardness and mistakes in playing are*
> *always due to a lack of concentration.*
>
> Wanda Landowska, *Landowska on Music*

CONCENTRATION AND THE GUITAR

The expansion of your guitar-playing awareness was the subject of the last chapter. Among other things, we discussed the value of being quietly but keenly aware of what is happening here and now in your playing. Since this kind of awareness is central to successful playing, it is worthwhile to explore it further. In particular, let's look at the logical extension of this awareness, which is being able to concentrate exclusively on one aspect of your playing. It should be obvious that good concentration is vital for the serious performing guitarist. But what can be done about it?

You probably have asked yourself at one time or another, "Is it possible to improve my concentration and, if so, do I have to force my mind to do it or is there an easier way?" Fortunately, almost everyone can improve their concentration to a great extent with very little effort. In an indirect way, the techniques for settling the mind and relaxing the body described in Chapter 2 will help you to concentrate better. This is because when the mind is quiet it is easier to focus it on something. However, in a more direct way, you can cultivate still more powerful concentration with the psychological and physiological approaches in this chapter—even if you can concentrate well now. Before going on to these new ideas, let's define concentration and its stages.

Natural Concentration

The dictionary definition of concentration is "exclusive attention to one object" or "directing (one's attention) to one point." To this definition it should be added that concentration is an easy, natural phenomenon when the mind gains happiness from it. If the mind is relatively quiet and you give it something enjoyable to focus on, then the mind will take to it spontaneously. This is called *natural concentration*.

Stages of Concentration

Now let's consider the various stages of concentration that people have experienced. The first stage is actually not concentration at all. It is the stage where your mind jumps about from one object to another like a "mischievous monkey." This is the stage of *diffused awareness* which you experience when you are trying too hard or are fatigued, frustrated, or overfed. In this stage, it is impossible to keep your mind on the fingerboard or on the sea of black dots on your music. Your mind acts like an ordinary light bulb that diffuses light in all directions without any special focus. To alleviate this condition, you can *let go* of excess conscious effort and self-criticism as was suggested in Chapter 2. If that does not work, then the best thing to do is to rest or do something that does not require much attention.

The second stage of concentration comes when the mind is settled enough to focus part of the time on some object, such as when you listen easily to some background music. This stage can be called *intermittent concentration*. In this stage, the mind roves around like a searchlight; it periodically focuses on a certain point but it is not steady.

In the third stage the mind is very settled and you are able to focus it sharply on one object to the exclusion of everything else. This stage is frequently called *one-pointed concentration*. It can be compared to the highly coherent state of light generated by a laser in which all the light waves are of one pure color, all the waves are in phase (all lined up together), and all the light is focused in one narrow beam. Many guitarists have experienced this state, or something close to it, when they are working on a delightful new piece of music or when they are absorbed in playing a favorite piece. Even a call for dinner is not heard because the attraction of the music is so great. At this point, you are so absorbed in the music that you lose awareness of yourself and your surroundings. You seem to become identified with the music. It is very interesting that time seems to slow down in this one-pointed state and thus, even though the piece you are playing may be fast, there seems to be plenty of time to play all the notes easily. This stage of concentration is a powerful one. If you have it a good deal of the time, then you will derive much benefit from your practice and will be able to play with few mistakes. However, there is a higher form of concentration that produces even better results.

The fourth stage of concentration is when you are able to focus one-pointedly on the music—as in stage three—but, paradoxically, you do not lose awareness of yourself and your surroundings in the process. This does not mean that you must *consciously* think about yourself and your audience and the music. Instead, you have an effortless awareness of these outer experiences of music and people and at the same time a deep sense of inner calmness. At this stage—which can be called *dynamically relaxed concentration*—there is complete harmony between you and the object. Your mind is in the

balanced state of dynamic relaxation (see Chapter 5) where it is sharply focused on the music and yet you feel totally relaxed. You are focusing just
enough—no more, no less. A number of guitarists have experienced this
stage and report that their playing flows effortlessly when they are in it. They
say that such an experience makes all the work of guitar playing worthwhile.

The unique character of dynamically relaxed concentration is that you
are able to focus sharply on one thing, like a laser, and at the same time, paradoxically, you are able to maintain a broad awareness of everything around
you—like an ordinary light bulb. In practical guitar terms, that means you can
focus sharply on some object, such as the melody in Tárrega's *Recuerdos de la
Alhambra,* and still be aware of the total sound of the piece, your inner calmness, and your audience. Dynamically relaxed concentration is the most natural and desirable form of concentration since you can enjoy awareness of all
the different levels of the guitar-playing situation at the same time. It is not
difficult to attain this state. It will come about automatically after you have
had some experience with the technique described below.

NATURAL CONCENTRATION:
THE PSYCHOLOGICAL APPROACH

The Natural Concentration Technique

Psychologically speaking, it is important to understand that concentration is
just a mental habit that everyone can easily develop with the proper technique. Everyone can already concentrate to some extent: it is just a matter of
refining that ability. So, if you feel that your concentration could be better,
there is something you can do about it.

In the natural approach to concentration there is no effort, no trying or
forcing involved. All of us have experienced that the mind can easily concentrate on something that is attractive to it. Thus, in the natural concentration
technique, *you focus your mind in a relaxed way on one attractive detail of your
playing*—such as the melodic line. This is the most fruitful approach because
the mind works best with one thing at a time. Of course, not every detail of
playing that needs to be practiced will seem equally attractive at first. However, after a bit of experience with this easy technique, these details will become more interesting since you will become more aware of the subtle aspects
of what you are doing. If you use this technique properly, you should find it
increasingly easier to concentrate.

You may say, "This is all well and good, but what if my mind wanders
even when I attempt to focus on one detail of the music?" At that point, the
procedure in the natural concentration technique is to bring the mind *gently,*

not forcibly, back to the melodic line or other detail. Patiently bring it back every time it wanders. Let go of any kind of straining or trying hard to concentrate because it will only make the mind wander all the more. That means letting go of excess self-criticism and unnecessary commands from your conscious mind such as "you must concentrate." It also means letting go of the physical manifestations of straining to concentrate such as frowning, clenching your jaw, or tightening your leg muscles. Such things only make concentration more difficult and waste energy.

Thus while the aim of the natural concentration technique is to focus your mind sharply on just one aspect of your playing, it does not use force to accomplish that goal. By using this natural technique systematically in your guitar study sessions, you will gradually develop the ability to focus with one-pointed concentration on whatever you want. With further practice of the technique, you will eventually experience the highest stage of concentration, the dynamically relaxed stage. Keep in mind that the higher stages of concentration cannot be forced. They must be allowed to develop gradually and naturally. Ultimately, dynamically relaxed concentration will manifest itself spontaneously in your performances without any conscious effort.

In the process of developing natural concentration, it is possible to be too relaxed about focusing your mind. That extreme is just as much to be avoided as being too controlled. The ideal in concentration is that delicate "middle way" where you focus the mind without focusing, so to speak. That means concentrating just enough—not too much, not too little. If your mind seems to wander excessively in spite of using the techniques presented in this and the previous chapter, then you may find it helpful to try the physiological approach described later in this chapter.

It should be added here that *very slow practice* is one of the best ways to relax and improve your concentration. When you practice slowly, you have plenty of time to focus on just one aspect of your playing. (See Chapter 7, "Slow Is Fast.")

Points of Mental Focus

You can apply the natural concentration technique to the following detailed areas when you practice and play: finger movements, melody, harmony, rhythm, formal structure, and inner meaning. In order to concentrate on these things, you can use your three senses of sight, sound, and touch as well as your intellectual understanding and emotional sensitivity.

If you know your music by heart, you will find that practicing with your eyes closed is an excellent way to concentrate on the various aspects of your playing. This approach is particularly useful to help you keep your mind on the sound of the music and the feel of the fingers because you do not have visual distractions. Now let's consider the different possible points of focus.

Finger Movements   The contemporary piano virtuoso Earl Wild said that one of the most important things he tells his students is to look carefully at what their fingers are actually doing. Then the students can be sure that the fingers are doing everything properly. This is also good advice for the guitarist. That awareness should be sharpened so that the player can see and feel his finger movements very clearly. Many students *look* at their fingers but they do not *see* what is happening because they are not concentrating. As a result, they often miss very obvious mistakes.

It is very helpful to look carefully at each detail of the movements of the left hand. Focusing exclusively on the left-hand fingers for part of your practice time is important because it will help you discover technical flaws and clumsy movements. As you are watching the left hand, always remember to ask yourself if your finger movements are natural and flowing. In performance, although it is necessary to pay some attention to the left-hand fingers, it is best to put your main attention on the musical expression. By the time you are ready to perform, you should know the piece so well that you can trust your fingers to do their work without much supervision.

For practice sessions, a very good but much neglected area of visual focus is the right hand. Normally, guitarists are too busy watching the left hand. Unfortunately, the right hand and arm are often great sources of mistakes and tension. Therefore the intelligent guitarist will do well to look closely at the right hand when practicing. Many students only look at the right hand from above and as a result do not see what the fingers are doing; they see only the back of the hand. It is a good idea to put your head down close to the fingers so that you can see exactly which fingers are being used and how the strokes are actually being made. Become aware of any mistakes and awkward fingerings. This can be very revealing! Continually ask yourself if the fingers are working naturally and effortlessly. Players often do not learn to be acutely aware of the right hand until they play a piece with intricate right-hand passages such as those in Figure 3–1 from Alonso Mudarra's *Fantasia X*.[1] The players discover that if they do not concentrate on working out every detail of the right hand in such passages, they simply will not be able to play them. The right-hand awareness and precision gained from working on such pieces as *Fantasia X* should be applied to every piece.

The sense of touch in your hands and fingers is another area on which you can concentrate. Even if you are just practicing the simple two-octave C scale from Segovia's *Diatonic Major and Minor Scales* (Washington, D.C.: Columbia Music, 1953), be very aware of what happens in your left hand. Feel

---

[1]The fingering for this piece is not what Mudarra indicates in the original score, but it is by far the most popular one because it produces an unusual harplike sound. (If he were alive, Mudarra might even find it interesting because his piece is supposed to imitate a harp player.)

Figure 3–1 Alonso Mudarra, *Fantasia X*

the increase and decrease of pressure of the fingers against the thumb and fingerboard as you play each note and release it. If you have to change positions in the scale, focus on the relative tension or relaxation in the hand as you make the shift. Many technical difficulties can be solved by putting your attention on this area.

For study sessions, the sense of touch in the right hand is a good place to focus your mind—especially the feeling of the rest strokes you use to bring melody and rhythm into the foreground. In Figure 3–2, for example, study No. 16 from *25 Melodic and Progressive Studies*, Op. 60 by Carcassi (London: Schott & Co.), try feeling the distinct sensation of playing full-sounding rest strokes on each of the melody notes (stems up) in contrast to playing soft free strokes in the accompaniment.

Figure 3–2 Matteo Carcassi, Op. 60, No. 16

Feel the initial contact of each melody finger as it goes across the string, as it produces the sound, as it contacts the adjacent string, and as it releases its tension. (See Chapter 5, "Play–Relax for the Right Hand," for a description of the right-hand strokes.) Do your fingers have a good sense of where the strings are? Do you feel much scraping, grinding, or other resistance from the fingernails as you play? Or do the fingers glide across the strings like butter? How does the sound relate to the feel? How about the speed of the stroke across the string? Is it quick or slow? How does your wrist feel during this process? How about your little finger? You will make many useful discoveries about your right hand and fingers when you become aware of how they actually feel while playing.

Melody Listening carefully to the principal melodic line (or lines) in a piece is the most useful point of focus for performance because it is normally the most compelling and most important detail of a piece for both the player and listener. Being able to focus on the melody is a vital musical skill for the guitarist. The guitarist must learn how to *balance the parts* in his pieces so that the important melodic lines are louder and in the foreground while the secondary parts are softer and in the background. In order to keep the mind interested, it is good for the player to focus on all the subtle movements of that melody. Carefully follow its direction and goals, its twistings and turnings, its peaks and valleys, its colors and shadings, its hurryings and hesitations. To get the mind even more interested in the melody, it is particularly good to focus—in a relaxed way—on something subtle, such as the variations in the quality of the tone as a melody is played on different strings. For example, the mind can become totally absorbed by focusing on the delicate difference between the sweet, mellow quality of a phrase played on the second string and the same phrase repeated with a brighter quality on the first string. Thus it is good to get to know the melody intimately. You will enjoy it more and you will find that concentration will become much easier.

Here is an example of how one student learned to focus on the melodic line. At one of his lessons, the student was playing through a pavan by Luis Milán. He was making many mistakes and hesitations. His concentration was in the "intermittent" stage—not steadily focused on one thing—so it was suggested that he should easily focus on the melodic line that was most important at any given time. First he decided what the important lines were. Then he focused on bringing them out and the result was quite striking: he made practically no mistakes and no hesitations. The musical expression was better and he enjoyed himself more.

One way of helping yourself to focus on the melody when you are studying a piece is to highlight the principal line or lines with a light-colored pencil or transparent felt pen. (Circling the melody notes with pencil will also do.) For example, the first sixteen bars of the Milán piece that this student was playing could be highlighted as shown in Figure 3–3.

Figure 3–3 Luis Milán, *Pavan No. 3*

You will probably discover that the mere act of focusing your attention on the melody will help you bring it out and thus balance the parts. However, that is often not enough. The simple exercise in Figure 3–4 will give you the technical means to bring out a melody in a clear-cut way.

Figure 3–4 Exercise to bring out the top note of a chord

In most cases the melody is in the top part of a piece; therefore the exercise is designed to help you bring out that part. In this exercise, we have taken the four-note C chord at the start of the pavan in Figure 3–3 as our example because it is typical of the chords in that piece as well as in many others. The basic idea is to play the block chord as an arpeggio with the three lower notes played very softly and the E melody note on top (with accent) played loudly. Be sure to stroke lightly with the thumb. At first the arpeggio is played slowly in eighth note rhythm and then, when you are able to bring out the top note more than the others, you increase the speed of the arpeggio to sixteenths, then thirty-seconds, and finally you play the chord as a block. The final unarpeggiated rendition of the chord should clearly bring out the melody note on the top. The exercise can be reversed and the low C bass note can be emphasized with the thumb while the three upper notes are played softly with the fingers. When you are able to bring out the top or the bass at will, then use the technique to bring out the various highlighted melody lines in Figure 3–3.

Rhythm   Another good area for mental focus is the rhythmical pulse of the music. Listen to the pulse carefully and feel it with your whole body. Enjoy the rhythm and let your body move freely with it. If the spirit moves you and you have a recording of your piece or can hear it in your head, then stand up and move with the rhythm by swinging your arms, walking around the room, or even dancing to it. Let yourself go, have fun with it, and do not mind if you are not as graceful as a ballet artist. The point is simply to focus your entire attention on the rhythm. You will find that involving the whole body will help you do that. It will also help you discover new ways of expressing the music.[2] To begin with, you can focus on the obvious level of the strong metric pulses of your piece. For example, you could put your mind on the first and fourth beats of each measure of a $\frac{6}{8}$ gigue by J.S. Bach. Giving yourself such a "ride on the rhythm" is very good for developing the sense of steady pulse that is necessary for musical playing. When you can focus clearly on the obvious rhythmic elements, then you can turn your attention to the more subtle levels, such as the upbeats, syncopations, and counter-rhythms in your piece. Using rhythm as a focal point is usually best for practice sessions since rhythm usually takes a back seat to melody in performances.

Harmony and Formal Structure   Another point on which to focus during study time is the harmony of your pieces. You can direct your attention to the alternation of tension and relaxation in the harmonic flow and to the way in which the harmonies move toward certain goals within a phrase or a section. For example, you can listen to and feel the tension and resolution of dominant seventh chords (or other dominant function chords) as they move to their tonics at phrase and section endings.

You can use your intellect to focus on the formal structure of your pieces. Listen carefully to the places where the principal sections of the music begin and end. Pay attention to the key changes. Listen for the principal and secondary climaxes. Listen for the contrasts and relationships between the various parts of the music. In short, let your mind follow the way in which the whole piece fits together. (See Chapter 9, "Analyze the Music," for more on harmonic and structural hearing and analysis.)

Inner Meaning   In this discussion of different points of musical concentration, we have moved from the outer physical level of the finger movements to the inner, more subtle level of the intellect. All these areas deserve your attention at one time or another. However, the even more subtle level of *inner meaning* in the music is more important than the rest. Inner meaning is a dif-

---

[2]For more on how to use body movements to help discover musical expression see Alexandra Pierce, "Characterizing Movement," Newsletter No. 6 of the *Institute for Holistic Education*, Spring 1980.

ficult term to define because it cannot be adequately expressed in words. It is the sum of all the refined emotions and spiritual qualities that the artist finds in his study of a piece and then expresses in his best performances. Every musician who aspires to true artistry discovers that this inner meaning is what he ultimately wants to focus his mind on because it gives the greatest joy to himself and his listeners. This highly refined inner meaning of music, as the great cellist Pablo Casals has said, is its most important aspect.

If a musician can focus on and project that subtlest level of music in his public playing, then he has set up the conditions so that he and his audience can actually go beyond that level and experience music in its purest and most enjoyable form. Naturally it takes time to refine yourself and your playing to the point where you are sensitive enough to focus clearly on this delicate level, but it is the most rewarding pursuit in music.

It is not possible either in practice or performance to force yourself to focus on the inner meaning of the music. First you must master the skill of natural concentration and gain command over all the more obvious aspects of the music. Then, when you play, you learn to let go and *allow* the inner meaning to come out. If you spend enough time studying the music and getting to know it intimately—careful listening to yourself is most important in this regard—then its deep inner nature will eventually reveal itself to you. Not infrequently it will come as a surprise. While you are playing a piece you know very well, you may suddenly pop into the state of dynamically relaxed concentration and the inner meaning of the music will express itself perfectly with virtually no effort on your part.

NATURAL CONCENTRATION: THE PHYSIOLOGICAL APPROACH

> *When hungry, eat; when tired, sleep.*
>
> Zen Saying

We have explored the *psychological* approach to improving concentration in some detail. That approach can be very fruitful by itself, but you can improve concentration even more by using the *physiological* approach as well. If the mind wanders too much, it is often the physiology that needs attention. Physiologically speaking, the main obstacles to natural concentration are stress, fatigue, and impurities in the body, particularly in the nervous system. Most of these obstacles can be removed by the approaches described in Chapter 2. Some of those approaches are discussed in more depth here; some are simply mentioned again for emphasis.

Some physiological ways of improving concentration are as follows:

1. Set up a regular routine.
2. When tired, sleep.
3. When hungry, eat.
4. Do physical exercise.
5. Learn to breathe properly.
6. Take it easy.

Set Up a Regular Routine

Being regular in your habits is very good for your concentration. A regular rhythm of going to bed, getting up, eating, working, and playing makes your mind clear and your life musical. Everyone knows the result of poor rhythm when playing music: The music comes out disjointed and is unpleasant to play or hear. The same applies to your daily routine: If it is not regular, then concentration is difficult and your activities are disjointed. Thus it is very helpful to establish some kind of organized daily routine—at least for your practicing. A practice schedule will help you to focus your mind and accomplish your goals. (See Chapter 7, "Set Up a Regular Practice Schedule.")

When Tired, Sleep

How well were you able to concentrate on your guitar studying today? Ask yourself this question and relate it to how well you slept last night. There is usually a strong correlation, although it is not always noticed. Concentration is definitely better if you have slept just the right amount of time. Too little or too much sleep results in scattered attention. In this matter of rest, it is good to listen to what your body is telling you. If it is urging "sleep!", then it is best to pay attention. One normally listens to the obvious requests from one's body but tends to ignore the subtle hints. When you look for the subtle messages, then you will make some interesting discoveries. You may find, for example, that if you get to bed one hour earlier—say, 11 P.M. instead of midnight—then you feel much better in the morning and your concentration is more powerful.

When Hungry, Eat

A few changes in your eating habits can bring great improvement in your ability to concentrate. The type, combination, quantity, and quality of the food you eat all have an effect on your mental clarity. It is difficult to say exactly what will be the best diet for a given person since everyone is so different.

The only really useful advice about diet is that you should eat what agrees with you and your guitar playing. In other words, eat pure, high-quality food and listen to what your mind and body say about it. If your mind is not clear with your present eating habits, then you might try altering your diet in a gradual way to include foods that do make it alert and powerful. Many musicians find that their concentration is best with a varied diet of fruit, nuts, vegetables, grains, dairy products, fish, and poultry and a limited consumption of red meat, fat, and sugar. Alcohol, caffeine, tobacco, and other stimulants, if used, should be used in moderation because they can adversely affect concentration.

One of the biggest factors in concentration is the quantity of food eaten. Eating too much or too little dulls the mind and weakens the body. Generally speaking, people in the affluent Western cultures tend to eat too much. The Russian-born pianist Vladimir Horowitz has refused to play evening concerts because too many people in his audiences eat a heavy meal beforehand and fall asleep during his performances—and his playing is not dull! Horowitz himself is an advocate of light eating—especially before performances. He has found that light eating tends to sharpen concentration.

Other well-known artists, such as Andrés Segovia and the violinist Yehudi Menuhin, also eat little or nothing for the one or two meals before they play a concert. With only a small quantity of food or none at all to digest, most of their energy can be focused on the music. I have tried this approach before my own performances and have found that it definitely improves my concentration. Practicing is also better if I do not eat too much beforehand.

When I found that I experienced better concentration by eating lightly before my concerts, I decided to try an extended experiment. A few weeks prior to a concert, I decided that I wanted to do everything possible to make it a big success. Because I felt that my concentration could be better, I thought it would be worthwhile to try following the Zen advice to eat only when really hungry. So I cut down on excess eating and, for a change, I let the subtle hints from my body be my guide. I paid attention when my stomach said that it had enough and I ignored "false hunger" pangs. I ended up eating much smaller amounts of foods than those to which I was accustomed. I drank somewhat more liquids and ate only small quantities of the richer, heavier foods.

The results of the experiment were excellent. After a few days of lighter eating I could focus my mind a great deal better. In the three practice concerts and the real one, my mind was very clear and I made very few mistakes. Concentration was effortless and natural and, best of all, I was able to enjoy playing much more. I am not suggesting that everyone should try my experiment. After all, if you like to eat, the above ideas may seem very unappealing. But, if you are having difficulty concentrating, you might want to do your own experiment in which you eat only when really hungry—even if only for a few days.

Do Physical Exercise

We have already discussed the value of physical exercise and yoga postures in Chapter 2, so we will only say here that they will help you to have a clear mind if practiced regularly. A healthy, flexible body is the basis for a clear mind.

Learn to Breathe Properly

How you breathe has a considerable influence on your concentration. In the yoga literature, mind and breath are said to be intimately connected to one another.[3] Just a bit of self-observation will bear this out. When your breathing is very fine and regular (sometimes almost imperceptible), the mind tends to be clear and concentrated; when it is heavy and/or irregular, the mind tends to be muddy and diffused. So it is good to be aware of your breathing habits and be willing to change them if necessary.

To show how mind and breath are connected, let us look at the case of a young guitar student. He had a problem with excess muscular tension and some difficulty in concentration when he performed in front of an audience. He also breathed very heavily and irregularly while playing—which was quite distracting. He was simply unaware of his heavy breathing until it was pointed out to him. He did not stop this panting immediately, but as he became more aware of it he gradually began to breathe more easily and naturally. It was interesting to see that his playing became more natural and less tense as his breathing became lighter and more regular. His concentration also improved in the process and he made fewer mistakes in his subsequent student recitals. Now he has dropped the heavy breathing altogether and plays quite well.

Yogic Breathing Exercises The subject of how to breathe properly is somewhat involved, but the basic ideas are easy to understand. In order for your body to function properly, it is important to get plenty of fresh air into your system and get stale air out. Thus efficient breathing is a subject worth pursuing. In fact, in the yoga system of personal development, breathing is considered so important that it has been made into a science with numerous exercises and techniques.[4] We will just mention a few aspects of breathing here.

[3]*How to Know God: The Yoga Sutras of Patanjali*, trans. Swami Prabhavananda and Christopher Isherwood (New York: New American Library, 1969), section I, 31, 34 and section II, 49–51. See also Peter Hamel, *Through Music to the Self* (Boulder, Colo.: Shambhala Publications, 1978), p. 175ff.

[4]Swami Vishnudevananda, *The Complete Illustrated Book of Yoga* (New York: Pocket Books, 1972), chapter 8.

First let's look briefly at good breathing habits. How you breathe depends on the activity you are doing. For physical exercise or for cleaning out the lungs the breath should be regular and deep—but not labored. For concentration on guitar playing the breathing should be regular and very fine. The movement of the diaphragm is important in this process. In order to ensure that you breathe deeply and completely, the diaphragm should be lowered when you inhale. A simple way to do this is to let your lower abdomen "drop" before inhalation and then allow the lungs to be filled up with air from the bottom up. This is the way yogis, top athletes, and good singers breathe. It may take some time for diaphragm breathing to become automatic, but it is worth the time since it more completely oxygenates the brain and improves concentration. Remember not to force this new way of breathing on yourself. Do it as naturally as possible.

One of the simplest ways to cultivate more regular breathing is to breathe in time with your footsteps when you go for a walk. For example, inhale slowly and deeply for eight steps. Then exhale slowly and completely for another eight. Doing this for five or ten minutes at a time is healthy and should make you feel good. It is an excellent way to clear your head before a concert. Incidentally, it will also help to improve your sense of rhythm.

Another simple approach to improving your breathing and clearing your mind is to sit down, take a series of ten or fifteen slow, deep breaths and then hang your head between your legs. This has a soothing effect on your nerves and is therefore a good thing to do about fifteen minutes before playing a concert—especially if you have a bit of stage fright.

Most people do not realize that they breathe through only one nostril for extended periods of time. The yogis say that, if you breathe too long through only one nostril (more than a few hours), it usually means that there is some imbalance in your system that will disturb mental clarity or physical health. In order to prevent such imbalances and increase mental clarity, the yogis recommend *alternate nostril breathing* which is done as follows: Assume a comfortable, upright sitting position and close the left nostril with the second and third fingers of the right hand. Then breathe out through the right nostril very slowly and silently. After that, breathe in through the right nostril in the same way. Then place the thumb on the right nostril, uncover the left nostril and breathe out of it. Following that, breathe in through the left nostril and then start the cycle over again. The breathing should be deep, but very slow and silent with no straining. As previously mentioned, the breathing should be done from the abdomen, that is, let the abdomen drop and fill the lungs from the bottom up.

This is an excellent exercise to do for about five or ten minutes before a performance. It not only clears and calms the mind, but it also takes your attention away from worrying about the performance—particularly if you count each breath.

Take It Easy

For guitar playing it is best to take a relaxed approach and avoid unnecessary strain on your nerves. Allow yourself some silent time during the day when you do nothing. Take things as they come and do not race around trying to do more than you can comfortably handle. This does not mean that you should never put yourself in challenging situations, but it is not good to subject yourself constantly to stressful overloads. Such overloads frequently cause loss of concentration. If you take it easy—but not too easy—during your study time and during the day's activities, then concentration will not require much effort.

SUMMARY

The ability to concentrate in a relaxed but powerful way is a fundamental skill for successful guitar study and performance. With good concentration, little time and energy is wasted in practice and fewer mistakes and lapses occur in performance. Everyone already has the ability to concentrate to some extent; all one needs to do is sharpen that ability with simple methods. Mind-settling techniques are a good preparation for concentration because they reduce excess mental activity.

There are at least four stages of concentration: diffused, intermittent, one-pointed, and dynamically relaxed. The dynamically relaxed stage is the highest one. In this stage you can focus sharply on one thing and simultaneously maintain broad awareness of yourself and your surroundings. The natural concentration technique is a simple but powerful *psychological* approach to dynamically relaxed concentration. It consists of developing the habit of focusing your mind in a relaxed way on one attractive detail of your playing at a time. If your mind wanders, you simply bring it back gently. Force does not work. On the other hand, you cannot just let the mind wander at will. Focus the mind just enough—not too much, not too little.

You can use the natural concentration technique to focus on various technical and musical points in guitar study and performance. In performance, the main melodic line is normally the most useful point. However, as you become more proficient in concentration and more mature in musicianship, the inner meaning of the music will eventually become your prime focus.

There are several *physiological* ways of improving your concentration that are very effective: a regular routine, sufficient rest, a good diet, physical exercise, proper breathing, and taking it easy.

When you have mastered the skill of natural concentration and can focus clearly on whatever you want, you will be well-prepared to learn how to achieve the state of dynamic relaxation in all aspects of guitar technique. Your sharpened awareness will help you to know when you have found the proper balance of tension and relaxation required for that desirable state. The state of dynamic relaxation is so important to natural guitar playing that the next two chapters are devoted to ways that will help you develop it.

4.

Dynamic Relaxation

balance the opposites
in sitting and hand positions

Whatever the art you may wish to
learn . . . there is one thing that every good
teacher will always say: Learn to combine
relaxation with activity . . . .

Aldous Huxley, *The Art of Seeing*

The Tao of the sage is work without effort.

Lao Tzu, *Tao Te Ching*

THE BALANCE OF OPPOSITES

In order to understand the state of dynamic relaxation, consider the playing of the master guitarists. How does a great artist make playing look "so easy that it appears he is doing nothing"? There are a number of things the artist needs to study in order to accomplish that goal. In the last two chapters, we discussed two areas that are important for effortless playing: increased awareness and the ability to concentrate. The fine artist has developed his awareness and concentration to a high degree and therefore is able to discover all the subtle ways of playing beautifully with minimum effort. Thus he does not have to work so hard in performance. If an artist did have to work hard to play every piece, he would probably be exhausted before the end of a concert.

As an artist sharpens his perceptions, he becomes aware of one of the most important elements of music making: the need to *balance opposites.* You probably recall from Chapter 1 that some of the most ancient teachings of the world emphasize the value of this balancing process. They state clearly that the greatest success in any undertaking comes to those who have put the various tendencies in their lives into balance. This idea certainly applies to the finest and most successful musicians.

One of the main reasons why the great artists of the guitar can play effortlessly is that they have achieved a finely tuned balance of opposites in their lives and their playing. Everything the artist does with his mind and body needs to be balanced; all extremes must be avoided. The balance between tension and relaxation, doing too much and doing too little, must be established. With respect to sitting and hand positions, this means finding the proper balance of forces between opposing muscle groups and between muscles and gravity. When the balance has been found, no energy will be wasted in maintaining the positions. In accordance with the principle of least action, the tension should be the minimum amount needed to produce the desired result.

With respect to playing movements, balancing the opposites means that the tension used to press the strings with the left hand or make the strokes with the right hand should not be too much or too little. Also there should be a relaxation, however slight, after (or sometimes during) each movement of the arms, hands, and fingers to balance the tension of that movement. When tension and relaxation alternate in a balanced way, the movements of playing tend to flow effortlessly. (See Chapter 5.)

The balancing of opposites, as we saw in the last chapter, can also be extended to the area of concentration so that the player focuses his mind on his playing to just the right degree—not too much, not too little. A balance must also be found in the practice room. A fine artist knows that he must work just the right amount. Overpracticing is just as harmful as under-practicing. Further, there should be a balance of opposites in the interpretation of the music. (See Chapter 9.) Finally, the great artist will seek balance in every aspect of his life. If there is no balance in his life and his playing, the artist will be either too relaxed or too tight when he performs. Then both he and the music suffer. If the balance is there, everything goes well.

The commonly held idea that playing should be totally relaxed is not a balanced approach. Both sitting and playing definitely require a certain degree of tension.[1] Too much relaxation tends to produce a disorderly sitting position and imprecise movements. One piano teacher illustrates this point graphically. First he sits at the keyboard and announces that he is going to relax. Then he proceeds to collapse in a heap on the floor! From this example it should be clear that total relaxation is not the answer for masterful playing. Instead, tension and relaxation should be balanced and should come in just the right amounts at the right times and places.

Dynamic Relaxation

When there is a dynamic balance between the opposites of action and rest, tension and relaxation, then a perfectly poised state of mind and body is created. This is a state that the most successful people in music and other fields are consciously or unconsciously seeking. The twentieth-century writer Aldous Huxley coined the expression "dynamic relaxation" to describe this state. Others have termed it "work without effort," "action in inaction," or "stillness in movement." This paradoxical state is a middle way wherein you do only what is necessary to produce a desired result—no more, no less. You are dynamically involved in activity and yet remain perfectly relaxed.

When a guitarist achieves complete dynamic relaxation—which happens fairly often among fine artists—then playing seems to go by itself. This result is what psychologists call "flow" or a "peak experience."[2] You feel that

[1]Otto Szende and Mihaly Nemessuri, *The Physiology of Violin Playing* (London: Collet's Publishers, 1971), p. 25.

[2]Abraham Maslow, *Toward a Psychology of Being* (New York: Van Nostrand Co., 1968), p. 89.

you are in perfect rhythm with the pulse of the music. Little effort is involved and the act of playing is intensely enjoyable, even ecstatic. Guitarists in this state sometimes say that they feel so good that it is like floating one foot off the ground. They report that everything seems to go right in their playing. Just about everyone has experienced this beautiful, natural state at some time in music, dancing, sports, walking through the woods, or even driving a car. When a musician has such an experience, it is a joy not only for himself but also for his audience.

Dynamic relaxation produces musical results because, when you are playing the guitar in that state, you are playing in harmony with natural principles. Nature is supporting your playing in every possible way. Since you are using little effort to play, you are in accord with the principle of least action or minimum effort. Also, since tension and relaxation are in balance, you are in accord with the principle of dynamic equilibrium. Other natural principles such as gravity and leverage support you as well.

Cultivating Dynamic Relaxation

At first, dynamic relaxation may seem to be rather elusive. It often appears to be an ability that fine guitarists have simply inherited and that is not accessible to less fortunate mortals. However, although some players may be able to experience that state more readily than others, it is possible for everyone to have it if they are patient and cultivate it properly. In his book *The Art of Seeing*, Aldous Huxley makes an important point about dynamic relaxation. He says that it is "that state of the body which is associated with normal and natural functioning."[3] Thus, the guitarist should not think that dynamic relaxation is some strange, unattainable state that only certain people achieve. It is simply the normal state in which we should always be. Many of us need to relearn how to let our minds and bodies function normally and naturally so that we can play the guitar with ease. It is good to do whatever we can to promote this natural state of dynamic relaxation. As Aldous Huxley says

> Whatever the art you may wish to learn—whether it be acrobatics or violin playing, mental prayer or golf, acting, singing, dancing, or what you will—there is one thing that every good teacher will always say: Learn to combine relaxation with activity; learn to do what you have to do without strain; work hard, but never under tension.[4]

Summarizing what we have already said about dynamic relaxation for the guitar, it means such things as

---

[3] Aldous Huxley, *The Art of Seeing* (New York: Harper & Brothers, 1942), p. 37.
[4] Ibid., pp. 36–37.

1. using just the right amount of left-hand finger pressure—no more, no less,

2. making right-hand strokes with just enough tension—not too much, not too little,

3. relaxing the arms, hands, and fingers to compensate for the playing movements,

4. balancing the body and using just the right amount of energy to maintain the sitting position—no more, no less,

5. concentrating your mind on your performance only as much as necessary to play well, and

6. balancing the opposites in your interpretations.

Let It Happen

If you have not yet experienced dynamic relaxation in your playing, then the ideas in this chapter and the next will help you set up the conditions for it to happen. At first, the majority of players will need to do some deliberate study of how to balance tension and relaxation in body and mind. But, after a certain amount of work on this, it will be necessary to let go of conscious study and *allow* dynamic relaxation to happen. Do not try too hard to achieve dynamic relaxation because it is a natural state that cannot be forced. Give the natural intelligence of the body a chance to produce the dynamically relaxed state automatically. It may surprise you to see how much it can do without much help from your conscious mind.

If you have already experienced some taste of dynamic relaxation, then you will find that the systematic techniques described here will allow it to be a more *regular* experience instead of a haphazard one. The techniques should also deepen the experience for you. The long-range results of cultivating dynamic relaxation are effortless guitar technique and improved musical interpretation. But the most satisfying result is that you have the joy of feeling that you are "one foot off the ground." Now let's explore the practical application of dynamic relaxation to the sitting position.

SITTING POSITION

Finding a Good Position

Before you can play with ease, you must establish a good sitting position. In spite of what people may tell you, it makes a good deal of difference how you sit. It is not a trivial matter. The guitarist should have a regal, but not arrogant bearing in his sitting position to fit the important role he has in making good music. When most fine players perform, their sitting positions are balanced and "dynamically relaxed." They avoid extremes of all kinds. They look natural and comfortable with the instrument. They give a sense of steadiness without rigidity, of flexibility without flaccidness. In such a position, the player is like a healthy tree. His torso, seat, legs, and feet are stable like the trunk and roots of the tree while his head, arms, hands, and fingers are flexible like the branches and leaves that can give in the wind. Thus the player presents an appealing picture of "action in repose."

There is no one right way of sitting, but most of the finer players use similar positions for concert work. What is described here is a position that is used by some of the best players who have studied with Andrés Segovia. This position is both technically good and aesthetically appealing. As described below, it is good for most players, but some changes may be necessary to adapt it and make it natural for players with certain physical characteristics, such as unusually long arms, legs, or torso. Of course there are alternative sitting positions that may be better for some players. For example, some concert players who put the left foot on the stool in the usual manner place the upper bout of the instrument instead of the waist on the left thigh. Others put the right foot or even both feet on the footstool instead of the more customary left foot. Some guitarists have even dispensed with a footstool altogether and sit with both feet on the floor; they support the guitar on a special cushion that straps to the left leg.[5] The interested player can try out these seating options if he so desires, but we will limit our discussion to one position that has been proven to be effective by many players.

Dynamically Relaxed Sitting

With a bit of familiarity, the dynamically relaxed way of sitting will feel quite natural. When done properly, it requires little or no effort to maintain. The key to the position is balancing the various muscle forces involved. A certain amount of experimentation is necessary to find the best way of adjusting the body for each individual.

Taking up the position can be broken down into several steps. While going through these steps, keep in mind that the photographs here give static views of what is a dynamically balanced situation, so they must be taken as only an approximate guide to the actual position. Now sit well toward the front of an armless chair with your back straight. Relax and let your arms and neck hang loosely for a few moments as in Figure 4–1. Closing your eyes will relax you even more. It also helps to shake the arms and shoulders to make sure that they are at a low level of tension. The shoulders should not be hunched or tilted. Now, keeping your back straight and bending from the waist, lean forward and backward and from one side to the other. This will help you find the balance point of your sitting position.

[5]This cushion is currently available from Guitar Works, P.O. Box 8085-S, Rockville, MD. 20856.

Figure 4–1 Sitting position: relaxing without guitar

Figure 4–2 Sitting position: adjusting position without guitar

Now lift your head up as in Figure 4–2. To achieve a comfortable straightness of the spine, imagine your head being held up by a string, not rigidly, but rather like a puppet.[6] Make sure you have found your center of balance so that you are using the least amount of energy to maintain your position. You should feel a strong center of gravity where you sit; you should be able to move the upper part of your body in any direction with ease and still feel rooted in that center of gravity. The legs should also be relatively free to move. The position should be stable and flexible at the same time. If it requires too much effort to maintain and is not comfortable, then make whatever changes are necessary. Remember that an uncomfortable, unbalanced position makes it difficult to make good music.

The Footstool

Now put the footstool (the adjustable type is best) directly in front of your left foot and place the foot on it (Figure 4–2). Make a rough adjustment of the height of the stool for your comfort. If it is too high, you may feel as though you are being pushed backward and that your left leg is being cramped; if it is

---

[6]See Alexandra Pierce, "Body and Performance," *Piano Quarterly* (Spring 1974), 4.

too low, then you may feel that you are falling forward. Find the height of the stool that is right for you (usually somewhere between five and eight inches off the floor, depending on the length of your legs and the height of the chair). Now place the lower right leg under the chair and balance it easily on the ball of the foot as in Figures 4–2, 4–3, and 4–4. Again check to see if your sitting position feels balanced and centered.

Holding the Guitar

At this point, pick up the guitar and place it gently on the left thigh (Figure 4–3). *Receive* the guitar easily rather than clutching at it. Again make sure the spine is straight, then lean forward from the waist slightly and meet the guitar (Figure 4–4).

Figure 4–3 Sitting position: front view with the guitar

Figure 4–4 Sitting position: side view with guitar

Notice that the guitar leans slightly back toward you and balances your forward leaning. The guitar is then supported by the left thigh, the right thigh, the chest, and the right forearm. Now it is appropriate to make a further adjustment to the footstool so that the neck of the guitar is at about a thirty-five degree angle with respect to the floor. The head of the guitar will be approximately at ear level. Part of this adjustment can be made by raising or lowering the right thigh since the lower bout of the guitar is sitting on it. The head of the guitar should not be too high because then the left arm will be so high in lower fingerboard positions that the blood circulation will be impaired. It is also quite awkward to make descending shifts up a steep incline. If the head of the guitar is too low, then it becomes awkward for the left hand to play in the upper fingerboard positions and the right arm becomes cramped because it is too high and does not get the best circulation.

There is another subtle adjustment to be made with the left leg. Many players let the leg lean to the left in an unbalanced way, which can cause back pain and technical problems. It is better to have the leg turned slightly inward. For this, it may be necessary to place the footstool somewhat more to the left. Then let the left knee lean inward toward the right leg. It is important not to hold the leg in this position with muscular force, as many players unconsciously do, because it is an unnecessary source of tension. If the leg is allowed to lean inward slightly, it normally will require no effort to support it. Also, for the sake of aesthetic appearance, it is good to keep the legs reasonably close together; in fact, it usually works out well to have both legs turned slightly inward. The composer Igor Stravinsky said that one of the important things not taught in music schools is that violinists should not sit with legs wide apart because it is so unattractive. Guitarists take note!

The guitar should be embraced gently, like a close friend. It should not be crushed up against oneself, but rather allowed to breathe and vibrate freely with full resonance. In Figure 4–4 you can see that only the top edge of the guitar touches the chest, not the entire back of the instrument. It is easy to demonstrate that, if you hold the back of the guitar tightly against the chest, the sound vibrations are damped and thus the sound is weaker. Only the relaxed weight of the right forearm is necessary to keep the guitar from falling off your lap; there need be no extra pressing of the instrument with the right arm. Such pressure is a waste of energy and creates unneeded tension. This pressure may also force the guitar to be pulled in too much to the right, which means that the fingerboard would be pushed too far forward. This causes problems of cramping for the right arm and hand as well as an awkward position for the left hand. It is better to have the face of the guitar either parallel to your chest or even turned slightly to the left. That allows the left hand to operate in a more relaxed way.

You need have no concern about the guitar slipping out of your grip if you are sitting properly. If you feel a need to hold the guitar very tightly, even though you seem to be sitting properly, it may be that you are overly anxious about your playing and are trying to *control* it too much. This difficulty may be due to a faulty right-hand technique. Many players feel that they will not be able to control the notes with the right-hand fingers if they do not hold the hand rigidly and press the guitar tightly against them with the forearm. Such problems usually disappear when the player stops trying so hard and learns how to use the right hand in a natural way. Remember that the fingers of the right hand should do most of the playing; the arm and hand should just give quiet support to the fingers and do not need to be held rigidly in place. Some firmness of the arm and hand is all that is necessary.

Sitting Straight

The significance of sitting with the spine straight and the chest out should be emphasized for several reasons. For one thing, sitting straight requires less effort than slumping. When you are slumped over, you have to fight gravity because it pulls the body down in many places; however, when you are sitting straight, gravity only pulls the body down along the axis of the spine. Another reason is that, when the spine is straight, the chest is more expanded and it is much easier to breathe properly. When the breathing is right, the mind is more alert and musical phrasing comes more naturally. The guitarist who is hunched over his instrument with his head hanging down and his nose following every move of the left hand cannot breathe properly. Thus he becomes tense and has technical difficulties. A further reason for sitting straight is that, if the spine is bent or twisted very much, the many nerves coming from it to the hands and other parts of the body get pinched. That can cause weakening of the muscles, to say nothing of backaches. The resulting physical discomfort is distracting and consequently leads to mistakes in performing. Slouching or excessive twisting of the spine can also have the effect of hindering the free flow of nerve energy between the body and the brain. This can inhibit mental clarity as well as bodily functions.[7]

The sitting position has a strong effect on your attitude toward playing the guitar for other people. A balanced, upright, "royal" position in which you lean slightly forward both looks and feels good. It tends to give you more confidence and less concern about "controlling" the instrument. On the other hand, hunching yourself over the guitar and trying to control every note makes playing an unnecessary struggle. It tends to produce a feeling of tension and a lack of confidence and does not make a good impression on audiences. However, in the "royal" position, the player is relaxed and open like a king who looks quietly down on his subjects—the fingers—as they go about their work. The player, much like the king, is not concerned about every little movement of the fingers, but rather is focused on the overall flow of the music. In such a dynamically relaxed position, playing becomes much easier. From the audience's point of view, the player will appear completely in charge of the situation.

[7]See Swami Vishnudevananda, *The Complete Illustrated Book of Yoga* (New York: Pocket Books, 1972), p. 69.

Now that you have a picture of dynamically relaxed sitting, let's discuss how you can achieve that state in your hand positions.

BALANCING THE RIGHT HAND

Natural Position

As in other aspects of guitar playing, the dynamically relaxed approach to the right-hand position avoids extremes. The position should look and feel as natural and balanced as possible. It should not involve bizarre twisting, bending, or excess tension. Such a position is based on the normal way you use your hand every day, that is, grasping or gripping various items. A good example of normal use is the way you grip the handle of your guitar case when you carry it. The fingers curl around the handle and the wrist is straight with respect to the forearm. People tend to prefer this position because it gives the greatest muscle balance and leverage and thus requires the least effort. All you have to do to prove to yourself that this is the strongest position is to try carrying the guitar case with the wrist bent in any direction away from the straight position. The relative weakness and discomfort should be immediately apparent.

You can apply the basic idea of the natural, straight-wristed grip to the right-hand position of the guitar. Let's start by placing the upper part of the right forearm on the upper bout of the guitar. Then make a fist as in Figure 4–5. Do it as if you are gripping the handle of your guitar case. Figure 4–6 shows the same thing without the guitar.

Figure 4–5 Right-hand position: side view of fist with guitar

Figure 4–6 Right-hand position: side view of fist without guitar

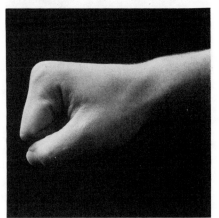

Notice that when you make a fist without thinking about it too much, you do not bend the wrist and strength is maximum. Notice also that the fingers are very strong in the curled position. However, for guitar playing it does not work well to hold the fingers in such a tightly curled way. Thus we will just use the fist as a natural starting point and then modify it somewhat so that the hand forms a natural position for playing. First, allow the fist to open easily so that the fingers retain a moderate, natural curvature—not too much, not too little—and then put the thumb on the fourth string and the index, middle, and ring fingers on the first three strings as in Figure 4–7. Figure 4–8 shows the position without the guitar from the side. Figure 4–9 shows another view. Notice the gentle, natural curvature of the fingers and the only slightly bent wrist. This position should not be interpreted too rigidly. Although extremes should be avoided, some bending of the wrist may be useful. For example, some players may find that the hand will work better if the wrist is bent slightly to the right; others will find it most comfortable to have a slightly greater arch in the wrist, that is, the hand will bend down somewhat toward the fingerboard.

Figure 4–7 Right-hand position: front view of typical position with guitar

Figure 4–8 Right-hand position: side view of typical position without guitar

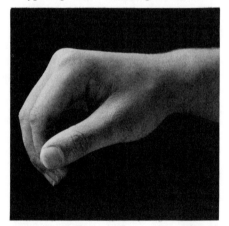

Contrary to what is often said, it is not always appropriate to line up the knuckles of the right hand exactly parallel with the strings; the angle of the knuckles in relation to the strings should be adjusted for each person according to the shape of the nails, length of the forearm, and so on. Since most guitarists' fingernails work best when the strokes are made off the left-hand side, the most comfortable position is usually one that is slightly angled to the left as in Figure 4–10.

Figure 4–9 Right-hand position: side view of typical position with guitar

Figure 4–10 Right-hand position: front view showing angle of knuckles to strings

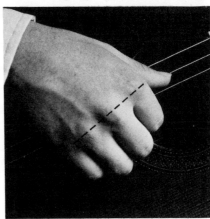

Stacking

A point that is often overlooked in the hand position is that the fingers tend to work best if, as in the fist, they are stacked very close to each other instead of being separated. In fact, a great deal of the time they can actually touch each other, particularly at the tips. This close-knit operation of the fingers has many advantages. First, it is a natural, relaxed position. When most guitarists hold the hand as in Figure 4–8, the fingers naturally tend to stack together. The fingers tend to be stronger in this position since there is no excess tension. Second, if the fingers are stacked close together at the tips, then it is easy to "plant" (that is, prepare) them accurately as a single unit on the strings before playing arpeggios or chords (see Chapter 5, "Planting the Fingers"). Third, stacked fingers make it easier to play all the notes of a block chord simultaneously. When you try to play block chords with unstacked fingers, the tendency is to inadvertently arpeggiate them. Finally, stacked fingers allow the player to focus his energy on the right hand in exactly the way he wants so that he has more control over musical expression.

Thumb Position

The right-hand thumb position often is a source of problems for the player; therefore, it requires some special consideration. Each player must determine the best position for his thumb, depending on its length, nail shape, and flexibility. Always keep in mind that whatever thumb position is finally chosen, it should not take the hand very far from the dynamically relaxed position we have described. The typical relationship between the thumb and fingers is illustrated in Figure 4–11, where the thumb and fingers are placed on one string.

Figure 4–11 Right-hand fingers on one string

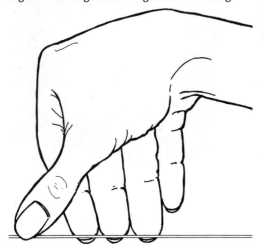

Note that the thumb is somewhat to the left of the fingers so that thumb and fingers do not get tangled up with each other. Players with long or short thumbs will usually need to vary the position slightly. The distance between the thumb and fingers will tend to be greater if the thumb is longer and less if the thumb is shorter. It is usually best to have a moderate distance between them. Then there is enough room for the thumb to operate independently and yet be close enough to the fingers so that the thumb and fingers can work together as a relaxed, compact unit.

For most playing, the wrist should not be too high or too low—that is, it should be bent only slightly—or it will hinder the efficient use of the thumb. If the wrist is too high, then neither the thumb nor the fingers will work very well because the tendons in the wrist will be strained. If the wrist is too low, then the thumb will be too far from the fingers and will not work so well with them; also the thumbnail will not be in the best position to produce a good tone. The appropriate height for the wrist varies with the player but usually falls in the range of four to five inches measured perpendicularly from the soundboard to the top of the wrist. A certain amount of experimentation is necessary to determine the normal wrist height for each player. It should go without saying that the wrist height may sometimes have to deviate from the normal according to the technique required by the music. (See, for example, the technique described in "Right-Hand Speed" in Chapter 5.)

Common Right-Hand Problems

Now let's consider the most common problems that students have with the right-hand position. They all result from inappropriate tension and/or extreme positions of the wrist or fingers. These positions deviate too far from the dynamically relaxed model just described. They are not comfortable and do not result in good playing. Some of the common difficulties as you would see them from the sitting position described in this chapter are:

1. bending the wrist too far to the right and extending the thumb too far to the left
2. having too much arch in the wrist, that is, holding it too high above the fingerboard
3. separating the fingers from each other, especially at the tips
4. curling up the fingers too much
5. straightening out the fingers too much
6. pressing the forearm too hard against the instrument

These extreme positions usually cause muscle cramps, aching tendons, lack of control of the right-hand strokes, and poor tone quality. Such extremes should be avoided. It is good to check your position for any of these distortions or excess tensions. This can be done by using a mirror. Another way to check is to place the guitar face up on your lap, then put the hand in position and look at it carefully.

If you avoid the extremes of position and apply the ideas we have discussed, you should be able to find a dynamically relaxed position for the right hand. Such a position should not be difficult to find because it is based on the typical, natural way we use our hand when we want to grip something. The exact details of how to position the hand will vary slightly with each individual; thus, the intelligent player will not try to copy the position exactly as described or as shown in the photographs but rather will adapt it to the special configuration of his own hand. Keep in mind that the position should feel comfortable when you play, look relaxed and graceful, and bring you good musical results.

BALANCING THE LEFT HAND

Natural Position

Many players experience considerable left-hand fatigue and usually blame it on "lack of strength." Although it is true that the left hand must be stronger than the right, brute strength is not required. Far more important is to find efficient ways of positioning and using the hand. It must be used with "more skill than strength" as Fernando Sor would say. Thus the basic position of the left hand, like that of the right, should be a balanced, dynamically relaxed one that uses the minimum energy and yet gives the hand its greatest power. Also like the right hand, the left hand should feel comfortable and look graceful. For those reasons, it is good to avoid all extremes in the way you normally hold the hand. To further lighten the left-hand burden, it is best to take advantage of every natural principle available to you, such as gravity and leverage. You will find that the left hand has the most strength and leverage when you use the same principles that were used for the right hand. That means that the normal position should be based on the straight wrist and naturally curved fingers.

The simplest way to find a good left-hand position is to begin as we did with the right hand, by making a fist without bending the wrist as in Figure 4–12.

Figure 4–12 Left-hand position: making a fist with straight wrist

Figure 4–13 Left-hand position: natural uncurling of the fingers

If you want to demonstrate to yourself that the straight wrist gives the strongest left-hand position, try the same experiment that you did with the right hand. Keep the fingers tightly curled and try bending the wrist gradually in all different directions. Because of the pinching and bending of the muscles and tendons as you bend the wrist, you will probably notice some weakening of the strength of the fist. Now try holding the fist with the wrist straight. It should be obvious that it requires the least effort to make the fist with the straight or only slightly bent wrist.

Figure 4–14 Left-hand position: placing fingers in relaxed position

Figure 4–15 Left-hand position: placing fingers in typical position

Now take your "straight-wristed fist" and place it with the palm parallel to and close to the fingerboard. Then open it easily as in Figure 4–13 so that the fingers are naturally curved and close together, much like the right-hand fingers in Figure 4–8. This is important for the strength of all the fingers but especially so for the little one. Now place the opening of the hand so that the thumb is under the fingerboard and the fingers sit naturally on the fingerboard starting at the fifth fret as in Figure 4–14. Then spread the fingers out so that each one is next to a fret (Figure 4–15). Do not try to force the hand into this position. Let your hand find its own comfortable position. If the fingers do not reach the frets easily at this point, do not be concerned. Just place them as close to the frets as they will go without straining. The ability to stretch them will come with practice. A stretching exercise such as the one in Chapter 5 can also be of help.

The natural left-hand position just described can be considered as your strong, relaxed "home base" position which, while not the only one you will use, is best for much of your playing. The hand should always return to that position as soon as possible after making some necessary deviation such as a full bar or an especially long stretch that requires bending of the wrist and/or straightening of the fingers. The "home base" position is powerful because it works in accordance with the natural laws of leverage in physics. When the wrist is straight and the fingers are properly curved, a complex lever system is formed that has the greatest mechanical advantage.[8] Figure 4–16 shows an end view of this optimal position.

[8]Otto Szende and Mihaly Nemessuri, *The Physiology of Violin Playing*, p. 17. See also Charles Duncan, *The Art of Classical Guitar Playing* (Princeton, N.J.: Summy-Birchard, 1980), pp. 4–8.

Figure 4–16 Side view of left hand showing optimal leverage position

It should be added that the left-hand deviations of which we have spoken usually work best if they do not depart too far from the shape of the hand in the "home base" position. For example, when you make a full bar, it takes less energy to play it if the wrist is bent no more than necessary.

Balancing the Thumb Against the Fingers

In the natural, fist-derived left-hand position, the role of the thumb is important. It serves as a balance, guide, and support for the fingers and thus it is vital that it be properly placed. Some players suggest an exact position for it, usually under the fingerboard opposite the spot between the first and second fingers as in Figure 4–17. In this picture, notice that the tips of the first and fourth fingers are not as perpendicular to the fingerboard as those of the second and third. This is a perfectly natural position and is due to the structure of the hand. Just so long as these fingertips exert their pressure nearly perpendicular to the board, there will be excellent leverage and the hand will feel strong.

The position of the thumb in Figure 4–17 is fine for most playing, but it is still better to find the special balance point for any given left-hand configuration where you feel that the thumb supports the fingers in the strongest way. For the majority of position changes, the thumb should *move with the hand* and

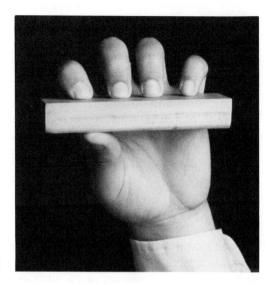

Figure 4–17 Front view of left hand showing finger and thumb positions

maintain its balance point with the fingers. Some experimentation will determine the balance point for various positions. The thumb usually works best when the tip segment is bent *away* from the palm as much as possible so that you are playing on the ball of the thumb. Playing with the tip segment bent in toward the palm is awkward and requires too much tension.

Minimum Effort and the Gravity Technique

It is not necessary to squeeze hard with the left-hand thumb and fingers in order to play well. However, a certain amount of tension is required in the fingers to maintain their curvature and to press down the strings. In accordance with the principles of least action and dynamic relaxation, it is best to find the minimum tension needed to produce clear notes. A way to find this proper muscular tension is to do simple exercises that allow you to experience the extremes of tension and relaxation. Then you will be able to tell more easily where the optimum tension point is. Try the following: Play any musical passage and press continuously as hard as you can with the left-hand fingers. Pay attention to how your hand and fingers look and feel. Are they strained or relaxed? How do the hands feel? Now play the piece with the fingers just barely pressing the strings so that none of the notes (except open strings) actually sounds. Again pay attention to the look and feel of the hand and fingers. Now play the piece again with just enough pressure to make the notes sound clearly. How do the fingers look and feel now?

After you go through these different levels of tension on the left-hand fingers, you should be more aware of how it feels and looks to

1. have too much tension,
2. have too little tension, and
3. have exactly the tension necessary.

Obviously you can apply this same approach to such things as individual bar chords and other left-hand formations. You can also practice this approach on nonguitar activities in order to increase your sensitivity to optimal tension levels. For example, check to see how hard you press down your pencil or pen while writing or how hard you grip the steering wheel of your car when turning corners. Try doing these activities with different levels of tension. See if you can perform them with precisely the amount of tension you need—no more, no less.

Another way to avoid excess tension and squeezing with the left hand is to practice with the thumb held away from the fingerboard. Most students are amazed that they can play that way. They do not realize that a considerable amount of force can come from just the downward pressure of well-curved fingers. Only in occasional cases, such as certain bar chords where the notes would not otherwise be clear, is it necessary to squeeze very much.

One of the major reasons why you do not have to squeeze hard in order to play most of the notes is that you can use the force of gravity to save you a tremendous amount of left-hand energy. For most left-hand situations, little effort is required to play the notes if you let the fingers sink into the strings next to the frets, using the weight of the left arm as the main pressure source. Of course the fingers must still have some minimum amount of tension on them to retain their curvature. In any case, instead of having to *squeeze out* the notes with brute force, you can *hang* on them and get the same results with less effort. For example, when you play a six-string E major chord (from bass to treble: E, B, E, G♯, B, E) in the first position, try hanging on it instead of squeezing it and see how much easier it is. This "gravity technique" can be used to good effect in almost every aspect of left-hand playing including scales, chords, and bars.

Common Left-Hand Problems

At this point, let's look at the faults in the left-hand position that come up most frequently.

1. bending the wrist more than necessary
2. breaking of the natural curvature of the fingers by letting the first or middle joints collapse, particularly in the little finger
3. playing on the sides of the fingers instead of on the very tips
4. leaning the fingers too far in the direction of the nut

5. cradling the neck in the space between the thumb and first finger, with the thumb sticking out above the fingerboard
6. playing with the tip segment of the thumb toward the palm instead of away from it
7. squeezing too hard with the thumb and fingers
8. holding the knuckles too low in relation to the fingerboard
9. keeping the line that goes through the knuckles too far from being parallel to the strings

All of the above problems of the left hand can result in excess tension, fatigue, and poor control over the finger movements. As with the right hand, there are always some deviations from the basic dynamically relaxed position that are perfectly fine. As we mentioned, some bending of the wrist is necessary, particularly for full bar chords and long stretches, but it should be kept to a minimum. After such deviations, the player should always come back to the basic straight-wristed position as quickly as possible in order to keep the hand quiet and relaxed.

Bar Chord Position

Fernando Sor recommends that one should "be sparing of the operations called barring and shifting."[9] The principal reason for avoiding bars is that playing them requires more effort than not. However, there are frequent occasions when bars are the best or only solutions for playing certain passages. So, if you have to use bars, why not look for the easiest ways of playing them?

A common mistake in playing bar chords is to hold the first finger literally like a straight bar. Unfortunately, the leverage provided by that position is not very great and thus it requires a considerable amount of energy to play the bar. However, if the first finger is curved to some degree, then you will have much more leverage and will need much less energy to play the bar. For example, the full six-string bar is much easier to play if the first finger is bent somewhat at the middle joint. It also helps to bend the base joint of the finger considerably so that the palm is close to the fingerboard. A sample of the curved full-bar position is shown in Figure 4–18.

The curved position can be used to special advantage in certain cases where some of the chord tones are held down by fingers other than the bar finger. In such cases, the bar finger only needs to exert pressure on those notes not pressed by the other fingers. In the five-string bar (a C minor chord) in Figure 4–19, the first finger is not only curved but is only pressing two notes, thus saving a great deal of energy.

[9]Fernando Sor, *Method for the Spanish Guitar*, trans. A. Merrick, Da Capo Reprint Series (New York: Da Capo Press, 1971), p. 48.

Figure 4–18 Full bar with curved index finger

If the second, third, and fourth fingers are raised, the strings that are under them will sound dead because the bar is just barely touching them; the first finger is curved such that it exerts pressure only on the fifth and first strings. This special technique can be very helpful in many situations. For a bar chord piece such as Sor's Op. 29, No. 1 (No. 19 in Segovia's edition of Sor Studies), the energy that can be saved by using this technique on many of the chords, particularly B♭ in the first position, means the difference between playing it in relative comfort on the one hand and suffering through it with aching muscles on the other.

Figure 4–19 Partial bar with curved index finger

There are other energy-saving techniques for bar chords. You can use the gravity technique that we discussed earlier in this chapter and "hang" on the chords instead of squeezing them. This works best when combined with the curved bar finger described earlier. In this way of playing, you let the flesh of the bar finger roll up close against the fret and let the weight of the arm supply much of the needed pressure; thus little of the pressure comes from squeezing. To save energy, remember that the minimum bend in the wrist for a given position is generally best because the leverage is greater with less bending.

Another energy saver is to bar only the number of strings necessary. Why bar six strings when five will do? Occasionally you may come to a situation where you would like to use a smaller bar (four or five strings) but decide to play a full bar anyway. This is because one of the strings is not pressed down properly by the smaller bar because of lack of flesh on the finger at that point (usually at the middle joint). Thus it is better to play the full bar so that the note will sound properly. This tactic may also prove useful when the full bar would serve as a preparation for what is needed in the next measure or two. One final way of saving energy is to lay the second finger on top of the first during full bars where the second finger is not needed for other notes. This trick will spare you much fatigue in long pieces.

Before we leave the subject of bar chords we should mention the so-called *half-bar*. This type of bar usually covers from two to four strings. For most players, the half-bar should take little energy if played with the first finger bent rather sharply at the middle joint. Finally, as with the full-bar, it is easier to *hang* on the half-bar rather than to squeeze it.

SUMMARY

The guitarist who wants to play effortlessly will be an eager student of dynamic relaxation. Being able to achieve the state of dynamic relaxation in mind and body on a regular basis is one of the major keys to success with the guitar. It is not some mysterious state but is simply the state in which mind and body are functioning normally and naturally with minimum effort. That "normal" state often seems supernormal because many people do not experience it regularly. It is a state that people need to recapture. It can be cultivated on the guitar by seeking those positions and movements that are physically natural for the player, that is, those that require the least effort. In this chapter, we have discovered some natural positions for sitting and for the right and left hands. If you study these positions carefully and see how they apply to your particular physical characteristics, you will be able to find your own dynamically relaxed way of sitting and holding the hands. It is not necessary to try to follow the positions described in this chapter exactly. However, it is good to hold to the principles of balance, naturalness, and minimum effort for whatever variation of the positions you may choose.

You will know when you have found dynamically relaxed positions because they are stable, comfortable, and produce good results for your playing. With such positions, you will have a strong foundation for ease of execution and you will be one step closer to playing the guitar with the ease of the masters. The next chapter will take you another step on the way to effortless playing. It will present a technique that will help you learn the valuable skill of relaxing between the notes. With that skill you will be able to achieve dynamic relaxation in the actual movements of playing.

5.

The Play-Relax Technique

*use the spaces
between the notes*

> *Cut doors and windows for a room;
> It is the holes which make it useful.
> Therefore profit comes from what is there;
> Usefulness from what is not there.*
>
> Lao Tzu, *Tao Te Ching*

> *I constantly asked myself [about technique],
> "What is the most natural way of doing this?"*
>
> Pablo Casals, *Joys and Sorrows*

DYNAMICALLY RELAXED PLAYING MOVEMENTS

Much has been written about how to play the notes on the guitar but little about how to relax in the spaces between the notes. It is important to realize that you cannot master the notes until you have mastered the spaces. This is because music, like most natural phenomena, consists of alternating waves of activity and rest. If you are not aware of the resting phase, you have missed half of the music. Thus there is a need to balance opposites by learning how and when to relax as well as learning how and when to play. Unfortunately, many guitarists are so involved in the physical and mental activity of playing that the spaces between the notes are rushed over or not even noticed. The result is excess tension, fatigue, and a "breathless," nonmusical way of playing. However, the moment you become aware of the possibilities for micro-, mini-, and macro-relaxations in those spaces, that is the start of dynamic relaxation and masterly ease in your playing. That awareness will also help your playing "breathe" and become truly musical.

In Chapter 4, we have already discovered dynamically relaxed ways of sitting and holding the hands. In this chapter, we will use the Play–Relax technique to find dynamically relaxed ways of making the actual playing movements. The Play–Relax technique is a simple, natural approach to guitar practice that helps the player take advantage of the spaces between the notes. It should be emphasized that the Play–Relax technique is a *practice* method. It is not something you should think about in performance. If the technique is used properly in your practice sessions, then the results will show up automatically in your performances. The basic premise of the Play–Relax technique is that, in order for guitar playing movements to be efficient and nonfatiguing, there must be a relaxation to balance out each exertion of the hands and fingers. The relaxation may be just a fraction of a second (micro-relaxation), a few seconds to a minute (mini-relaxation), or more than a minute (macro-relaxation). Whatever the case, some relaxation between the notes is necessary to compensate for the muscular tension of playing.

The balance between playing and relaxing is critical. It is much like tight-rope walking. Mistakes result if the balance is tipped too far in either direction. However, if playing and relaxing are distinctly and rhythmically alternated using the Play–Relax technique, a good balance between the two states will be created. This eventually leads to effortless, dynamically relaxed playing and fewer mistakes.

Some of the finest musicians both past and present, such as the pianist Ferruccio Busoni (1866–1924), the contemporary violinist Yehudi Menuhin, and the guitarist Leo Brouwer, have used a practice approach similar to the Play–Relax idea. Menuhin, for example, suggests letting go of effort completely, or almost completely, between violin playing movements such as bow strokes.[1] Brouwer recommends such things as releasing tension on each left-hand finger very quickly after it plays a note of a scale. Other fine guitarists also use this approach, although it is seldom discussed. The reason this approach can be applied successfully to various instruments is that it works in harmony with the basic nature of the human nervous system. The nervous system operates in accordance with the natural law of cyclic action and rest (periodicity). The transmission of information in the nervous system functions in an action or rest, on or off, "play" or "relax" manner with nothing in between. As the biophysicist Eugene Ackerman puts it:

> The spike potential [the electrical nerve impulse] is an all-or-none response. Either there is a transmitted spike or not . . . the neuron acts in a similar manner to a flip-flop electronic circuit such as used in counters and digital computers . . . the neuron is either in the conducting or non-conducting state; nothing is transmitted in between. This analogy seems so strong that it is hard to avoid describing the computer in anthropomorphic terms and the nervous system in terms of a digital computer.[2]

The muscle cells contract and relax in an on-off manner similar to the nerve cells. The Play–Relax guitar practice method is parallel to and compatible with the on-off functioning of nerve cells and muscle fibers. This method emphasizes making very distinct "on" and "off" movements with the fingers. Many guitarists, including some advanced players, make "fuzzy" movements, that is, they do not focus on clear-cut application and release of tension on the fingers at the precisely appropriate moments. The most common faults are:

---

[1]Yehudi Menuhin, *Violin and Viola* (New York: Schirmer Books, 1976), p. 41. See also Franzpeter Goebels, ed., *The New Busoni: Exercises and Studies for the Piano* (Wiesbaden: Breitkopf & Haertel, 1968), p. x.

[2]Eugene Ackerman, *Biophysical Science* (Englewood Cliffs, N.J.: Prentice-Hall, Inc., 1962), p. 80.

1. keeping too much tension on the fingers too much of the time
2. failing to release finger tension in a quick, distinct way after it is no longer needed

Thus many players spend too much time in the "on" or "half-on" states and not enough in the "off" state. There is no balanced alternation between the states. It should be mentioned that, even among the best players, it is normal to have a slight amount of baseline tension in the muscles even when they are in the relaxed "off" condition. That seems to be a necessary part of good muscle tone. However, many players almost never relax to that baseline state and thus become easily fatigued.

The main point here is that, when you make a right-hand stroke or press down a left-hand note, you need to concentrate on producing one clear impulse in the nervous system and the muscles at precisely the right time. Then the movement will be made with the least possible effort and will create the best possible effect. What you want to avoid is having too many nerve firings and muscle contractions going on at inappropriate times. Then, immediately after the movement has been completed, there needs to be an equally clear impulse to release the tension that created that movement. Good playing requires precise, coordinated signals from your mind to your fingers. The exercises in this chapter will deal not only with relaxation but also with coordination and precision of movements.

ENTRAINMENT: PLAYING IN PERFECT RHYTHM

A vital part of the Play–Relax approach is learning how to play in precise, regular rhythm. Why? It is simply easier to play in good rhythm. Let's examine this further. The human body and nervous system are constantly pulsing with many on-off rhythms such as the brain waves, heart beat, breathing, and the blinking of the eyes. Some of these rhythms are orderly and some not so orderly, depending on the state of the individual. However, even if some of the more superficial rhythms are in disorder, there seems to be order at a deeper level of the person. In his inspired book, *The Silent Pulse*, George Leonard hypothesizes that deep within everyone there is a perfect rhythmic pulse.[3] He feels that when conditions are right, the perfect rhythm within you manifests itself in your activities and enriches you with a "peak experience."[4] In music, for example, it would manifest as an exhilarating, effortless performance.

[3]George Leonard, *The Silent Pulse* (New York: Bantam Books, 1981), p. xii and p. 107ff.
[4]See Abraham Maslow, *Toward a Psychology of Being* (New York: Van Nostrand Co., 1968), p. 89.

One of the conditions that can help bring out your perfect inner rhythm is the frequent experience of an orderly external pulse. This pulse can come from various sources such as live or recorded music, hand clapping, foot tapping, or a metronome. As good musicians know, such a regular pulse is of great help during study sessions. It is a tool that can organize the rhythms of your nervous system so that your playing will have rhythmic authority. Ultimately, it will help integrate your inner rhythm into your playing.

A regular pulse seems to be very attractive to the nervous system. It appears very likely that such a regular rhythm—especially in connection with certain kinds of music—has the power to make the brain waves synchronized and coherent. When this comes about, there is less "noise" in the nervous system, that is, there are fewer random firings of neurons. As a result, the musician or music listener experiences a sense of harmony and peacefulness.

When a person who is listening to or playing some music that has a regular pulse becomes completely "locked in" to the rhythm, we can say that *musical entrainment* has taken place. Both mind and body are affected by this process: The mind becomes absorbed in the music and the body often moves with it. Entrainment is not just a musical phenomenon. It is a universal scientific occurrence that comes about when two or more vibrating systems are close to one another and are pulsing at nearly the same rate. Under those conditions, the vibrating systems become entrained and start to pulse at *exactly* the same rate. Nature apparently favors having systems pulse exactly together since that takes less energy and thus is in accord with the principle of least action. A nonmusical example of entrainment occurs when two radio oscillators are in close proximity and have nearly the same frequency of oscillation. The two oscillators will tend to pulse together at the same frequency, usually the higher one of the two. Another striking example of entrainment in music is when all the members of an orchestra act as a harmonious unit and play perfectly in rhythm with each other.

Entrainment is thus a common but very important phenomenon of which the guitarist should become keenly aware. With the help of a metronome, entrainment should be consciously cultivated when doing the Play–Relax exercises in this chapter. In fact, for almost all aspects of practicing, whether exercises or pieces, it is good to learn how to "entrain" your nervous system and your fingers with the steady pulse of a metronome. (Do make sure that your metronome is steady!) After some practice in strict time, you will "lock in" to the rhythms of your exercises and pieces and they will start to play themselves.

We have strongly emphasized the value of the metronome, although many players do not care for it. The metronome should not be regarded as a distasteful, mechanical discipline, but rather as an important tool to help you establish effortless, rhythmical playing. It is definitely not recommended that the metronome be used constantly. Natural musical rhythms, after all, are not precisely metronomic. The metronome can even hinder the natural rhythms if used too much. Thus, part of your practice time should be spent without it. However, it is best not to neglect it altogether. Keep in mind that many of the world's best concert guitarists practice *frequently* with the metronome and recommend it highly to their students.

One of the greatest benefits of learning to play in good rhythm is that it helps to balance out the opposites in your playing. When you play with a steady pulse, the opposite tendencies of rushing ahead of the beat and dragging behind it are evened out. Playing with a steady pulse also allows you the time to relax between the notes. Then tension and relaxation become balanced. When these balances are achieved, you will feel a certain ease and will be focused more on what is happening *now* in your playing instead of being anxious about what just happened or what is yet to come. Now we will see how to apply the Play–Relax idea to the right hand.

PLAY–RELAX FOR THE RIGHT HAND

Dynamically Relaxing the Fingers

The Play–Relax technique can be applied very effectively to various right-hand movements. However, before we discuss the actual technique, it is necessary to know about *finger tension* and the technique of *planting*. First let's look at finger tension.

To achieve dynamic relaxation in the fingers, they must have a proper balance of tension and relaxation. When the fingers are not playing, they should be naturally curved and relaxed. (See Chapter 4, Figure 4–8.) There should be no more tension used than what is needed to keep them in position. When the fingers actually make the strokes, the guitarist must learn how to put just the right amount of tension on them—no more, no less. When a stroke is made, the amount of tension in the finger is normally a kind of "firm elasticity"—somewhere between rigidity and looseness—like a branch on a healthy tree. That means that there should be enough tension so that, when the finger goes across the string, it retains a slight curvature and does not collapse. In particular, make sure that the middle and the tip segments of the fingers have enough tension on them so that they have good leverage and do not collapse as they go over the string. Insufficient tension creates considerable difficulties with control of tone and technique.

With respect to finger tension, probably the most common error is to keep the upper and middle segments firm and relax the tip segment completely as in Figure 5–1. This is done in the belief that the finger will go over the string more easily. However, keeping the tip segment completely relaxed usually works only for those players whose fingertips do not bend backward.

Figure 5–1 Overrelaxed right-hand fingertip

For most players, when the fingertip is completely relaxed, it is too loose for controlled playing. It is something like trying to play tennis with a rubber racket. With the loose fingertip, the nail takes too long going over the string, snags frequently, and often creates a bad-sounding click. Also, without some firmness of the tip, it is very difficult to have any control in fast passages since it takes the over-relaxed fingertip too long to return to playing position after a movement.

The opposite extreme of having too much tension on the finger is just as awkward as not having enough. That also results in poor control of tone and technique besides being painful. If you do become aware of excessive tension in the hand or fingers, remember to stop and let the hand relax before continuing. The real secret of using the fingers properly is to go the middle way and use enough tension so that the finger does not collapse during the stroke but not so much that it does not give at all. In fine playing there will naturally be some variation in the fingertip tension according to the express-ive quality of the tone desired by the player, but it will be somewhere be-tween the extremes. After some experimentation with finger tension, you will be able to maintain a balance between control and flexibility, power and deli-cacy with respect to the right hand. When you achieve that balance, you will experience dynamic relaxation in the fingers and it will feel exactly right.

Planting the Fingers

The preparation of the right-hand fingers by "planting" or placing them on the strings before playing the notes is a hallmark of all the best schools of guitar technique. The preparation of finger movements is not peculiar to the guitar. "Planting" on the guitar is analogous to the manner in which fine pianists prepare their fingers by placing them on the notes of scale passages or arpeggios before they play them. Good violinists also prepare their bow-strokes by placing the bow on the strings just before playing wherever it is musically and technically feasible. The advantages of a similar kind of preparation for the guitarist are many. When a player uses the planting approach, he can develop a very fine control over tone, technique, and expression that is otherwise not possible. As you will see, planting is also important for the Play–Relax practice approach.

It is difficult to produce a consistently good tone and be accurate with the right-hand strokes without planting. If you swing or bat at the strings from even a short distance away, you never know for sure if you will strike the strings. Even if you do strike the strings, you will not be certain what part of the fingertip will strike them. Thus you will not know what kind of tone will be produced with each stroke. Sometimes the fingertip will hit the string at just the right spot with the right combination of flesh and nail and the tone will be good. However, more often than not, the spot that hits the string will be either all flesh, which produces a dull thump, or all nail, which often snags and creates a tinny sound.

Planting wherever technically and musically feasible helps the guitarist avoid the pitfalls of inaccuracy and poor tone control. It is best to plant the fingers on the strings *in a precise groove* on each fingertip before making the strokes. For each type of nail and nail shape, the planting groove will be at a slightly different angle. (See "The Art of Caring for the Nails" in Chapter 6.) At that point, the combination of flesh and nail will go over the string with least resistance and maximum beauty of sound. Because most nails release most easily when the stroke is started from the left side of the nail, it is usually best to plant the fingertip at an angle such that the string is seated snugly in the groove between the flesh and the left-hand side of the nail. Figure 5–2 shows how the planting of a typical four-note arpeggio looks from the underside of the strings. Figure 5–3 shows the planting grooves in the fingertips created by pressing on the strings. (Once you have discovered the right place for the planting grooves, you can draw lines on them with a pen so that you can check if you are planting on the right spot.)

When one first learns about right-hand planting, it is necessary to do it consciously and carefully. However, after a while the fingers will tend to set themselves up on the strings very naturally and automatically just before the strokes. Planting in advance of playing is possible most of the time. It can be used to great advantage for playing melodic passages, scales, arpeggios, tremolo, and block chords. We will discuss all these applications in this chapter.

It is not always desirable to plant the right-hand fingers in advance because this will tend to cut notes too short, particularly for legato playing where the notes should receive as much of their written value as possible. To

Figure 5–2 Fingers planted on the strings seen from underneath

Figure 5–3 Planting grooves in the fingertips

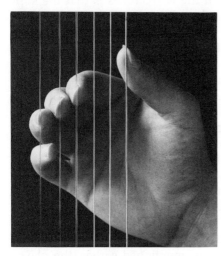
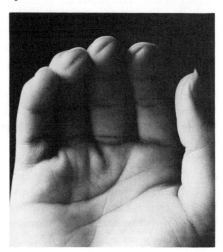

maintain a legato sound, it is often necessary to wait until just a microsecond before making the strokes to plant the fingers.

In addition to the uses we have already described, planting can be very helpful for stabilizing the right hand. For fast scales and arpeggios, it is particularly helpful to plant the right-hand thumb on one of the bass strings *whenever you can*. Thus the *i m a* fingers will have a solid base from which to make their strokes. (For examples of where to plant the thumb, see "Arpeggios" and "Right-Hand Speed" later in this chapter.)

Although it is useful to plant the thumb on the bass notes to stabilize the fingers, it is sometimes equally useful to plant the fingers on the treble strings to stabilize the thumb. For example, the thumb may have to play an extended passage by itself or may have to work in combination with *i*. In the latter case, for example, the thumb will be more stable if you rest the *a* or *m* finger (or both) on one of the treble strings—provided that it does not cut off any notes that should sound.

From this discussion of planting it should be clear that it is a valuable technique. It has many applications and will make a great contribution to the security of your playing. Now we will move on and see how planting is applied in the Play–Relax way of making right-hand strokes.

Play–Relax Rest Strokes

The Snap Stroke   Among the finer guitarists there are two basic ways of making right-hand rest strokes (*apoyando* in Spanish). One, commonly called the *supported* stroke, is most often used for playing fast scales securely. The other, which we will call the *snap* stroke, is usually used for emphasizing particular notes. The main difference between the two strokes is that the supported stroke is actually allowed to rest on the adjacent string while the snap stroke strikes it and is allowed to bounce off. We will discuss the snap stroke now and consider the supported stroke in the "Fast Scales" section later in this chapter.

Although the snap stroke has been used for years by the best guitarists, it is not as widely known as the supported stroke. It is a very useful musical technique and it embodies the Play–Relax idea. It has two important elements. The first, which we have just discussed, is that you plant the fingers on the strings before you make a stroke; the second is that the stroke is made very quickly ("snapped") and is almost instantaneously followed by a clear-cut release of tension.

To do the snap stroke well and keep the hand relaxed, it is important to be able to turn the finger tension "on" and "off" very fast, much like the high speed, on-off operation of a computer. The more you approach this kind of clear-cut, on-off operation in your fingers, the more relaxed they will be, whether you play fast or slow pieces. (As we mentioned earlier, the player may apply many subtle degrees of tension in the right-hand strokes for variety of tonal expression. However, these variations in tension are generally made in the *attack* on the strings, and thus, after the stroke has been made, there can still be a clear-cut "turning off" of the finger tension.) Many guitarists have difficulty turning the fingers on and off quickly and completely enough. The inability to turn them off seems to be particularly prevalent and it results in a carryover of excess tension from one stroke to the next. The simple exercise shown in Figure 5–4 will help resolve that difficulty.

To make a snap rest stroke in the Play–Relax style, try the following:

Figure 5–4   Play–Relax exercise for snap rest strokes

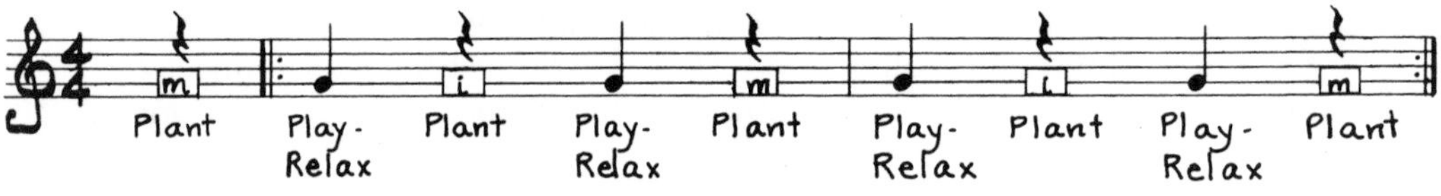

At this point, do not be much concerned about the rhythm. Start by placing the thumb on the sixth string to stabilize the hand. The actual stroke is done as a two-step process: first "plant," then "play–relax." Now, on the first quarter rest, say "plant" as you place the *m* finger on the G string. Plant the finger in that precise groove on the fingertip which produces the best tone and least resistance, usually near the left side of the nail. (See Figures 5–2 and 5–3.) Next, hold the first two joints of the finger firmly in a slightly curved shape as in Figure 5–5. As we mentioned in the section on finger tension, these two joints flex very little during the stroke. The main movement is made by moving the entire finger from the top or knuckle joint. Now say "play–relax" as you make a vigorous, *very quick* stroke. The fingertip should move slightly downward toward the soundhole and slightly left or straight back toward the adjacent string (see the arrow in Figure 5–5).

Now comes the more unusual part of the Play–Relax snap stroke. Let the finger strike the adjacent string, releasing all tension immediately. Allow it to *pop* back to a natural position as is shown with the dotted lines in Figure 5–6. Be careful not to let the back of the nail hit the plucked string during the release. The release of tension on the finger should happen almost at the same time as the stroke is made—hence, "play" and "relax" are put together as "play–relax." The sign that you have released the tension quickly is a slight muscular twitch in the hand as you finish the stroke. The slight movement is normal and should not be inhibited. The hand and fingers should have a flexible and free-floating feeling after the stroke. However, the hand should not fly up in the air! It should move less than an inch for normal playing.

Figure 5–5 The snap rest stroke (showing direction of stroke)

Figure 5–6 The release of tension after a snap stroke

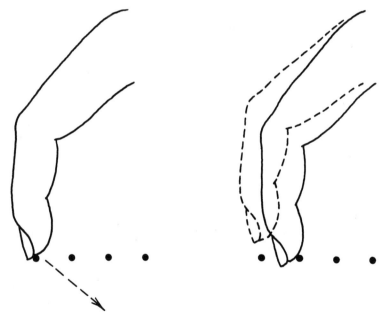

After you have made the stroke with the *m* finger, be sure to let go of the tension as quickly as possible. Feel the relaxation completely. Do not rush over it. *The relaxation between the strokes is just as important as the stroke itself.* It may help to exaggerate the "letting go" by allowing the hand to hang loosely from the wrist after each stroke. In a short time, you will become aware of how to release the tension quickly and the exaggeration will not be necessary. When you come to the quarter rest, plant the *i* finger gently on the string so that the previous note is cut off in a staccato manner. Now play the next stroke in the same way and continue the exercise.

When you can do the exercise easily, then start using the metronome at about ♩ = 50 so there is a click on the rests as well as on the notes. This tempo may seem slow but it will give you plenty of time to be completely conscious of what your fingers are doing and whether you are releasing the tension completely between the notes. The regular alternation of "play" and "relax" with the metronome will make the hand feel very comfortable, like walking at a steady pace. After a while the Play–Relax response will come automatically because it is so natural. It will form the basis of playing with minimal tension.

When doing the above exercise, keep in mind that the Play–Relax snap stroke is done very fast in the same way as one flicks or snaps the fingers. You just start the stroke and let the rest of it happen. Think of it as a sudden release of energy like a lightning bolt rather than something that you force out. (To get the idea of this fast stroke, some students find it helpful to blow a quick puff of air out of their mouths right at the moment of making the stroke.) The actual energy expenditure of each stroke is a burst that only lasts an instant; if done properly, the finger and hand will feel relaxed both before and immediately after the stroke. It will feel as if you have done almost nothing to produce the stroke because it happens so quickly. However, the sound of the stroke can be very powerful, depending on how strong the initial playing impulse was. With this technique you are truly doing less and accomplishing more.

Many of the best players use the snap stroke in order to emphasize certain notes. Later in this chapter, in the section called "The Uses of Rest and Free Strokes," we will discuss specific applications of this stroke.

Thumb Rest Stroke   The principal movement of the thumb comes from its base where it is connected to the hand. Little if any movement should come from the other joints. If the tip segment of the thumb bends backward to some degree, then it usually is best to straighten it out and hold it firmly in that position in order to control the way the nail goes over the string and thus control the tone quality.

As with the fingers, the thumb is planted on the strings in a precise groove on the tip before playing. For most players, the groove will be on the flesh just behind the middle of the nail when viewed from the top and it will release from the left-hand side (Figure 5–7). The nail should be firmly seated against the string. The thumb rest stroke is made by a quick push somewhat downward and inward: downward toward the soundhole and the next string and inward toward the index finger (Figure 5–8).

Figure 5–7 Planting the thumb on a bass string

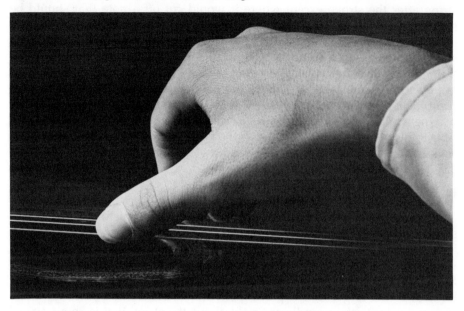

Figure 5–8 Thumb rest stroke (showing direction of stroke)

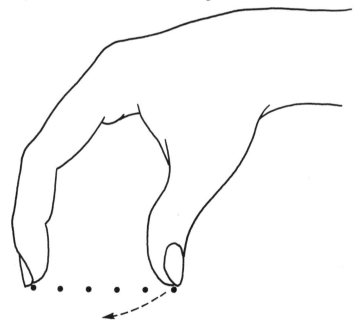

For stability of the hand, the thumb can rest lightly against the next string after the stroke except where it would cut off a note that should be sounding. The movement should be done in a clear-cut Play–Relax manner, so that the tension on the thumb is released almost at the same time that the stroke is made. Because of its weight and its direction of movement, the thumb can gain some assistance from gravity to make the stroke; in fact, you can even put some of the weight of the hand and arm into the stroke if you want. This is particularly useful for bringing out a single line bass part or playing a full sounding chord with a thumb stroke. For tonal variety, it is possible to play a thumb rest stroke with the flesh instead of the nail; for this the thumb is rotated forward somewhat so that the nail is out of the way.

Play–Relax Free Strokes

Single Free Strokes The free stroke (*tirando* in Spanish) is done in two steps in a way analogous to the rest stroke: first "plant," then "play–relax." It is best to do it from about the same hand position as the rest stroke. In this way, the movement of the hand will be minimized when switching back and forth between the two types of strokes. For the best leverage, the top joint or knuckle of the finger that is playing should be located at a point on a line perpendicular to the soundboard right above the string that is being played (Figure 5–9).

Figure 5–9 Free stroke (showing direction of stroke)

Figure 5–10 Release of tension after a free stroke

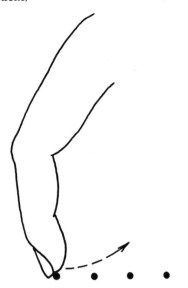

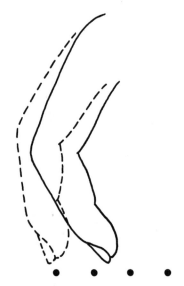

Single free strokes can be practiced using the same exercise that was used for the rest stroke (see Figure 5–4). When you make the free stroke, you use a technique very similar to that of the snap stroke. The free stroke is started by planting the finger on the string in the same groove on the fingertip as for the snap stroke (see Figure 5–2). Also as in the snap stroke, the first two joints should have enough tension to keep the finger in the slightly curved shape shown in Figure 5–9. To maintain control over the stroke, avoid letting these two joints collapse during the stroke. The main movement of the finger should come from the top joint while the first two remain firm. Thus the whole finger moves as a unit and provides maximum power.

The actual stroke is executed in the same *lightning-quick,* Play–Relax manner as the snap stroke. It first moves slightly downward and backward, also like the snap stroke (see the dotted line and arrow in Figure 5–9). But then the fingertip moves over the top of the adjacent string at a very shallow angle instead of striking it. Then, after the stroke, the complete release of tension should follow so quickly that it seems that playing and relaxing happen simultaneously. A slight muscular twitch will indicate the tension release. The finger ends up in the dotted line position in Figure 5–10. If you keep the finger firm and move it from the top joint, the stroke should feel very easy. You will be merely *pushing* the string. Remember that, if the top joint of the playing finger is not on a perpendicular to the string, you will have a tendency to *pull up* on the string instead of just pushing it back. The pulling up is done in order to avoid hitting the adjacent string. You will also have a tendency to pull up if the finger is curved too tightly. Pulling up on the string is not particularly good because it usually results in excess tension in the tendons on the back of the hand and in the snagging of the nails.

The Thumb Free Stroke   The thumb free stroke is made by first planting it on the correct spot on its tip. The spot may be somewhat different than for the rest stroke. For the stroke, the first joint of the thumb is held firm. The main movement comes from the large joint. The stroke is normally made in a downward direction so that the thumb barely clears the next string (Figure 5–11). The stroke is made quickly with an immediate release afterward as in the rest stroke. A slight circular motion after the stroke is quite natural. This movement is frequently helpful because it will bring the thumb back to its starting point, thus preparing it to play further notes on the same string.

In order to obtain a thumb free stroke with a strong "punchy" quality, some players plant the thumb slightly *under* the string and then make a powerful flick outward and away from the strings. If your thumb joints are very elastic, there can be some flexing of the tip segment right at the end of this stroke to make the "flick." This slight flexing can be used to advantage to control the exact movement of the string.

Figure 5–11   Thumb free stroke (showing direction of stroke)

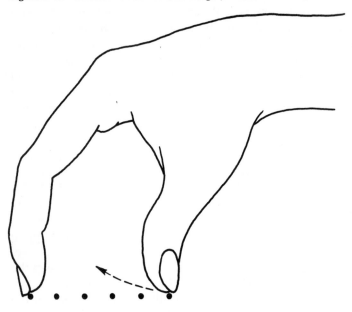

The thumb free stroke as described here is the normal one that makes use of the crisp nail sound, but it is also possible to play free strokes with the flesh of the thumb for a soft, muted tone quality.

Chords   Figure 5–12 presents a simple Play–Relax exercise to give you the feeling of easy, yet strong free strokes on chords.

Figure 5–12   Play–Relax exercise for right-hand block chords

The technique is virtually identical to that of the single free strokes. On the first quarter rest, say "plant" as you place the thumb and the three fingers on the chord. Be sure to "stack" the fingers together at the tips (see "Stacking" in Chapter 4) and find the precise grooves on the fingertips where the tone is best and the nails do not catch. Also be sure not to curve the fingers too tightly. Now say "play–relax" as you make a very fast squeeze movement. The thumb will move toward the first string and the fingers move back toward the palm. As in the single free strokes, the motion consists of *pushing* the strings rather than pulling them up. The instant the chord is played, the tension should be totally released. The sign of correct release will again be a slight twitch of the hand as you allow the fingers to spring back naturally to a relaxed position over the strings.

Remember to feel the relaxation after the stroke clearly. When you come to the next quarter note, say "plant" again as you place your fingers on the strings and deliberately cut off the previous notes. Continue the exercise slowly as long as necessary to learn to make quick movements and quick relaxations. When you can do this exercise easily, start using the metronome at a slow speed to make the Play–Relax movements rhythmical and precise.

Arpeggios   The Play–Relax approach can be used with arpeggios in a way similar to free stroke chords. Take a simple arpeggio as in Figure 5–13.

Figure 5–13   Play–Relax exercise for right-hand arpeggios

For the moment, let's play the exercise without the metronome. The first thing is to plant *p i m a* on the strings and leave them there until you play the notes. (Be watchful about this. Many players plant the fingers carefully but then unconsciously pick one or more of them up just before they play!) The planting process should be done at the beginning of each arpeggio as shown in Figure 5–13. The *i m a* fingers are actually planted at the same time as *p* plays the C bass note. This process of planting arpeggios gives great security and accuracy and is therefore standard with most fine players.

The strokes in this exercise are made in the same way as in the previous free-stroke exercises except that the thumb does a rest stroke. Remember to keep the fingers slightly curved, make quick strokes, and relax each finger immediately after a stroke.

Now on to the exercise. With the fingers planted, make the *p* stroke on the low C and quickly relax it, letting it rest on the fourth string. The thumb can remain on that string until a new arpeggio begins in the next measure. For arpeggios, remember that your technique will be most secure if you stabilize the hand by anchoring the thumb on a bass string wherever you can. Now make a quick *i* stroke on the G and relax the finger immediately. Be sure not to pick up the *m* or *a* during the *i* stroke. Now play the C with *m* and relax it while the *a* remains planted. Next, play the E with *a*.

At this point, you have used up the fingers that you had originally planted. Of course *p* is resting on the D string but the other fingers are up in the air. This may give a feeling of insecurity for the descending part of the arpeggio. However, you can make things more secure by doing some subtle planting as follows: *At the same time* as you make the *a* stroke on the E string, plant the *m* on the B string. Then, at the moment you play the *m*, plant the *i* on the G string. Continue planting in this same way for the rest of the arpeggio. At the start of the next and each succeeding measure, repeat the whole process of planting and playing that we did up to this point. The last measure is of course shorter and simpler than the previous ones.

After you feel comfortable with the above exercise, try it at a slow tempo with the metronome and gradually increase the speed as you are able to relax more quickly. When you do the exercise or any other arpeggio, keep in mind that one of the keys to fluent, accurate arpeggios is always having a *clear-cut relaxation between the strokes*—even if it is only a micro-relaxation. It is also important to relax the whole hand as well as the fingers between the strokes. After a while, the fingers and hand will automatically relax at almost the same time as you make the strokes. Ultimately, you will be able to play fast arpeggios without much tension at all. In fact, they should be very easy.

You can use the Play-Relax approach for almost any arpeggio with excellent results. For example, the technique is useful for the rapid arpeggios in Villa-Lobos' *Preludes No. 2* and *No. 4* and *Etudes No. 1* and *No. 11*. Incidentally, it is often much easier to play quick arpeggios if you play them closer to the bridge rather than over the soundhole. At the soundhole, the strings feel as loose as rubber bands and thus are hard to control at rapid tempos. At the bridge, the strings are stiffer and snap back quickly after being struck. You may find that new strings or higher tension strings may also help to solve this problem of looseness.

The Uses of Rest and Free Strokes

The sound of these two principal strokes is somewhat different. The rest stroke tends to be more full-bodied, "fat," and powerful, while the free stroke is a bit thinner in character. Students often have a particularly thin-sounding free stroke with *i m a*. Thus there is an awkward contrast when they switch from one type of stroke to the other. Professional players cultivate a free stroke that is almost as full and powerful as the rest stroke so that the contrast is not so pronounced. This is important because the free stroke is generally used more often than the rest stroke.

Guitarists often ask where to use rest strokes. As a general rule, the player should be very discriminating about which notes he plays with rest strokes. They should only be used on relatively important notes because they tend to sound accented. Many guitarists use rest strokes on every possible note—even relatively unimportant ones—in order to obtain a full sound. Unfortunately, playing all rest strokes results in a heavy, plodding sound and every note is made to seem equally important. And, since this creates only one level in the hierarchy of musical values, the result is monotony. There are no high or low points, no goals in the musical lines—something like the unending flatness of Kansas.

The best way to discover how to use rest strokes is to study very carefully the natural contours and musical sense of each piece you play. Listening carefully to live or recorded performances of fine players will also give you many ideas about where rest strokes can be most effective. You will find that concert artists frequently use the *snap* stroke in melody and accompaniment pieces such as Sor Studies 3, 5, and 6 in the Segovia edition and Villa-Lobos' *Etude No. 8*. (See also Chapter 3, Figure 3–2 for a Carcassi example.) Most of the treble melody notes (stems up) in these pieces can be brought out beautifully with full-sounding snap strokes while the accompaniment is played with light free strokes. The snap stroke is also used to begin a phrase or to accent single-note high points of a phrase. Further, snap strokes work well for rhythmic accents. They are also good for bringing out the peak notes of arpeggios to give the arpeggio a distinctive shape. Another use for the snap stroke is playing unaccompanied or sparsely accompanied melodies where maximum fullness of sound is desired.

The main use of the *supported* stroke is for playing fast, vigorous scales where security and accuracy are paramount. (These strokes are described later in this chapter under "Fast Scales.")

Free strokes are used for the majority of the notes—for accented and unaccented melodic notes, accompaniments, arpeggios, and light, fast scales. Also, since they have a somewhat lighter sound and are easier to play at speed, free strokes are the dominant strokes in fast pieces; rest strokes are used sparingly for special accents. In any case, remember that a good free stroke is essential for high-quality playing.

Naturally there are variations on these basic strokes. There are light and heavy varieties of both strokes that are applied according to different musical needs. Light rest strokes of the supported type, for example, are often used to play fast scales. The supported stroke gives security because the fingers have constant contact with the strings and the lightness allows the fingers to move quickly. Heavy free strokes, on the other hand, may be used to accent a melodic line that cannot be brought out with rest strokes.

The Side Stroke

This stroke is a variation on the free and rest strokes we have already discussed. It is used for special expressive purposes and is usually done with the fingers, not the thumb. Segovia and his students have shown how effective this stroke can be. It can bring out an important note in a particularly lush way or give an especially sweet, full sound to each note in a slow melodic

passage. The stroke is made by playing across the string at a considerable angle, either to the left or to the right. Figure 5–14 shows a side stroke moving to
the player's left. The dotted line shows how the finger travels along the string
for a short way before it releases.

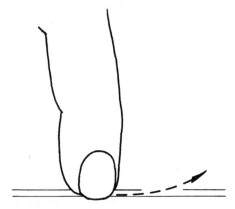

Figure 5–14   Right-hand side stroke

The effect is that of a very wide finger going across the string. This produces
an especially soft sound because the high harmonics are attenuated by the
broad surface of the attack. The string in this case is literally "caressed." The
sound is delicately coaxed out of it rather than strongly encouraged. The side
stroke can be done with either rest or free strokes on single notes or chords.
However, it is usually done with rest strokes on single notes.

Tremolo

Many players have difficulty achieving a good tremolo when they play such
pieces as Tárrega's *Recuerdos de la Alhambra* or E. Sainz de la Maza's *Campanas
del Alba*. The Play–Relax approach can be helpful here. In fact, in one form or
the other, a number of prominent players recommend it to their students. Figure 5–15 illustrates one way you can do it.

Figure 5–15   Play–Relax exercise for tremolo

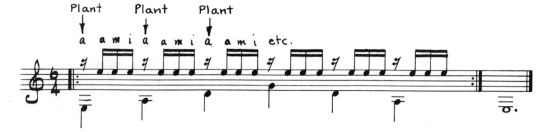

This simple type of exercise does not involve the left hand and thus you can more easily concentrate on the tremolo. In this tremolo practice method, the *a* finger is planted on the first string at the same time as *p* plays the bass note. Whenever possible, *p* plays a rest stroke and is allowed to rest on the adjacent string to stabilize the hand. Once the *a* finger is planted, the other fingers seem to have no trouble finding the string. Many students have developed a perfectly accurate and even tremolo this way.

Slow, conscious practice of the exercise in Figure 5–15, starting with the metronome at about ♩ = 88, will develop the precision and evenness of movements needed for the tremolo when it is played up to tempo. The practice of planting the *a* finger is what assures the accuracy of the tremolo at high speed since that finger, although it will not be consciously planted, will be trained to stay very close to the tremolo string. The other fingers will tend to follow the ring finger.

Some players recommend planting *every* finger to make sure that each one learns to find the right string. This completely staccato approach starts off as above by planting *a* along with *p* and then the process is continued. The *m* finger should plant at the same time as *a* plays and *i* should plant at the same time as *m* plays. Finally, *p* should plant as *i* plays. The additional planting in this approach may be just the thing to make your tremolo perfectly accurate.

You can try both these methods of tremolo practice and see which one works best for you. Whichever practice method you choose, each finger should make a vigorous free stroke of equal loudness and, as in the previous exercises, the fingers should relax as completely as possible after the stroke.

For the tremolo to have its proper effect, it must be played quickly—at least ♩ =144 (four notes to a beat). At that tempo, the listener gets the impression of a continuous thread of sound rather than individual notes. The tremolo practice methods we have described—especially the second one—tend to produce a choppy, staccato sound at slow speeds, but as you increase your speed, the choppiness will gradually disappear. One way to gain speed and yet retain accuracy is to gradually increase your metronome settings using the tremolo exercises we described. However, players who try to increase their speed by this "one-notch-at-a-time" method often have difficulty getting past a certain tempo because they are trying too hard to control each note of the tremolo.

Another and perhaps better way to increase speed is to alternate the slow, careful practice with "letting the tremolo happen." "Letting it happen" means that you play the tremolo at the fastest comfortable speed without trying to control the accuracy—even though it may sound a bit messy at first. The idea is to gain the fluidity that is necessary to play the tremolo fast. Sooner or later, the player will have to "let the tremolo happen" anyway in order to play at tempo, so he may as well practice letting it go shortly after he starts working on it. With this combined approach, the accuracy and evenness of the slow practice and the fluidity of the fast practice will eventually come together in a beautiful, dynamically relaxed tremolo.

PLAY–RELAX FOR THE LEFT HAND

Dynamically Relaxing the Left Hand

The Play–Relax practice strategy can be just as useful for the left hand as for the right. This approach can be applied to almost every aspect of left-hand playing: chords, scales, slurs, stretching, legato, speed, and coordination of the left hand with the right. The principal idea of the Play–Relax practice technique for the left hand is a simple one: Learn to release the finger pressure as completely and quickly as possible after each note or chord has been played. This way of practicing is completely in accord with the principle of minimum effort. You learn how to relax the fingers and the hand at every opportunity so that you do not become fatigued. You also learn to focus your energy only on those fingers that you actually need to play the notes; the others "play dead," so to speak. Further, you learn to use just the right amount of tension in the fingers when you play. When the fingers have the right tension and are properly curved, then the first two joints will not collapse and you will have good control over your playing. If for some reason you experience too much tension in the left hand while practicing, remember that the Play–Relax idea is to stop and release that tension before continuing.

An important adjunct to the Play–Relax approach for the left hand is a technique that violinist Yehudi Menuhin calls "pussyfooting." Pussyfooting on the guitar, as the name so graphically suggests, means that, with the exception of ascending slurs, the left-hand fingers should not be slammed against the fingerboard as if pounding nails. Rather the fingers should be allowed to fall gracefully of their own weight onto the board and then the required pressure should be applied. Even ascending slurs should not be any more forceful than absolutely necessary. This "pussyfooting" approach saves the player much energy and cultivates greater left-hand sensitivity and accuracy.

Now let's look at how the Play–Relax practice technique can be applied to make left-hand movements easier and more effective.

Legato Chord Sequences

Guitarists frequently have difficulties playing chord sequences legato (connected) and in rhythm without wearing out the left hand. The crux of the problem is that many players put too much tension on the hand during the sequences. The difficulty is often compounded by lack of coordination between the two hands.

A good approach is to do the exact opposite of the legato that you ultimately want. Thus you play the chords in the sequence with a deliberate staccato in the Play–Relax manner. You can do this by placing an eighth or a quarter rest between the chords during which you relax the left hand and fingers as much as possible, but leave them lightly resting on the strings. During position shifts, it is good to keep the fingers either on or very close to the strings. Also, the changes of position should be made with light, distinct movements. There should be little pressure on the strings during such changes. (See "The Art of Making Connections" in Chapter 6.)

It is important to plant the right-hand fingers on the chords just before playing them to give the left hand a brief silence during which it can change chords and relax. The planting also ensures that the two hands will be coordinated.

We can use the following excerpt from *Pavan No. VI* by Luis Milán to illustrate how to apply the Play–Relax idea to chord sequences. Figure 5–16 shows the passage as usually written.

Figure 5–16   Luis Milán, *Pavan No. 6*

To develop the "on-off" Play–Relax response, you can practice the passage with quarter rests inserted between the notes as in Figure 5–17.

Figure 5–17   Play–Relax chord exercise based on Figure 5–16

You can start working with the metronome beating quarters at about ♩ = 60 with special emphasis on relaxing during the rests. To gain the maximum effect from the exercise, play the study with both hands doing staccato, that is, plant the right-hand fingers and release the left-hand pressure quickly after playing each chord. You should find that practicing this way is much less tiring than the usual method of applying continuous pressure.

Practicing chord sequences in this manner lays the foundation for legato playing. The clear-cut staccato technique helps you to establish precise, coordinated movements with relaxation in between. When you have learned the movements well, you can play more and more legato by gradually shortening the space between the chords until they are sounding for almost their full value. There will always be spaces between the chords, but they can be made almost imperceptible. The Play–Relax approach trains you to take advantage of these tiny spaces so that you have a very brief yet significant relaxation of the fingers. Playing legato in this way is not so tiring as the constant pressure method that many players use. (For more on this, see "Staccato and Legato" in Chapter 6.)

Now let's look at a special Play–Relax technique that is useful for making smooth left-hand changes. Here we will use it in a melody and accompaniment piece. When you change chords in such a piece, it is particularly important to make the breaks between the notes in the main melodic line as small as possible. That is, after all, the most prominent part and it should sing out smoothly. However, there can occasionally be larger breaks in the less prominent parts, during which some of the fingers get a chance to relax and prepare for a smooth chord change.

Figure 5–18 presents an example of how to use Play–Relax in the last two bars of Tárrega's *Adelita* to make a legato left-hand chord change. Most players try to make the change legato by holding on to *all* the notes of the B7 chord as full quarter notes until the last instant before moving to the E chord (Figure 5–18a). Unfortunately, although it seems logical to hold all the notes for their full value, this approach does not always work well. In this case, the player is forced to make a jerky, disconnected movement from B7 to E which causes a distinct break in the melodic line.

Figure 5–18   Play–Relax legato technique in Tárrega's *Adelita*

The remedy for this awkward change requires only a slight shift in thinking. In this example, since the main musical interest is in the D♯ to E in the treble melody, that is what really needs to be legato. It is not necessary to make all the notes of the two chords connect perfectly. A good overall legato effect can be produced by playing the chord as shown in Figure 5–18b. First, play the full B7 chord with a bar at the beginning of the beat. Then, after the chord has had a chance to sound for three quarters of the beat, remove the bar but leave the fourth finger on the D♯ for its full value. While the fourth finger is holding the D♯, you can easily prepare the first two fingers to play the E chord in the next measure. In order to get a really "seamless" connection between the D♯ and E, hold the D♯ long enough so that it actually sounds along with the E for a fraction of a second.

This approach is musical because the melody comes out virtually unbroken. The approach is also relaxing because the first three fingers of the left hand get a brief rest before going on to the next chord. The slightly shortened accompaniment in the bass is not really disturbing since the main attention is not on it. Play–Relax chord changes of this sort are found frequently in the playing of fine guitarists. This approach can be used in many of your chord changes to make them flow both technically and musically.

Slurs and Stretching

The Play–Relax concept works very well as a practice technique for various kinds of left-hand movements. The main idea is to rest between repetitions of left-hand exercises and passages. Take the typical slur exercise in Figure 5–19 as an example.

Figure 5–19   Play–Relax slur exercise

The exercise starts in the ninth position and is moved down the fingerboard one position at a time to the first position. Typically, such exercises are played continuously, that is, without breaks between the positions. This creates a considerable amount of tension and fatigue. If you use the Play–Relax technique as in Figure 5–19 and take a one-beat rest before each position change, you can avoid the excess tension build-up.

Play–Relax slur practice is of great value for both beginning and advanced players. It is not the only way to practice slurs, but it is a good preventive against excess tension. It also prepares the hand to play continuous slurs or other movements with greater ease because, as in the previous Play–Relax exercises, the hand and fingers learn to take micro-relaxation breaks between the notes. In this case, the breaks are taken during the position shifts. It is helpful to go back to this method whenever tension appears.

Play–Relax is very useful for stretching exercises. Such exercises, if done in the conventional way with no breaks, can be damaging to the muscles and tendons of the left hand. The exercise in Figure 5–20, which has a rest after each stretch, is quite effective and causes less strain for the player.

Figure 5–20   Play–Relax stretching exercise

The method is similar to the way yoga postures are done. It is a kind of yoga for the hands. You develop the flexibility of your fingers by stretching them out, holding them for a short period, and then letting them relax. The key expression is "short period." You stretch the fingers just a bit beyond the point where you begin to feel a strain and then stop. For this exercise, therefore, you should descend only to the fingerboard position where the stretching starts to be uncomfortable and then stop there. Let the progress be gradual and painless. The flexibility will come.

PUTTING THE HANDS TOGETHER

Fast Scales

Sooner or later you will realize that one important challenge is to get your two hands to work together. Coordination and synchronization of the hands is important for all areas of playing, but nowhere is this more important than in fast scales. If the hands are not exactly synchronized in a speedy scale, you will know it immediately because the scale will come out in disarray. For that reason, working on scale speed is one good way of developing and testing the coordination of your hands.

Playing scales quickly is not a problem once the guitarist knows the best ways to practice. There are several necessary ingredients to fast scale technique. The most important one, which we have already mentioned, is coordinating and synchronizing the hands. The hands and fingers must also be in a dynamically relaxed state. It is especially important that the middle and tip segments of the right-hand fingers be curved and firm enough so they do not collapse during the rapid strokes. The left-hand fingers need to be curved and firm as well. The fingers of both hands also need to have micro-relaxations between the notes to avoid excess tension. Another important part of fast scales is anchoring the right hand in some way so that it has stability and leverage. Further, the movements of both hands should be as quick, accurate, and small as possible. Finally, after disciplined practice, the player must be able to let go and allow the scales to come out at high speed in a relaxed way. Now, before we get involved with synchronizing the hands, we need to look at some specific ways to develop speed and accuracy in the right hand.

Right-Hand Speed

The Supported Stroke   The Play–Relax approach can be used effectively to achieve right-hand security and speed. The exercise in Figure 5–21 incorporates this idea.

Figure 5–21   Play–Relax exercise for the supported rest stroke

This exercise is similar to the one in Figure 5–4, but here we use the *supported* rest stroke instead of the snap stroke because it gives greater security for fast scales. In the snap stroke, as you may recall, the finger is allowed to recoil freely from the adjacent string—a technique that is a bit loose for high speed scales. In the supported stroke, on the other hand, each finger is allowed to rest on the adjacent string after the stroke (except on the sixth string). Thus there is continual string contact in this kind of stroke, which is what gives you security.

The alternation of *m i* rest strokes is the most common way of playing fast scales, so we will use it in our exercise. First, rest the thumb on the sixth string to anchor the hand. Now plant the *m* finger on the G string (at the eighth rest) and play it with a quick, vigorous stroke. Then, allow the finger to come to rest on the adjacent D string after the stroke, releasing the finger tension in the process. Avoid letting the finger bounce. It should remain sitting on the D string for security. At the same time that you make the stroke with the *m* finger, plant the *i* finger on the G string in a ready position. This will create a staccato effect which is just fine for practicing this stroke. Now make the *i* stroke, let it come to rest on the D string, and plant the *m* finger simultaneously on the G string. Continue the exercise in this way until it feels comfortable. In this process, try to keep your finger movements as small as possible.

Stabilizing the Right Hand   It is good to emphasize the importance of anchoring the thumb in some way for fast scales. Usually the thumb rests on one of the bass strings. You can also anchor it on the soundboard temporarily when starting scales on the sixth string. Another way to stabilize the hand is to lay the thumb sideways across the bass strings. (The latter way has the often desirable effect of stopping unwanted ringing of the strings.) Flamenco guitarists have a further way of stabilizing the hand for fast scales. In addition to resting the thumb on a bass string, they also position the right-hand wrist down fairly close to the soundboard for greater leverage. Both lowering the wrist and resting the thumb on a bass string will be helpful in the following exercises.

Right-Hand Speed Bursts   When you have become comfortable with the supported strokes in the exercise in Figure 5–22, you can start to build up your right-hand speed. (Before starting the exercises, make sure your nails are done well so they do not snag.) The conventional way of increasing speed is to move up the metronome a notch at a time. This usually works, but for many people the Play–Relax approach works better. The Play–Relax way is not to begin with long "speed runs." Instead, you start with short, quick bursts of *i m* or *m i* alternation with rests in between as in Figure 5–22.

Figure 5–22   Right-hand speed burst exercise

With your thumb resting on the sixth string and wrist lowered, play this exercise as fast as is comfortable. Do it with the metronome for rhythmic precision. Do not work too hard to play fast. *Let* it happen rather than trying to force it. You will find that it is best to play somewhat more lightly when you are aiming for speed. The vital parts of the exercise are the rests. Let the hand and fingers relax as much as possible during these rests. You can make up your own exercises along these lines with varying numbers of notes per beat and varying speeds. In order to integrate accuracy with speed, you can alternate the slow, staccato practice with the practice of speed bursts. This will eventually produce dynamic relaxation in the right hand. When you are comfortable with short bursts of strokes, do longer and longer bursts until they extend to the length of whatever scales you want to play.

Synchronizing the Hands

Now that you have some ideas about developing velocity for the right hand alone, let's see how to develop it in a coordinated way for both hands. We can start with a simple chromatic scale exercise as in Figure 5–23.

Figure 5–23   Exercise for the synchronization of the two hands

For the moment, let's focus on the left-hand part. Each left-hand finger movement can be practiced with the same kind of staccato Play–Relax method as in the chord exercise in Figure 5–17. You play ("P") each note and then relax ("R") the finger immediately after its note has sounded, thus cutting the note off. For minimal movement in the ascending scale, let the left-hand fingers sit lightly on the string after they have played. It is not necessary to move them until it is time to play on the next string.

Left-hand playing in the Play–Relax way is quite easy since you actually apply pressure on a note with only one finger at a time and that pressure is released quickly as soon as the note is finished. At any given time, the three fingers that are not playing learn to do almost nothing—they "play dead" if you will—and thus get maximum relaxation between the notes. This relaxation is crucial for playing at high speed. You will find that the more quickly you can relax each finger between the notes, the faster you can play scales.

Now let's see how you can synchronize the hands in the preceding scale exercise. The synchronization is based on planting the right-hand finger just before the left-hand finger presses down its note. To begin, plant *m* on the low E and then play it. On the eighth rest, immediately after the *m* has played, plant *i*. Exactly on the second beat, place the first left-hand finger on the F and play it with *i*. After the F has sounded, release the pressure on the first finger. Then, on the eighth rest, right after *i* has played, plant *m*. When you arrive at the third beat, place the second finger on the F♯ and play it with *m*. Continue the exercise up the chromatic scale to the fourth fret on the first string.

At first, play slowly through this exercise with the metronome at ♪ = ca. 100 (clicking eighth notes) emphasizing the release between the notes. As you become more comfortable with the movements, increase the speed until the scale is going well with eighth notes at about 200. Then try playing the scale with the same staccato, Play–Relax approach but with the metronome clicking quarter notes (no rests in between) at 100. Speed up as it feels comfortable. Even after much practice, at a certain speed it will become very clumsy to keep on playing staccato. At that point, you will be ready for doing high speed exercises.

With careful practice of this exercise (or any other scale) in the Play–Relax manner, coordinated movements for scales will become automatic. Then you will not have to think about them when you are playing fast. The coordination that comes from the slow Play–Relax process is the basis of fast playing. When you play quickly in this manner, the clear-cut, on-off movements are still taking place, but in very rapid succession. If the movements are not clear-cut at speed, then the coordination will break down. It is time to go back to the slow practice!

Speed Bursts for Both Hands   Once you have established right- and left-hand coordination with the slow, staccato scale practice, you can build up speed. You can do this gradually with the metronome or by alternating the slow practice with quick, light practice as you did with the right hand alone. If you choose the latter, work on short bursts of notes with both hands together. Take the first position chromatic scale (or any other desired scale) and play a small part of it very quickly, relax, repeat, and go on to another part. Figure 5–24 shows one way of doing this.

Figure 5–24   Play–Relax chromatic exercise for fast scales

You can take each small segment of the scale and practice it separately in the same way. When you practice in this manner, the fingers will not get tense and the scales will be more accurate. When you feel relaxed and secure playing the short segments at speed, try stringing longer and longer segments together until you can play the whole scale. You might do it as in Figure 5–25.

Figure 5–25   Continuation of the exercise in Figure 5–24

Another Play–Relax tactic for practicing fast scales is to play as shown in Figure 5–26.

Figure 5–26 Another exercise for fast scales

The point of this exercise should be clear. When you are learning to play a fast scale, it is often best not to try to race through the entire scale at the same speed but rather to play a short group of quick notes and then relax on some slow ones. This method can be applied to any scale. Once you are comfortable with the pattern in this exercise, you might want to gradually increase the number of quick notes that you play consecutively—say eight sixteenths instead of four and then twelve, sixteen, and so on. In that way, you can easily gain speed without straining. If the exercise gets to be a strain at any point, just reduce the number of quick notes you play consecutively.

Figure 5–27 is a final example of how you can use the Play–Relax approach for scales.

Figure 5–27 A fast scale exercise taken from Villa-Lobos

H. Villa-Lobos, *Etude No. 7* from *Douze Etudes Pour Guitare*. Copyright © 1953 and reprinted with permission of *Editions Max Eschig*, owners of the work.

Here we can use the techniques from the previous chromatic scale exercises (Figures 5–23 to 5–25). Start off slowly using the Play–Relax approach. The actual effect of the technique is approximately as shown in Figure 5–28—at slow speed, of course.

Figure 5–28 Play–Relax approach to Figure 5–27

When the fingerings and coordination have been solidly established at the slow tempo, then take short sections and play them as fast as is comfortable. (Alternatively you can work up the speed a few metronome notches at a time.) You can start with this fragment (Figure 5–29).

Figure 5–29   First fragment of the scale in Figure 5–27

Play the fragment quickly and with good rhythm. Then relax as soon as you are finished. When that is comfortable at tempo, add on another fragment (Figure 5–30).

Figure 5–30   Next fragment of the scale in Figure 5–27

If the coordination of the hands is not right, go back to the slow Play–Relax practice. In any case, continue this chaining of segments until you have the entire scale at speed. This method will bring you to a rapid tempo in a short time. Remember, when you are playing the entire scale at speed, that it is best to *let the scale happen* and not try to force it to go faster than it will comfortably go.

After you have worked on the Play–Relax approach for a while, there is another technique that will help increase your scale velocity. This is a mental technique called *visualization*, which is discussed in Chapter 8.

PLAY–RELAX FOR PRACTICING
AN ENTIRE PIECE

The emphasis so far has been on application of the Play–Relax idea to improve specific parts of your exercises and pieces, such as scales, chord sequences, and slurs. However, Play–Relax can be useful in practicing through an entire piece. This can help you establish precise finger movements without having to use constant left-hand pressure. This approach works well on most pieces.

Using Play–Relax to practice a piece involves making on-off staccato movements wherever possible. That means lifting up the left-hand fingers after each note or chord and planting the right-hand fingers wherever possible. It is a way of studying that will not fatigue you as much as the usual way. The clipped staccato sound is not the most musical, but the energy you save is worth it. Obviously, practicing this way all the time would be very boring, but it is an effective method to use part of the time.

It is particularly effective to use Play–Relax when practicing an entire arpeggiated piece that can be put into block chords.[5] Sor's Op. 6, No. 11 (Segovia edition No. 17) is a good example. The original has a similar arpeggiated texture throughout (Figure 5–31).

Figure 5–31   Fernando Sor, Op. 6, No. 11

The arpeggios can be arranged into three or four note block chords and then played as follows (Figure 5–32):

Figure 5–32   Figure 5–31 arranged in block chords

Left-hand pressure is released between the chords. When you practice the study as shown, you will not only find it very relaxing, but the left-hand movements and the simple underlying chord structure will also become clear. It goes without saying that this idea can be applied to other arpeggio pieces with a similar structure, such as Tárrega's *Estudio Brillante,* Carcassi's Op. 60, No. 3, Giuliani's Op. 48, No. 5, and Villa-Lobos' *Etude No. 1* and *Prelude No. 4.*

As you can see, the Play–Relax staccato approach works well with block chord textures. However, this approach is not limited to block chords. It can be used for almost any kind of musical texture. For example, you can use it for pieces that are based on counterpoint, such as the Fugue from J.S. Bach's *Sonata No. 1* for solo violin (BWV 1001). Naturally it will not always be convenient to play staccato on every note of such pieces, particularly where you have open strings, slurs, or arpeggios. You need not be concerned about these notes. Every single note does not have to be staccato. Just plant your fingers

---

[5]In Goebels, *The New Busoni,* p. 73, Busoni recommends that students play the arpeggiated Prelude XV from *The Well-Tempered Clavier* first as block chords, then as arpeggios.

and cut the notes short with the left hand wherever it is feasible to do so. This technique will help you coordinate your finger movements as well as control the articulation of the notes. As you may know, good use of articulation (legato and staccato) helps clarify contrapuntal structure by controlling the length of the notes. Counterpoint can become very muddy on the guitar if the notes are allowed to ring longer than is appropriate.

SUMMARY

The state of dynamic relaxation can be cultivated specifically for guitar playing movements by using the Play–Relax practice technique. The technique consists of making distinct, regular alternations of playing and relaxing in the fingers. This technique is effective because it is done in a rhythmical, on-off manner that is parallel to the way the nervous system works. The nervous system seems to favor entraining itself with such rhythmical Play–Relax movements because it involves less effort. When the technique is practiced properly, these movements are balanced. For every exertion, there will be a corresponding relaxation. The relaxation between the notes is especially significant. You learn to take full advantage of the space between the notes, however small, to get the greatest possible relaxation. In this way, you learn to balance the playing with relaxation. When that balance is just right, then playing becomes effortless.

The Play–Relax technique is a valuable method for practicing scales, arpeggios, slurs, chords, and entire pieces. There are, of course, other applications that we have not mentioned which you can imagine. You might use it, for example, to relax the fingers quickly between the strokes of the *rasgueado* (a technique derived from flamenco guitarists that involves strumming the strings with one or more of the right-hand fingers). In any case, since the technique emphasizes relaxation between the notes, it makes guitar practice much less tiring. When it is combined with planting of the right-hand fingers, the Play–Relax approach also produces efficient, precisely coordinated finger movements. With this technique, the emphasis is on "doing less and accomplishing more" in your practice sessions.

When you use the Play–Relax technique, it is good to keep in mind that it is just one of a number of practice methods. While it is very effective, it is not meant to be used to the exclusion of other methods. It should be clear that Play–Relax is not meant to be used when you actually perform. In performance, the benefits of deliberate Play–Relax practice should come through, but in such an automatic way that you do not have to think about it.

If you regularly cultivate a balance between playing and relaxing with the Play–Relax technique, it will help you experience dynamic relaxation on a regular basis when you perform. In that state, your hands and fingers will work with the least possible effort. When conditions are right, your pieces will seem to play themselves. You will not be playing them with conscious effort. Instead, the natural intelligence of body and subconscious mind will play them through you. When this happens, performance becomes a complete joy and involves no strain on the player.

Now that you have some of the basic ideas of an effortless, natural guitar technique, it will be fruitful to look into some refinements of that technique. That will be the topic of the next chapter.

6.

Refining Your Guitar Skills
pay attention to the details

I have always regarded technique as a means, not an end in itself. One must, of course, master technique; at the same time, one must not become enslaved by it. One must understand that the purpose of technique is to transmit the inner meaning, the message of the music. The most perfect technique is that which is not noticed at all.

Pablo Casals, *Joys and Sorrows*

There is a great difference between something solidly sewn and something timorously adjusted.

Wanda Landowska, *Landowska On Music*

As in other worthwhile endeavors, playing the classical guitar well requires close attention to technical details. If you do not take care of the details, they will come back to haunt you when you perform. Thus, the wisest course is to take care of as many fine points of technique as possible before a performance. However, when polishing your technique, always keep in mind that, as the cellist Casals said, the aim of technique is not technique itself, but to bring out the inner meaning of the music in a natural, unostentatious way. Now let's look at some ways of refining your technical skills.

REFINING THE RIGHT HAND

Tone Concept

A good classical singer in the Western/European tradition aims at producing the best possible quality of sound. He will not be able to uplift his listeners if his voice is hoarse and scratchy. Similarly, the good classical guitarist works toward producing the best possible tone quality with the right hand. He attempts to refine his tone to the point where no coarseness or impurity remains. Thus the player has a concept of a beautiful tone and then tries to produce it on the guitar.

What is the tone concept of the major concert guitarists today? These artists all use their fingernails to produce the tone since the nails offer brilliance and variety of tone color. This is not to say that playing with only the flesh of the fingertip has no value. Rather it appears that the use of the relatively soft flesh tone is generally better suited to instruments such as the lute which are oriented more toward small audiences and less toward great tonal variety. In any case, the normal nail tone associated with the finest concert guitarists is clear, round, sweet, and ethereal in character. It has no harshness, scratchiness, thumps, or clicks. It is pure. Segovia says that this "physical beauty of sound . . . is not the result of stubborn will power but springs

Note: Some of the ideas on nails, articulation, and vibrato from Charles Duncan's fine book *The Art of Classical Guitar Playing* (Princeton: Summy-Birchard Music, 1980) have been very helpful for this chapter.

from the innate excellence of the spirit."[1] This is the kind of tone that can be completely enchanting to both player and listener. Every guitarist should aim for such a beautiful, clear sound. Do not be easily satisfied. Experiment with your tone until you obtain the desired sound. Remember that whether you play *piano* or *forte* the tone should still be good. The Russian composer Scriabin admonished his piano students that, even when they wanted to play a powerful *forte,* they should not make it sound like a "falling chest of drawers." The same obviously applies to the guitar.

Your first concern in producing a good tone is to get a clear concept of that tone in your "inner ear." The best way to get this concept is to *experience* the beautiful sound of a good player either live or on record. Listen carefully to that sound many times. Then close your eyes and imagine the sound as clearly as possible. When you have a clear idea of the sound in your head, then it will not be so difficult to actually produce it on the guitar. The other important concerns in tone production are the right-hand strokes and the nails. We have already discussed right-hand strokes in Chapter 5. At this point we will consider the nails. As you work on the nails, listen carefully to your tone and constantly try to improve it.

The Art of Caring for the Nails

In the same way that a singer's vocal cords influence his voice quality, a guitarist's nails intimately affect his tone. The shape and finish on the nails must be just right or the result will be clicks or roughness in the tone. Improperly shaped nails also result in their catching on the strings, thus impeding the flow of the right-hand finger movements. In order to avoid these difficulties, the guitarist needs to learn the delicate art of nail care. Each player must ultimately learn it for himself since all nails, like hands, are different. However, there are some ideas about nail care that can be helpful. Most guitarists will find that once they know the correct principles, they will have little problem getting the nails to work. Others may find that it will take more time and experimentation before they discover how to do the nails in the best way. In any case, no one should despair about their nails even if they present some difficulty at first. There is a way to take care of almost every nail problem. Some of the best concert guitarists have overcome such obstacles, so there is no reason why others cannot do the same. Now let's go directly to the heart of the matter.

Shaping　Caring for the nails is best done in three steps: shaping, sanding, and buffing. In the first step, the nail is given a rough shape with a "diamond dust" file (made with bits of synthetic gems), which is available in most drug stores. Emery boards are a poor second to diamond dust files. The common all-metal files are not satisfactory at all because they rip the layers of the nails apart and leave the edges ragged.

[1]Andrés Segovia, *Diatonic Major and Minor Scales* (Washington, D.C: Columbia Music, 1953), p. 1.

In filing the nails, one of the first questions that comes up is how long they should be. The nails work best when they are filed neither too long nor too short, that is, short enough to avoid catching and long enough to provide the right amount of resistance and to strike the strings when the fingers are moving quickly. The usual recommendation is that the nails, when seen from the back side, should be about one-sixteenth of an inch above the flesh (Figure 6–1). The thumbnail is usually somewhat longer—about one-eighth of an inch (Figure 6–2).

Figure 6–1 Suggested fingernail length

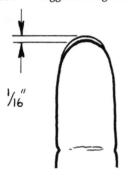

Figure 6–2 Suggested thumbnail length

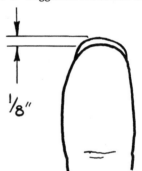

A general principle in shaping the nails is to avoid irregularities and sharp peaks. Most nails should have *slightly rounded* surfaces that more or less follow the contour of the fingertip. The slightly rounded shape allows the nail to pass over the string with just the right amount of resistance. When "planting" or placing a properly rounded nail on the string (see "Planting the Fingers," Chapter 5), it touches the string on its left side and at the end of the stroke it releases easily from about the middle of the nail (Figure 6–3).

Many players make the mistake of leaving a sharp peak somewhere on the nail. Thinking that the nail will go across the string more easily, they often file down the left side (the normal playing side) of the nail too much, thus leaving too much of a peak in the middle of the nail. However, with the left side too short and a peak in the middle that is even a bit too sharp, the nail often tends to snag even more. This is because the stroke begins at a rather low point on the left side of the nail. Thus, before the nail can release from the string, it has to ride up a relatively long way to its peak. If the peak is too high, the nail may hook very badly. The general remedy for the problem is to let the left edge of the nail grow somewhat longer and to file the peak down so that the top edge is slightly rounded. (Some nails work best when the top edge looks almost flat.)

Not all nails will work with the slightly rounded shape just described. Nevertheless, even if the nail requires an angled shape in order to function properly (see Figure 6–10), the corners should be slightly rounded to prevent snagging and bad tone.

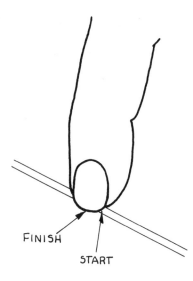

FINISH

START

Figure 6–3 Placement of the nail and fingertip on the string

Since each player's nails are unique, the exact way of filing them will vary. Also, since each individual nail may have a slightly different contour, it will have to be filed a bit differently from the others. In any case, you can start the rough shaping process by holding the file firmly in the left hand and placing the nail against the file as shown in Figure 6–4.

Figure 6–4 Nail-filing technique

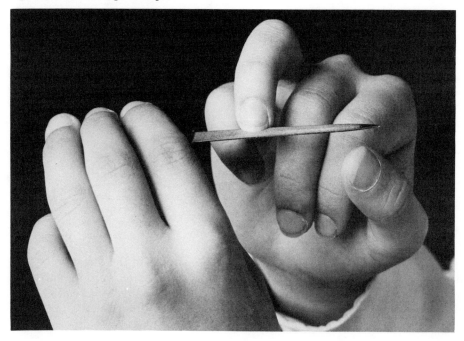

When seen from the side, the nail should be filed with the tip segment of the finger at no less than a 70-degree angle (Figure 6–5). With at least a 70-degree angle on the playing edge, the nail tends to release easily from the string. With a smaller angle, the nail often snags because it must ride up a greater distance before releasing.

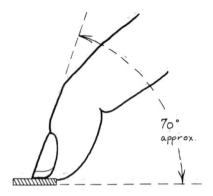

Figure 6–5 Side view of nail-filing angle

When looking at the nail from the front, the lateral angle of filing will depend on your natural nail shape. If the nail has a relatively regular curvature with the high point in the center (Figure 6–6), then the nail should be filed with the fingertip in a perpendicular plane to the file (Figure 6–7).

Figure 6–6 Nail with regular curvature

Figure 6–7 Filing a nail with regular curvature

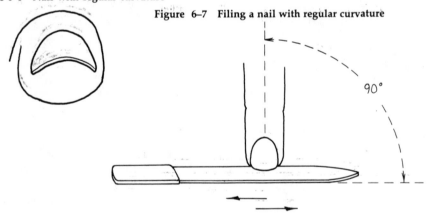

The nail should be filed with short, brisk strokes in the direction of the arrows so that most of the nail edge, particularly the center portion, ends up sitting almost in a straight line on the file. Then, as we suggested earlier, the corners should be rounded off slightly to avoid snagging.

If your nail curvature is irregular (something like Figure 6–8), then the perpendicular filing will generally not work very well. The same holds true for nails that have very little curvature (as in Figure 6-9).

Figure 6–8 Nail with irregular curvature

Figure 6–9 Nail with little curvature

In these cases, you can experiment with filing at different lateral angles until you find the one where the nail passes over the string with the correct amount of resistance and produces the best tone. The exact angle of filing will depend on nail curvature and how the strokes are made. It is good to avoid extreme angles to prevent snagging. Many nails will work well if they are filed with a *slight* slope down toward the playing side (Figure 6–10).

Figure 6–10 Filing nail with slope down toward playing side

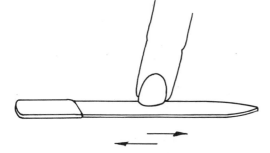

Figure 6–11 Filing nail with slope down toward nonplaying side

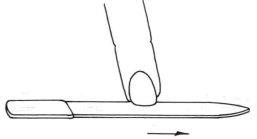

Some players may find to their surprise that their nails work best if they are sloped down somewhat in the *opposite* direction from the playing side (Figure 6–11). Thus the higher side of the nails is the playing side. Whatever the direction and angle of the slope, file the edge of the nail straight across. Then gently round off the corners.

It is good to make sure there is a proper angle on the playing edge of the nail—no matter what the shape—so that it will pass over the string as smoothly as possible. To do this, run the playing surface gently across the file several times in the direction of the arrow as shown in Figure 6–12. Do it just as if you were making a stroke and the file were a string.

Figure 6–12   Giving a proper contour to the nail

If difficulties persist after trying these nail-shaping ideas, see the section "Special Nail Problems" on page 124.

Sanding   The nail-sanding process is done with fine finishing paper. This step removes most of the roughness left by the file. 600 grade silicon carbide paper works very well for this purpose. One way of working with this paper is to wrap a piece tightly around your file and then, in a manner similar to that in which you filed the nails, to sand the entire playing edge with light strokes. Use the paper to round off the playing edge further and thus reduce the chance of snagging. In this sanding process, make sure to remove all the remains of the rough filing, especially for the underside of the nails. Players are frequently careless about this and wonder why their tone is not good.

Buffing   The final step of caring for the nails is buffing or polishing. A chamois nail buffer (available in drug stores) is one of the better polishing agents, although you could also use a well-worn piece of 600 grade finishing paper or a fresh piece of 800 grade paper. Rubbing the nails vigorously on one's trousers also works, although not quite as effectively as a chamois buffer. The entire playing surface of the nail should be rubbed with the chamois or other buffing material. Make sure not to miss the underside. The entire playing surface should end with a *glassy smooth* finish. You can test for smoothness by running your left-hand thumbnail across the playing surface of each nail. Every bit of roughness and every nick should be removed so that the nail does not catch and the tone is silky in quality.

The Thumbnail   A well-shaped thumbnail is a vital asset to the guitarist. If you make the stroke properly, the thumbnail will produce clearly articulated bass notes that project well in a concert situation. If the nail is not shaped properly or is not used with care, there will often be too much flesh striking the string. As a result, the bass sound will be muddy and it will be difficult to tell where the notes begin and end. The muted flesh tone has its place as a special effect, but it is best to use the clear nail tone for normal playing.

As with the fingernails, the thumbnail should be filed according to its natural contour. If, when viewed from the end (Figure 6–13), the nail curvature has a high point in the middle, it usually works best to file the nail with the thumbtip perpendicular to the file. File the nail so that the middle part sits on the file in a straight line (see Figure 6–7). Then round off the corners as usual. Thus, from behind, the nail will have a somewhat squarish appearance (Figure 6–14). This may seem like an odd shape for a nail, but some players get good results with it.

Figure 6–13 Thumbnail with regular curvature

Figure 6–14 Thumbnail with regular curvature after filing

If the nail has an irregular curvature (Figure 6–15) or has little curvature (Figure 6–16) when viewed from the end, then, as with the fingernails, you should experiment with filing the slope of the nail in different directions and with different angles.

Figure 6–15 Thumbnail with irregular curvature

Figure 6–16 Thumbnail with little curvature

In many cases, it works best to file the nail with the slope going down somewhat toward the left-hand playing side. From behind, the nail would look approximately as shown in Figure 6–17.

Figure 6–17 Thumbnail filed with slope down toward playing side

Figure 6–18 Thumbnail filed with slope down to nonplaying side

Depending on the curvature of the nail, it may work better to file the thumb-nail with the slope in the opposite direction (Figure 6–18). Thus, the playing side should be the highest. Since a good nail tone requires that the nail give a certain amount of resistance, this reverse slope may be the only way to get it. In any case, a certain amount of trial and error is necessary to determine the optimum slope direction and angle. Again, be sure to round off the corners of the nail. Now the nail should be sanded and buffed like the others.

Special Nail Problems   The majority of nail problems can be handled by keeping them clean and filing them properly. However, there are certain difficulties that require special treatment, such as weak nails that break or tear, and very flat, irregular, or hooked nails.

Some players complain about weak nails. Since nails are made of protein, the best approach for most people is to improve the nail from within by making sure there is high-quality, well-assimilated protein in your diet. Gelatin is sometimes recommended as a protein source. However, other sources—such as milk products and poultry—are better because, unlike gelatin, they are complete proteins, which are fully utilized by the body. If the internal approach is not enough, there are some external nail preparations on the market that may be helpful. The best kinds are made from natural ingredients that soak into the nail and strengthen it. If you use one of them, avoid those that contain formaldehyde because they will "pickle" your nails and make them hard and brittle; this often results in a harsh tone. Another solution for weak nails is to use a commercial nail hardener that coats the surface, but such preparations also tend to make the tone rather hard. To avoid the hard sound, do not put the hardener on the very tip of the nail near the playing surface. Avoid leaving the hardener on the nails for long periods or they will weaken. Periodically take off the hardener with nail polish remover and let the nails "breathe" for a day or two.

Even with the best of precautions, nails may sometimes break or tear. Thus it is important to have some way of fixing them. Usually the most effective way of repairing a tear is to glue the torn parts with one of the "super" glues presently available. Ladies' nail repair kits may also help. After the repair, apply one or two coats of a good nail hardener. Even if a nail has been torn off completely, it is sometimes possible to glue it back on. If that does not work, then there are two kinds of false nails that can be glued on. Some are especially made for guitarists,[2] while others are meant for ladies; the former are best, but the latter may do in an emergency.

Now let's look at a description of a special method used by some concert artists to deal with nails that have irregular or little curvature. In the former case, the nails are "wavy" (see Figure 6–8). In the latter case, the nails are

---

[2]Special plastic nails for guitarists called "Player's Nails" are currently available from Balkan Music, 99 Pond Ave., Suite 224, Brookline, Mass. 02146.

almost flat when viewed from the end (see Figure 6–9). The difficulty with very irregular or very flat nails is that they often present too much resistance to the string and tend to catch too easily as one makes a stroke. The special angled filing that we discussed earlier may take care of this problem, but for stubborn cases there is another way. It is not as natural as one might like, but it works.

The process is as follows: If the nails are hard, soak them in warm water for about ten or fifteen minutes to soften them. Now pinch the sides of each nail between your left thumb and index finger so that the middle is formed into a more rounded, regular curvature (see Figure 6–6). Generally, a nail with a rounded, regular curvature does not create as much resistance as the flat or irregular nail in going over the string. After pinching and reforming, the nails will usually stay in the new shape for a short while. However, to ensure that they remain that way for several days, give them two coats of a commercial nail hardener, preferably one with nylon fibers for strength. Put one coat on sideways across the nail and the other lengthwise. Let the first coat dry thoroughly before applying the second and also let the second coat dry well before playing. Now file, sand, and buff the nail as suggested earlier. With the new curved shape and proper filing, the nails should not snag on the strings. This should be particularly noticeable in playing fast scales and arpeggios. If the tone is harsh, make sure the hardener is not applied too close to the playing edge of the nails.

Some players have nails that grow over the edge of the flesh and hook downward. This creates difficulties because the nails tend to catch on the strings very easily. One solution to this problem is to file the hooked part of the nail straight across and then round it off slightly at the edges. If you have a hook on the left-hand corner of the nail, it sometimes helps to file it off from the *underside* of the nail. If these ideas do not work, the player might try soaking and pinching the nails into a more arched shape and coating them with nail polish. If all else fails, the player can cut his nails all the way down and use the above-mentioned plastic nails that are made just for guitarists. One professional player was so dissatisfied with the nails on his index finger that he tried one of those special nails. He claims that it wears better and produces a better tone than the natural nail.

Tone Color

One way of refining your playing is to learn how to produce an attractive and varied palette of tone colors and then use them tastefully in your pieces. Tone color refers primarily to the quality of sound you produce with the right-hand strokes on the different strings. The particular tone color is largely determined by the presence or absence of certain harmonics above the fundamental note. On the classical guitar, tone color is a great expressive resource. You can produce many colors that sound like different instruments by striking the strings in different ways. Thus you can make the guitar sound like a "miniature orchestra."

An important concept in connection with tone color and other elements of interpretation is the establishment of a *normal mode of expression*. That means, for most music, that you establish one basic tone color and use others as occasional contrasts. If you change the color every other bar, or even every phrase, you will have nothing but constant contrast and the color variations will become meaningless. Therefore it is good to be discriminating in your use of tone colors.

Most guitarists are familiar with the different tone colors produced by striking the strings closer to or farther away from the bridge. There are also color variations that can be produced by playing the same passage on different strings. Some of the colors obtainable just by moving the right hand are: a nasal oboe sound close to the bridge; a brass sound midway between bridge and soundhole; what Segovia calls the full "natural voice" or normal sonority of the guitar at the edge of the soundhole nearest the bridge; and a very mellow, harplike tone at the edge of the soundhole nearest the fingerboard. Not everyone will agree with Segovia's idea of the normal sonority of the guitar, but it is something that the guitarist should think about. In any case, remember that if you want true color variations, you must have a normal color from which you can occasionally deviate so that there will be meaningful contrast.

The colors produced by playing the same notes on different strings are quite varied due to the differences in thickness and material of the strings. The color of open strings and the stopped strings in lower positions tends to be bright and clear while that of stopped strings (except the first) in upper positions tends to be softer and richer. Of course there is a clear difference between the nylon and metal wound strings. The former tend to be lighter and thinner in tone quality and the latter heavier and richer—although, when new, the metal strings have a certain brilliance.

Experiment with the colors on the guitar to get a feel for them. Take a short melodic passage and play it on different strings and with different right-hand attacks. Listen to the sounds with eyes closed so that you can focus on them clearly. Try making sounds that are "golden and round," "dark and velvety," "light and silvery," "sharp and nasal," or whatever you can imagine. Notice the subtle or not so subtle differences in the emotions that the different tone colors evoke. You will find that it is not necessary to move your right hand very much to produce several colors. You can do it by simply changing the angle with which you attack the strings. For most players, a straight-on attack (with the nail face parallel to the string) produces a sharp, metallic quality; a more angled attack (off the left-hand side of the nail) produces a softer, mellower tone. Of course there are many shades in between. An additional muted color can be created by playing with the flesh of the thumb.

The use of tone colors is most often left to the discretion of the performer, although modern scores are sometimes quite detailed in this respect.

The colors are usually indicated by words such as: *ponticello* (at the bridge), *tasto* (at the fingerboard), *dolce* (sweetly—usually near or over the soundhole), and so on.

Segovia has suggested that, if guitarists want to learn how to use tone colors properly, they will do well to study orchestral performances to hear how the various instrumental sounds are applied in a composition. The player can then see how he might imitate some of those sounds at appropriate places in his pieces. Needless to say, this guitar "orchestration" should be done with care and taste. A beautiful example of how tone colors can be taste-fully applied can be found in Segovia's edition of Turina's *Fandanguillo*. To the flamenco aficionado, the piece will evoke the sound of dancers and singers. However, for someone who has listened to much orchestral music, the piece will evoke the sounds of different instruments. The first few bars start off with sounds like a timpani on the fifth and sixth strings answered by brass on the first four strings (Figure 6–19).

Figure 6–19 Joaquin Turina, *Fandanguillo*

From *Fandanguillo* by Joaquin Turina. Copyright © 1926, B. SCHOTT'S SÖHNE, Mainz. Copyright © renewed 1954. Used by permission of the publisher, B. SCHOTT'S SÖHNE, Mainz.

Shortly afterward comes a passage that sounds like a string section playing pizzicato (Figure 6–20).

Figure 6–20

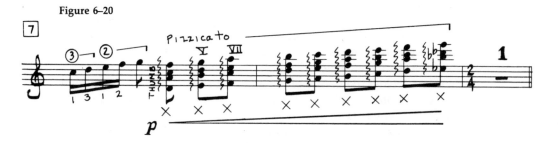

In measure 27 of the piece (Figure 6–21), there is a passage on the first three strings that sounds very much like trumpets and in bar 29 the same passage is echoed on strings 2, 3, and 4 where it suggests French horns.

Figure 6–21

There are other striking color effects in the *Fandanguillo* that you can undoubtedly identify. By exploring the colors, in this piece, you get some ideas about how to "orchestrate" other guitar works. Obviously such colors cannot be used in every piece. Each individual piece must be studied carefully to see how much "orchestration" would be appropriate. Many pieces need little or none, while others, like the *Fandanguillo*, can use quite a bit.

Staccato and Legato

Among the various technical means for expressing musical emotions, variety of *articulation* is one of the principal ones. Articulation chiefly concerns how notes are begun and ended. More specifically, it deals with whether they are *legato*, that is, smoothly connected with one another, or *staccato*, that is, separated from one another.

The best players cultivate a fine control over the total range of staccato and legato, from a brusque staccatissimo with clear-cut spaces between the notes to a soft legatissimo with very small spaces. In playing one piece, the artist may use many different shades of these articulations to express various feelings. The finer players are especially noted for making their legato so smooth that they make the guitar *sing* like a human voice. How these various articulation effects can be achieved will be our subject here.

Let's take a look at the nature of the guitar. It seems to be an instrument on which staccato comes easily. First, the notes on the guitar tend to die very quickly; second, it is easier to play if you do not hold the left-hand fingers down for the full value of the notes; third, it is easy to plant the right-hand fingers on the strings unconsciously and thus cut off the notes prematurely; and fourth, the guitar requires separate percussive movements for almost every act of playing. For these reasons, beginning players tend to play everything staccato. In itself, there is nothing wrong with staccato. In Chapter 5, we saw that the staccato Play–Relax approach is a good practice technique. In fact, as we shall see shortly, that technique can be useful for developing a good legato. Staccato also has its place in musical expression. However, continuous staccato is not a satisfying approach to music. Thus the sensitive guitarist will seek out ways to play smoothly as well as staccato.

Legato on the guitar is somewhat of a puzzle. Even when a professional guitarist plays as legato as possible, it still comes out somewhat staccato. As others have pointed out, this situation is not unique to the guitar.[3] In fact, the best legato that can be mustered on most instruments has at least a slight staccato component. However, for the reasons we have stated, it seems to be more difficult to reduce the staccato component on the guitar than on some other instruments. A near-perfect legato sound does not seem to be possible on the guitar in the same way as it is on the violin and other instruments. A good legato on the violin, for example, is relatively easy to obtain; a large group of left-hand notes can be nicely connected with one stroke of the bow. Legato on the guitar, however, requires a kind of "magic trick" where you somehow make it *seem* that you are smoothly connecting the notes. Actually there are staccato spaces between the notes since, except for slurs, each note must be played with a separate stroke of the right hand. Even left-hand slurs are not completely connected since the left-hand fingers have to hammer on or pull off each note separately at each fret.

It should be pointed out that, although a butter-smooth legato is not difficult on the violin, it is still not perfect. There are still minute breaks between the notes as the left-hand fingers and the bow direction change. On most instruments, no matter how intimately connected the notes may be, each one still has some vestige of independence because of the tiny space between it and the next one. It seems to be a basic feature of our reality that we must experience the world as alternating waves of action and rest, sound and silence. In fact, if we are not aware of these aspects, we are missing half of our reality.

Now let's look at how articulation is controlled on the guitar. And, in particular, we will look at how you can perform the "magic trick" of playing legato on a staccato instrument. There are two basic ways of controlling articulation. The main one is to use the Play–Relax idea from Chapter 5 and plant the right-hand fingers on the strings for varying amounts of time before playing the notes, depending on the degree of legato or staccato desired (see

[3]For an interesting discussion of staccato and legato on the guitar and other instruments, see the chapter on Articulation in *The Art of Classical Guitar Playing* by Charles Duncan (Princeton: Summy-Birchard Music, 1980).

"Planting the Fingers" in Chapter 5). The left hand can also play a part in articulation. Notes can be made more staccato or more legato according to how long the left-hand fingers hold them. Notes can also be played legato with left-hand slurs and slides.

It may seem paradoxical to suggest that you can produce a legato sound by planting the fingers in the staccato Play–Relax style. However, recall the idea from Chapters 4 and 5 that opposites can be balanced and reconciled. In this connection, we already mentioned that the bit of staccato that is found in the legato of even the best professional guitarists is somehow not perceived as breaking up the musical lines. In fact, the listener may even be fooled into thinking that the lines are continuous. Why is this so? The main reason seems to be that the notes and the spaces in between are alternating in an even, rhythmical pattern and are thus perceived as being smoothly connected. It is interesting to see that the opposite states of sound and silence alternate in a regular way to produce this pleasing effect.

Let's look at this guitar legato phenomenon more closely. As we mentioned in Chapter 5, the human nervous system works basically in rhythmical, on-off pulses. We also suggested that the nervous system seems to be attracted to a regular rhythm and apparently will synchronize or entrain itself with it. Thus we might speculate that the very even, rhythmical presentation of notes and spaces in the well-performed guitar legato produces even, rhythmical pulses in the nervous system of a listener. Most listeners seem to experience a soothing feeling from this legato. In comparison to the often disorderly rhythms generated by the noise and chaotic activity of everyday life, a regular rhythm is no doubt felt as quite relaxing. The musical effect is that "magic trick" we spoke of—perceived smoothness of the melodic line in spite of the silences. The silences do not seem to be disturbing at all. They apparently allow the nervous system to have a regular micro-relaxation after each note.

The most refined players create the illusion of a very smooth legato on the guitar mainly by waiting until the last instant to play the notes with the right hand. The fingers are planted to ensure accuracy and a good tone, but the planting takes place just a fraction of a second before playing. The strokes are made very evenly and in an easy manner. There must be the usual Play–Relax release of tension between the strokes. With respect to the left hand, holding down the fingers as long as possible and making smooth, quick left-hand connections between the notes also contribute to the illusion.

When all is said and done, you really need not worry too much about the technical means for producing legato. Probably the best way to play legato is to *think* legato—because legato is really something in your mind; that is, if you have a clear concept of the notes of a phrase being beautifully connected, then that idea will guide you to its physical realization on the guitar. (See Chapters 8 and 9 on the "Mind Over Fingers" idea.) For this purpose it is very helpful to *sing* the phrase that you want to make legato. Then play all the notes of the phrase in one breath, so to speak, as if you were singing it. You will find, as many have, that the technique of legato will come to your fingers naturally if you take the singing approach. If you are not clear what a good legato sounds like, listen to fine guitarists and fine singers.

Now let's look at how staccato and legato articulation are notated and then see how you can make use of it in your pieces. Frequently there are few or no written indications of articulation. The composer leaves it up to the discretion of the player. Sometimes a composer will indicate what he wants by simply putting the word "legato" or "staccato" at the beginning of a piece or passage. Or he may use various signs such as are given in Figure 6–22. The usual execution is given beneath the written notation.

Figure 6–22   (a) staccato and (b) legato articulations

written :

played (approx) :

A curved line over the notes signifies as smooth a legato as possible (Figure 6-22a). As you can see in the bottom staff, the way it is usually played is not perfectly legato. There are tiny rests between the notes, even in masterful legato playing. A curved line with dots over the notes (Figure 6–22b) indicates that there are slightly bigger spaces between the notes than in the last example. Sometimes short lines over or under the notes are used to convey the same idea. Dots over the notes (Figure 6–22c) conventionally mean that the notes are played staccato and should be given half of their written value. Wedges over the notes (Figure 6–22d) nowadays signify a very clipped staccato. The student should know, however, that the dot and the wedge were used interchangeably in the music of composers like Sor and Giuliani to indicate playing staccato with approximately half the value of the written note.

You can broaden your range of expression by exploring the different degrees of staccato and legato in Figure 6–22 in the melodic lines of pieces you know. First, try the articulations on single-note melodies to make things simple. It is best to start by playing the lines with a clipped staccato and then gradually move to the smoothest legato.

You can further extend your expressive capabilities by experimenting with various articulation patterns in your exercises and pieces. The following eight combinations of left-hand slurs and detached notes (Figure 6–23) are ones the guitarist will frequently encounter and use. Of course they can also be used on eighth or quarter note sequences. Similar combinations can be made with three-note figures.

Figure 6–23   Common articulations on sixteenth-note groups

Figure 6–24 is an example from Giuliani's *Grand Overture*, Op. 61 (bars 21–23), which shows three of the above articulations within a short passage.

Figure 6–24   Different articulations from Giuliani's *Grand Overture*, Op. 61

As an experiment, you might try changing the articulation patterns from those that Giuliani indicated. If you change them, what differences do you notice in the emotional impact? After some exploration of these articulation patterns, try making imaginative and appropriate use of them in your pieces. If you are not sure how to go about making up your own articulation patterns, one of the best ways to learn about it is to listen carefully to the recorded and live interpretations of the best concert artists (also listen to other good instrumentalists besides guitar players) and attempt to imitate what they are doing. That approach, along with experimentation on your own, will produce fruitful results.

Damping

An important technical and musical refinement is to get rid of extraneous sounds in your playing. A piece can sound very messy unless unwanted notes are stopped. There are several ways of damping such notes. Using the right-hand thumb is the most common way. The thumb can act much like the damper pedal on the piano. The most common unwanted notes are basses that ring too long, such as the ones in Figure 6–25 from *Pavan No. 1* by Luis Milán.

Figure 6–25 Damping example: Luis Milán, *Pavan No. 1*

If the first A bass is not stopped, it clashes with the next chord; if the E bass is not stopped, the following A chord is in second inversion instead of root position. The main result of these ringing bass notes is that the musical texture becomes muddy, making it difficult for the listener to follow the various melodic lines. Thus the player should become aware of these undesirable sounds and damp them. In the Milán example, it is easy to damp the first A bass if you play a light thumb rest stroke on the following E. The A is stopped by the thumb coming to rest immediately after the stroke. The (ˣ₅) after the low E in the second bar means to damp the fifth string. The first E bass must be stopped by a special movement of the thumb. The smoothest way of doing it is to "flip" the thumb back on the E (ˣ₆) the instant *after* the following A minor chord has been played; this damping movement is actually done in rhythm with the playing of the A minor chord. With this technique, the E briefly overlaps the A, thus connecting the sounds nicely. The second A is then cut by another light rest stroke on the bass of the E chord.

The approach of cutting off the unwanted note after the next note has been sounded can also be used to stop undesirable harmonics in the bass. Figure 6–26 is an example from Sor's Study Op. 6, No. 8 (No. 1, Segovia edition).

Figure 6–26 Damping example: Fernando Sor, Op. 6, No. 8

In this case, playing the E on the third beat of the first bar causes the sixth string octave harmonic to ring by sympathetic vibration. If the sixth string is not immediately damped with the thumb right after the F is sounded in the next measure, a dissonant minor second can be heard.

Frequently there is not enough time for the thumb to jump back to a previously struck string to damp it, so another way must be used. In the Carulli passage in Figure 6–27, for example, you first play the A and let the thumb come to rest on the D. Then, at the same time as you play the D, damp the A by touching it lightly with the flesh on the side of the thumb. In other words, you stuff the thumb between the two strings. This method is not always the smoothest, but it may be the only feasible one in some cases.

Figure 6–27   Damping example: Study, Ferdinando Carulli

Occasionally, it may be necessary to alter the right-hand position in order to damp several basses at once. This technique may seem a bit awkward at first, but the resulting cleanness of the sound makes it worth the trouble. This approach will get rid of undesirable harmonics such as the ones in the excerpt in Figure 6–28 from Sor's Study, Op. 6, No. 2 (No. 3, Segovia edition).

Figure 6–28   Damping example: Fernando Sor, Op. 6, No. 2

In this case, all three bass strings can be damped by laying the side of the thumb across them. Then the melody can be played with *a* and the accompaniment with *m i*. This approach can be used for part of this piece and for similar passages from other pieces. It should be clear that in the above Sor study the thumb will not lie on the three bass strings through the entire piece. It will move according to the music. Sometimes it will damp only one or two basses and sometimes it must play a bass note.

The thumb may also be used to damp the many undesirable string vibrations created by playing a scale. You can lay the thumb across the strings as in the previous example. It can move across the strings along with the scale playing fingers, either toward the treble or bass, depending on which way the scale is going. Another useful damping technique which allows you to make a clean break in the sound at the end of a phrase or at the end of a piece is to lay the fleshy side of the hand (on the little finger side) on all the strings near the bridge. Of course the left-hand fingers can occasionally be used to damp notes where it is not feasible to use the right hand. At times the flamenco technique of damping the strings with the stretched-out little finger of the left hand can prove useful.

Natural Right-Hand Fingering

An important principle in right-hand fingering is to use the fingers, as much as possible, in the natural position they tend to assume on the strings. One of the most common natural positions of the fingers is shown in Figure 6–29.

Figure 6–29 Natural right-hand position on E minor chord

Figure 6–30 Natural right-hand position on F major chord

That finger position suggests that it is most natural to use *i a* for the chord in Figure 6–30 instead of *i m* because the notes are separated by one string. It also suggests that string crossings (moving from one string to another) will often work better if the fingers move according to the way they are arranged in that natural position. In the following examples, an awkward fingering (Figure 6–31) and a more flowing one (Figure 6–32) are shown. The string crossings are shown in brackets.

Figure 6–31 Awkward right-hand fingering: Robert Johnson, *Alman*

Figure 6–32 Improved fingering for Figure 6–31

There are frequently several right-hand fingerings that will work for a given passage and it is sometimes difficult to decide which is best. One helpful idea is to choose the stronger combinations of fingers wherever possible. For example, *p i m* tends to be a stronger combination than *i m a* for most three-note ascending arpeggios. And for scales, *m i* or *a i* is stronger than *m a*.

Of course no generalization will always hold, so the ultimate criterion for a fingering is whether or not it works musically and technically.

A typical approach to right-hand fingering is to use alternation wherever possible, but although that works well a good deal of the time, it is often better to see what fingering naturally fits the music rather than to impose a planned, "logical" pattern. The harpsichordist Wanda Landowska said that when planned fingerings do not work " . . . I let the fingers find their own way. It is like an overflowing river returning to its bed."[4] This approach is often the best course for the guitar. For many passages, planned alternation may be best, but for others, repeating the same finger(s) is what the fingers naturally want to do. In the passage (Figure 6–33) from Scarlatti (L. 483) strict alternation is quite clumsy and does not follow the melodic rhythm pattern, while repeating the *m* finger does.

Figure 6–33 Use of repeated *m* finger: Domenico Scarlatti, *Sonata*, L. 483

There are numerous other cases similar to this one where it is better to let the fingers find their own natural pattern. By the way, in the Scarlatti passage you have an example of how the thumb can be used to cut the basses somewhat short for rhythmic incisiveness and expressive lightness. Although the basses are written as half-notes, they sound less ponderous played staccato as quarter-notes, at least in this passage. With shorter basses, the treble line also sparkles and stands out more clearly. The E's in the third and fifth measures are intentionally allowed to ring to give the feeling of release at the phrase endings. In baroque music, this practice of cutting notes short was rather common; thus when it is done as in Figure 6–33, it is in good style. Fine players often cut basses short in other types of music to achieve similar effects of musical clarity.

REFINING THE LEFT HAND

The Art of Making Connections

The image of a mountain stream flowing easily and gracefully downhill is a particularly good model for the left hand; all left-hand movements should have that fluidity and effortlessness. All awkward or excessive movements

[4]Copyright © 1965 by Denise Restout, ed., trans., assisted by Robert Hawkins. From the book *Landowska on Music* (New York: Stein and Day, 1964), p. 374. Reprinted with permission of Stein and Day Publishers.

should be avoided. Keep in mind that what looks good tends to sound good. The essence of flowing movements is making smooth connections between the notes.

Wherever possible, it is good to *deliberately prepare* the left-hand fingers before a movement is to be made. This technique is similar to the "planting" of the right-hand fingers before playing. There are several types of left-hand preparation. Two common types of preparation are the use of *guide* and *pivot* fingers. Somewhat less common is the *hinge bar.* Another form of preparation is through *fingerboard contact.* The technique of *visualization* is also useful. We will discuss the latter technique briefly here and in more detail in Chapter 8.

Guide Fingers Guide finger preparation involves lightly gliding the fingers on top of the strings to go from one position to another. In the excerpt in Figure 6–34 from the Rondo of Sor's *Sonata,* Op. 22, there are several examples of guide fingers.

Figure 6–34 Use of guide fingers: Fernando Sor, Rondo from *Sonata,* Op. 22

Moving from the first chord (D7) to the second (G), the first finger acts as a guide to bring the hand into a half-bar at the third fret. The first finger should stay in contact with the strings at all times during the shift. Then, going from the third (D) to the fourth chord (G), the fourth finger is the guide. From the fourth chord to the fifth (A7), both the first and fourth fingers act as guides. Finally, the fourth finger connects the last two chords.

Sometimes there is no obvious guide finger that can be used to make a smooth position change. However, a finger that will be needed in the next position can often be used as a guide by placing it lightly on the string it will play. This is done deliberately in the position before the change. In Figure 6–35, an excerpt from Bach's *Prelude in D Minor,* this more subtle type of preparation is shown.

Figure 6–35 Subtle use of guide finger: J. S. Bach, *Prelude in D Minor*

In both measures the third finger (in parentheses) is prepared for the shift by placing it on the fourth string before any movement is made.

Pivot Fingers   The second type of preparation, which makes use of pivot fingers, is often helpful in smoothing out the finger movements. A pivot finger is one that serves as a connection between two chords by holding down a note that the chords have in common. The example in Figure 6–36 from Milán's *Pavan No. 3* shows how the first finger acts as a pivot between the chords.

Figure 6–36   Use of pivot fingers: Luis Milán, *Pavan No. 3*

Hinge Bars   A special way of facilitating smooth connections is a technique called the hinge bar, of which there are several varieties. One example of how the hinge bar can be applied is in another passage from Milán's *Pavan No. 3* (Figure 6–37).

Figure 6–37   Hinge bar: Luis Milán, *Pavan No. 3*

In this passage, the F in the bass is supposed to be sustained through the whole measure. In order to do this and yet have good melodic continuity, you place the full bar at the beginning of the first measure to play the F on the first string. Then you pick up the basal segment of the bar finger to play the open E, but leave the tip segment on the low F so that it continues to sound. Figure 6–38 shows this "hinged" position.

Right after the "hinge" movement, the basal segment of the bar finger is put down again so that the C on the second string can be played. The use of the hinge bar here makes it possible to play the passage in a smooth, musical

Figure 6–38   Hinge bar in Figure 6–37

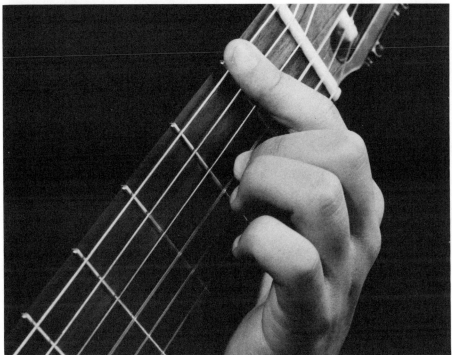

way. Any other way of playing it would involve clumsy movements and wrong note durations.

Another common variation on the hinge bar is to use the bent tip segment of the index finger either alone or in combination with another finger. This often facilitates position changes and makes otherwise awkward passages smooth. Figure 6–39, an excerpt from Giuliani's Op. 48, No. 18, uses the hinge bar in a typical way on an A major arpeggio.

Figure 6–39   Small hinge bar: Mauro Giuliani, Op. 48, No. 18

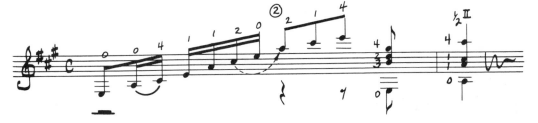

The advantages of playing the arpeggio in this way are several; it is easy to play the low C♯ with the little finger; it also allows all the notes of the A major chord to ring together, thus giving a full sound; and finally, the second finger, which plays the C♯ on the second string, can facilitate the change to the ninth position by sliding up the string. The bar appears as shown in Figure 6–40.

Figure 6–40 Small hinge bar in Figure 6–39

Another very useful variation on the hinge bar uses the flesh at the base of the index finger to make a partial bar to prepare a smooth connection between positions. For example, in the Sor study, Op. 35, No. 22 (No. 5 in Segovia's edition), the sequence of chord changes can be made very smooth with a hinge bar (Figure 6–41).

Figure 6–41 Another type of hinge bar: Fernando Sor, Op. 35, No. 22

The F♯7 chord in the first measure is played with a full bar. Then the hinge bar is made at the beginning of the second measure on the Bm chord. It is done by lifting all of the index finger *except the fleshy part at the base* off the F♯7 chord. Thus the chord is played with the first two segments of the finger up in the air while the flesh at the base of the finger holds down the F♯ on the first string (Figure 6–42).

Figure 6–42 Hinge bar preparation for Figure 6–41

This position allows the open D bass to sound. Now for the shift. First prepare the little finger for the shift by placing it lightly on the second string. Now the advantage of the hinge bar comes when you are easily able to slide the bar up to the fourth position and lay it down gently on the C♯7 chord (Figure 6–43). Without the hinge bar, the shift is not as smooth.

Fingerboard Contact   Having the left-hand palm lightly grazing the lower edge of the fingerboard most of the time is a good general way to smooth out left-hand changes. This technique is particularly useful in making connections from one position to another when there are no guide fingers to help you. With fingerboard contact, you always have a point of reference so that you know where the fingers are in relation to the fingerboard. It is something

Figure 6–43 Completion of hinge bar prepared in Figure 6–42

like touch typing where you have your fingers lightly resting on or near the home keys so that you know where the fingers are. Of course, just as it is not good to press the typewriter keys too hard, it is also not good to *clutch* at the fingerboard. A very light contact is quite sufficient. It is also a good idea to take the hand away from the fingerboard where the music permits and let it relax. The end of a phrase or section or the playing of open strings gives an opportunity for such a relaxation.

The Silent Connection Since we are discussing left-hand connections, let's dwell for a moment on how to make them sound clean. When you first heard the classical guitar, you probably heard some annoying squeaks along with some beautiful music. These noises are caused by the left-hand fingers sliding up and down the three bass strings. You may have noticed that even some of the best guitarists sometimes squeak rather prominently on record and in concert. You might conclude that these noises are an inevitable part of classical guitar. However, with a proper approach such string squeaks can be reduced considerably, if not eliminated altogether. It is especially important to be *conscious* of the squeaking. Many players become so used to it that they no longer hear it.

So, why do these noises come about? Because of the metal winding on the bass strings, it is relatively easy to make squeaks during position changes. If the strings are new and the fingertips are capped with hard, dry callouses, the noise problem may become quite noticeable. Be that as it may, the main reason that players squeak on the basses is that they are overly anxious about making their position changes secure. Thus, they press too hard on the strings with guide fingers during position shifts in order to keep close contact with them. The players seem to accept the resulting squeaks as the price of feeling secure about getting to the right place on the fingerboard. However, the anxiety about accuracy and the consequent noises are not completely necessary.

There are several ways to reduce bass string squeaks. One is to perform only on strings that have been "played in" for a while. This lubricates the string surface with skin oils and reduces the noise. Another possibility is to use "squeak-proof" strings. However, the presently available strings of this type that the author has seen, although they do not squeak, also do not last more than a day before they lose their resonance. Those players who have a squeaking problem that is caused by hard callouses will find it helpful to soften them with hand lotion.

One of the best ways to reduce bass string noise is to cultivate light, Play–Relax position shifts. We discussed shifting to some extent in Chapter 5, but it is worthwhile delving into it a bit more here. In this technique, you first press on the string(s) to sound the note(s) in the starting position. Then, just before you move to the new position, you release the finger pressure from the first position quickly and almost completely. The appropriate guide finger(s) should be sitting on the string(s) with practically no pressure. Now, just barely touching the surface of the string(s), you move the fingers in a swift, light manner to the next position. Then you press down to sound the note(s) in the new position. Thus the sequence is *press, release, shift, press*. The key to the technique is to skim over the surface of the string as lightly as a bird. This way of shifting reduces noise and gives the left hand a chance to relax more than if there were constant pressure on the string.

In many cases, it is possible to shift without touching the string at all. Instead, the fingers hover just a fraction of an inch over the strings as they shift. But how can you feel secure if you are not actually touching the strings while moving? Two ideas are helpful here. The first is to have a clear picture of where the fingers are supposed to land after the shift. This clear mental picture will help ensure your accuracy. (See Chapter 8, "Visualization for Left-Hand Movements.") The second idea was mentioned in the previous section, that is, as you shift, let your palm lightly graze the edge of the fingerboard to guide your hand. After some practice, you should be able to make noiseless or almost noiseless bass string shifts. This technique allows the music to come through pure and simple without distracting squeaks.

Natural Slur Technique

Some fine points of slurring are often overlooked. One such point is that the position of the left hand in performing slurs must not be conceived as a rigid one. Like other left-hand playing movements, the hand must be allowed to accommodate itself to each particular movement. An example of this is in playing slurs on the three nylon strings. It is often suggested that the palm of the hand always be exactly parallel to the fingerboard. However, for players with average-sized hands, it is actually much easier to do the slurs on the nylon strings when the little finger side of the palm is turned slightly away from the fingerboard. This gives the fingers more room to operate for the slurring movements. It is also best not to try to keep the slurring movements artificially small with the idea of saving movement because this often inhibits their free flow. Besides, in ascending slurs, the fingers have more power when they are cocked back further from the board and can build up more momentum before striking the strings. Some of the momentum comes from using the weight of the hand and a slight rotation of the forearm to play the slurs; the movement should not come solely from the fingers. It is also good to remember that the fingers should retain their curvature when playing slurs so that they have the maximum leverage. The joints should not be allowed to collapse. This is particularly important for the little finger.

Another point is that, in descending slurs, many players seem to have difficulty in making the slurred notes loud enough. This is often a result of not having prepared the left-hand fingers which stop the note(s) after the initial one that has been struck by the right hand. In the example in Figure 6–44, it is difficult to make the A sound properly unless the second finger is placed a short time on it before playing the B. To prepare this, the second and fourth fingers can be placed on their respective notes simultaneously.

Figure 6–44 Preparation of the left-hand fingers for a slur

Control over descending slurs can be further refined by a *push–pull* technique. You *pull* with the slurring finger and *push* with the stationary one. In the example in Figure 6–44 you can pull with the fourth finger and push with the second. This gives more leverage and hence more volume of sound to your descending slurs. There is also more room to make the slur comfortably because the pushing movement prevents the slurring string from being pulled too close to the adjacent string. This push–pull technique also prevents the common problem of bad intonation caused by pulling the strings sideways too much.

One final point about descending slurs will be useful. Many students tend to play descending slurs with very ponderous, slow motions and complain that slurs are difficult. However, if you pull off a note with a quick movement, your slurs will be more fluid and less fatiguing. The movement should be lightning quick, something like the snap stroke for the right hand. Be sure to relax the hand at least for a brief moment after each slur.

Vibrato

Vibrato is a special means of emotional expression where a string (or strings) is made to fluctuate in pitch by the left hand. There are two kinds of vibrato in common use on the guitar. The *standard* or longitudinal type, which is used by violinists, cellists and other string players, is created by the motion and friction of the fingertip. This causes the string to be moved back and forth along its length. This motion alternately shortens and lengthens the string and thus causes the pitch to fluctuate above and below the note being vibrated. The other type, which we shall call the *pull–release* vibrato, is made by alternately pulling the string toward the palm of the hand with one of the fingers and, keeping the finger lightly on the string, letting it return to its normal position. With this type the pitch also fluctuates, but only above the note vibrated, not below.

The vibrato can be a beautiful effect on the guitar if it makes sense in the context of the music you are playing. The finest players use vibrato with discrimination. It is not used on every note. Vibrato is best treated as an ornament to heighten the emotional intensity of certain notes and give them a lively singing quality. For example, it can be used to bring out the climactic note of a phrase or to emphasize the melody notes in a melody and accompaniment piece. Vibrato can also be used to help sustain a note. There is naturally a considerable range of expression available with the vibrato on the guitar and the best players exploit it. As the violinist Yehudi Menuhin says, "Vibrato must be as varied as the weather in England."[5]

The variety in the vibrato comes mostly from its two basic components: the fluctuation of the pitch and the speed. The guitarist should be aware of how much the pitch fluctuates in the vibrato because the effect changes according to the amount of fluctuation. It is generally good to have only minor

---

[5]Yehudi Menuhin and William Primrose, *Violin and Viola* (New York: Schirmer Books, 1976), p. 75.

deviations in the pitch or the effect will be overdone. Normally the deviation should not be much more than a quarter-tone on either side of the main pitch, although it may be somewhat more.

The speed of the vibrato should be varied according to the speed and emotional character of the music you are playing; the speed should also be related to the register in which you are playing. Generally, the quicker or more intense the music, the faster the vibrato; the upper register of the guitar also calls for a somewhat faster vibrato because of the greater intensity of higher pitches. The speed of the vibrato usually falls within the relatively narrow range of four to ten cycles per second. It is important to avoid extremes in the speed so that the vibrato will seem to be a natural, unobtrusive part of the music. A vibrato that is too slow for a given passage is just as undesirable as one that is too fast. A very slow vibrato may be fine for special effects but not for most of the standard repertoire; a very fast vibrato usually ends up sounding very nervous rather than intense as the player may have intended. A truly artistic vibrato should also have an even rhythm instead of a chaotic one.

The *standard* or longitudinal vibrato on the guitar is not difficult if it is approached in the right way. To practice this type of vibrato, it is best to sit with the guitar in the usual classical position. Since it is easiest to get results with the standard vibrato between the fifth and ninth frets, choose a note in that range. Now try the following exercise with each left-hand finger, starting with the first. Place the finger on the note as shown in Figure 6–45.

Figure 6–45   Standard vibrato

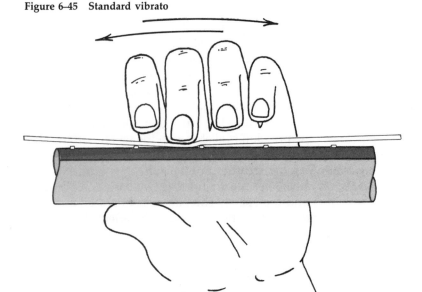

Do not press hard against the neck with the thumb. Many players find it better not to touch the neck at all. Lack of thumb pressure facilitates the hand and arm movements. Now put some pressure on the fingertip using the weight of the arm so that the tip stays in one spot close to the fret and does not slide up and down the string. The wrist should be held straight and firm. To make the vibrato, make small movements from side to side with the hand and arm together so that the finger moves back and forth like a rocking chair. The arm should be loose so that it can move freely. The upper arm need not move much; the forearm can move slightly more.

Since the evenness of the rhythm of the vibrato is important, the metronome can be put into service here. Try an initial setting of about 100. Each "back" movement and each "forth" movement should get one click of the metronome. When you have a regular vibrato going at 100, set the metronome faster by several clicks and repeat the exercise. Increase the tempo until you can vibrate evenly at 208, then set the metronome back to 100 and instead of each back and each forth movement taking one click, do "back and forth" on one click. The tempo can then be increased until the desired speed is reached. It is also possible to do the "back and forth" twice on each click and start at a slower speed.

When you are comfortable doing the vibrato on one note with each finger in this exercise, then a good further study is to play the Segovia scales[6] with a vibrato on each note. The D major scale is a good one to start with because it falls in the easiest register for the standard vibrato. Another perhaps more enjoyable exercise is to take only the melody line of a favorite study or piece and practice doing vibrato on every possible note.

The standard vibrato as described here is useful for a good portion of the fingerboard. However, the standard vibrato is difficult to execute on the first four frets mainly because it is difficult to move the hand and arm freely. In the lower positions the *pull–release* type of vibrato works better. The pull–release vibrato is executed by placing your finger firmly on a note and then alternately pulling the string to the side and letting it return to its normal position (Figure 6–46).

The pull–release vibrato also is more effective than the standard type for notes above the twelfth fret. Further, it is the only practical way to vibrate a single note in a chord being held by the left hand. This is often done in pieces such as Tárrega's *Prelude No. 2* in A minor where vibrato is done only on the melody notes in order to make them sing out beautifully over the accompaniment. The pull–release vibrato can naturally be applied to any note on the fingerboard, but many players prefer to use the standard variety wherever feasible because it can be more easily controlled and can create pitch fluctuations both above and below the vibrated note.

Be sure to practice the pull–release vibrato with even rhythm as you did

---

[6]See footnote 1 in this chapter for the publisher of these useful scales.

Figure 6–46 Pull–release vibrato

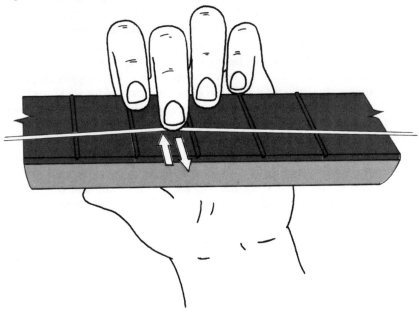

the standard one. It is also good to practice this vibrato on each note of a Segovia scale. Another way of studying this vibrato is to take a simple melody and accompaniment piece such as the Sor Study Op. 6, No. 2 (No. 3, Segovia edition) and play vibrato on every melody note. You will find that working with the pull–release vibrato will greatly increase your left-hand coordination and strength. It takes particularly good coordination to play a good vibrato on the first string without pulling the string off the board!

For further examples of how the vibrato can be used, see "Refine the Interpretation" in Chapter 9.

Natural Left-Hand Fingering

It is important to find the *simplest* possible left-hand fingerings that express the sound you want so that the music flows effortlessly and you do not feel stress and strain while playing. The Chinese Taoist idea of "yield and overcome"—the way in which water overcomes obstacles—is very useful for finding good fingerings. In other words, if you are running into obstacles with a particular fingering, do not try to play your way through the problems with brute force. It is better to yield and look for a simpler, more flowing fingering. Such fingerings are not always obvious, so some experimentation is needed. Try several different fingerings until you find the one that works best musically and technically.

One idea that helps to keep fingering simple is, wherever possible, to finger similar passages in a similar way. It is much less confusing in performance and it usually makes for greater unity of the musical sound.

In his *Method for the Spanish Guitar*, Fernando Sor has some helpful ideas for making fingering simpler and more natural. One idea is to do your fingering in "handfuls," or *positions*, whenever it is appropriate, that is, find fingerings that are compact and can be done in one position at a time. One position encompasses the four frets within easy reach of the four fingers. There are as many positions on the guitar as there are frets. The first position is at the first fret, the second is at the second fret, and so on. The location of the first finger determines the position. For example, if the first finger is at the fifth fret (or would be if you put it down), you are in the fifth position. Sor explains his idea of position fingering as follows:

> To consider fingering an art, having for its object to make me find the notes I want, within reach of the fingers that are to produce them, without the continual necessity of making deviations for the purpose of seeking them.[7]

Another one of Sor's ideas about fingering is "never to give work to the weakest fingers, whilst the strongest are doing nothing." He also suggests that, if a difficult position comes up, the most difficult part should be done by the strongest finger. If applied carefully, these concepts will save energy and result in much smoother playing. The stronger and more coordinated combinations of fingers are: 1 and 2, 1 and 3. Somewhat weaker and less coordinated are: 2 and 4, 1 and 4. Still weaker and less coordinated are: 2 and 3, 3 and 4. The approach of favoring the strong fingers wherever possible fits in well with the principle of least action or "doing less and accomplishing more."

One good way of keeping the hand relaxed is not to stretch out the fingers unless it is necessary. For example, in many cases the hand can be spared much excess tension if two-fret stretches are taken with the first and fourth fingers instead of the first and third—even though the third is a relatively strong finger. The basic idea is to keep the hand in a relaxed position with the fingers close together as much of the time as possible. Stretches obviously have to be made, but the hand should be allowed to come back to the relaxed state as soon as possible.

---

[7]Fernando Sor, *Method for the Spanish Guitar*, Da Capo Press Reprints (New York: Da Capo Press, 1971), p. 48.

Two fingering concepts will be very useful to you: *scale fingering* and *chord fingering*. The basic idea is that most melodic passages are scale- or chord-oriented or are a mixture of both. These passages sound best when they are played with the appropriate fingerings. In a scale that moves step-wise in seconds, the notes are usually played several to a string and sound more or less separated from each other. However, if the passage has a broken chord, that is, it skips through intervals such as thirds or sixths, then it is usual to play the passage with chord fingering on different strings so that the notes overlap and harmonize. Many guitarists make the mistake of playing such broken chord passages (known in baroque parlance as *style brisé* or "broken style" passages) with scale fingering. As a result, the passages are awkward to play and do not have a flowing sound. The beautiful sound of overlapping chord tones is lost. Figure 6–47 is an example of a chordal passage in the fugue from the Bach *Sonata No. 1* for solo violin with two differ-ent ways of playing it. Figure 6–47a shows scale fingering; Figure 6–47b shows chord fingering.

Figure 6–47 **(a) Scale fingering concept: J. S. Bach, Fugue from *Sonata in G Minor* for solo violin**
(b) Chord fingering concept: same passage as Figure 6–47a

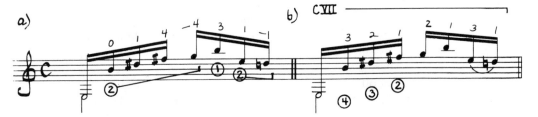

Straight scale passages are normally not done with chord-type finger-ing. However, the charming *campanelas* ("bells") effect from baroque guitar music (and music from other periods) with its overlapping scale tones is an exception to this.[8] In this effect, one scale tone is played on one string and the next one is played on an adjacent string. The tones alternate on different strings like this, giving the impression of simultaneously sounding church bells.

SUMMARY

There are endless refinements that you can make to your guitar technique so that playing is easier and more musical. The refinements mentioned in this chapter are certainly not the only ones that can be made, but they are some of

[8]For a description of baroque guitar *campanelas,* see Robert Strizich, "A Spanish Guitar Tutor: Ruiz de Ribayaz's *Luz Y Norte Musical* (1677)," *Journal of the Lute Society of America,* VII, 1974, p. 68ff.

the most important ones. Still more of them are discussed in Chapter 9 in connection with the interpretation of a piece.[9] Attention to such details makes the difference between rough and polished performances. The whole purpose of refining and perfecting your playing is to eliminate all distracting and irrelevant sounds and movements so that the pure essence of the music can come through. This process requires quiet, concentrated work and a keen awareness of muscles and music, but the end result is so attractive that it is definitely worth your time and energy.

In Chapters 4, 5, and 6 we have dealt with various considerations of guitar technique and music. In Chapter 7, it will be useful to see how you can go about studying these things in an organized and enjoyable way. In short, we will discuss the most natural ways to learn.

[9]For further discussion of musical and technical refinements, see Duncan, *The Art of Classical Guitar Playing*.

7.

Learning from the Masters

use natural study methods

> *We love to associate with heroic persons since our receptivity is unlimited; and with the great, our thoughts and manners easily become great.*
>
> Ralph Waldo Emerson, *Uses of Great Men*

ENJOY YOUR GUITAR STUDY

In Chapters 4, 5, and 6, we have dealt with the principle of dynamic relaxation, the Play–Relax practice technique and technical refinements. In this chapter we will consider some additional ideas about how to get the most from the guitar learning process with the least effort. In particular, we will deal with learning from master guitarists by imitation, structuring your practice sessions for best results, and solving guitar problems with master strategies.

One thing should always be borne in mind when you are studying the guitar: It is meant to be enjoyed. You can enjoy each moment of practice if you really want to. Even scale, slur, and arpeggio exercises can become things of beauty when practiced with care and musical feeling. If you are frustrated or bored during your practice sessions, then you are simply doing something contrary to nature. It is seldom the fault of the guitar. It is just that you are going too fast or trying too hard. You are living in the past or future—not in the *now*. When you are consciously focused on the present and are clearly aware of such things as the feel of the fingers on the strings, the quality of your tone, the phrasing of a melodic line, or the sensation of the rhythmic pulse, then studying will be a joy and you will always make progress in technique, musicianship, and personal life.

If you want to be as *conscious* as possible when you study, the best approach is to be physically rested and mentally alert. For that reason it is very helpful to quiet your mind and body before you start your practice sessions. The mind-settling and body relaxation techniques in Chapter 2 can be helpful. Even if you just close your eyes and relax all your muscles for a few minutes, you can greatly enhance your receptivity to learning new things.

IMITATIVE LEARNING

The Way Children Learn

The easiest and most effective way of learning anything—including the guitar—is by imitating someone who knows how to do it well. Shinichi Suzuki, the contemporary Japanese violin teacher, has pointed out that children learn their mother tongue extremely well in an effortless, natural way just by hearing it repeatedly and imitating what they hear. With his "mother tongue" music method, Suzuki has shown that children can learn to play music on the violin (and other instruments) in the same effortless way as they learn their own language.[1] That is, first they hear a piece of music many times. They also see it performed. Then, after some elementary technical training, they are encouraged to imitate on their own instruments what they have seen and heard. Note reading is not introduced until the children have been playing several years. People who have heard a few concerts of children trained in the Suzuki method know how successfully it works. The gypsies in Hungary train their young children to be musicians along the same lines as Suzuki, although less methodically. Very young children are given musical instruments—most often a small violin—and they are allowed to sit in with the local gypsy orchestra. They are encouraged to play along with the adults. They learn to play in a gradual, natural way by imitating what the musicians are doing. In spite of the lack of formal academic training, the children grow up to be very proficient musicians, as anyone who has heard them will attest.[2]

The imitative learning process of the young child is interesting to observe. From this observation anyone can gain insights about how to improve his own learning process. Normal, healthy children resemble innocent, receptive sponges that soak up new knowledge easily. For example, take a child who is just learning how to talk. The mother says "banana" and the child then tries to imitate this new bit of knowledge immediately with great delight. If the child cannot say "banana" right away he will not give up and will not have any hang-ups about it. The young child has no concept that anything is "impossible" and he does not "try hard" to learn. As long as the child is corrected in a gentle way, he will be flexible and simply drop the incorrect pronunciations and try new ones until he gets it right. Of course he is enjoying himself thoroughly in the process. It is all a marvelous game.

The imitative learning process of the child can serve as an effective model for learning how to play the guitar—for children or adults. Most gui-

---

[1]From Shinichi Suzuki, *Nurtured By Love* (Smithtown, N.Y.: Exposition Press, 1969), pp. 9–11, 49–54. © 1969 Shinichi Suzuki. Reprinted by permission of Exposition Press, Inc., Smithtown, New York.

[2]Leonhard Deutsch, *Piano: Guided Sight-Reading* (Chicago: Nelson-Hall, 1959), p. 63.

tarists have picked up at least a few good ideas by listening to and imitating the great artists. However, many players seem to spend a disproportionate part of their learning time staring at printed music, playing exercises, reading books, and analyzing problems. Although these approaches are certainly important for the classical guitarist, both beginning and advanced players can benefit greatly by spending more of their study time learning by imitation of good players. Imitation does not mean that you stop thinking for yourself. It means rather that you can increase your rate of progress by learning from the excellent musical and technical example of the finest guitarists.

To get a feeling for learning by imitation, just recall how easily and naturally you learned when you were a child. Cultivate the attitude of being receptive to any new knowledge that comes along. Be flexible like a child and let go of techniques or approaches that are not producing good results. For example, instead of focusing on how bad an old playing habit is, put your attention on the new one that you want to learn. Along these same lines, you can speed up the learning process by temporarily dropping your old repertoire—which carries the ballast of old habits—and learning new pieces. In all your studies, keep in mind what children know instinctively: Learning should be enjoyable and struggling or "trying hard" to learn does not produce good results. It is much more productive to regard the guitar learning process as a delightful game rather than as a form of drudgery.

The Master–Student Relationship

Imitation of successful behavior as a way of learning is certainly not anything new. It is the most ancient and most powerful way of learning, particularly in the form where the student apprentice spends some years studying with a master. This type of long-term teacher–student relationship is still with us in our Western culture to some extent. However, we have deemphasized it in recent times in favor of book learning, muddling through on our own, and casual, short-term teacher–student relationships.

The idea of the apprentice studying with and imitating a master has always been very important to the arts. This idea is particularly strong in India and other Oriental cultures. In these cultures, the master–student relationship is not taken as lightly as it frequently is in the West. This is because the goal of music instruction in these cultures is not just to create a few more musicians, but also to develop human beings with the highest personal and spiritual qualities. For example, when you study with an authentic Indian master musician, you usually go through an initiation and make a pledge that you will study with him for a certain number of years. Students are generally expected to live an orderly, disciplined life. Many Indian masters have their students live with them as long as they study so that they can attend to the student's development both as a person and as a musician. By such close contact with a true master, the student tends to absorb his high ethical and spiritual values. The method of musical training is not by reading notes. It is rather by directly imitating the playing of the master so that you absorb his technique and intuitive feeling for the music.[3]

Of course our culture is very different from that in India and the Orient and we should not copy exactly what they do. However, we can learn something from the importance they give to a strong master–student relationship. If such relationships were taken more seriously in our own culture, guitar students would tend to become better musicians more quickly.

There is much to be said for being a close student of a master. Many of the great men of Western music submitted to the discipline of studying with a master for a period of time. Beethoven, for example, studied with the classical masters Haydn and Mozart, among others. These influences are clearly seen in his early works. Beethoven then built upon what he had learned from these masters and became a master musician himself. An example of a master–student relationship in the guitar world is the one between the master Fernando Sor and his student Napoleon Coste. Coste was an excellent student who became a fine guitarist and composer. A similar relationship existed between Francisco Tárrega and Miguel Llobet. Llobet was a close disciple and friend of Tárrega who eventually became famous as a concert artist and arranger.

Learn from Master Guitarists

Learning by imitation can be done in several ways: (1) studying with a master player or teacher; (2) studying live and recorded performances. The best way is to study directly with a master in private lessons or classes. As an adjunct to direct study, the student should study the master player's performances, both live and recorded, as well as his musical editions. Of course the guitarist should leap at any chance to study directly with a fine player. There is nothing like being *in the presence* of a master guitarist who can show you a living, inspiring example of how to play well. In this way, you learn not only the more superficial aspects of guitar playing, such as how to do fingering, but you also learn on the more delicate levels of your being. In the presence of a master, you see, hear, feel, and spiritually sense how one goes about playing the guitar beautifully. In an immediate way, the master guitarist awakens you and leads you to a heightened appreciation of life and music.

If direct study with one or more master players is not possible or is rarely available, then you can gain a great deal by close study of their performances, recordings, and scores. You can also benefit by taking private lessons with a good local guitarist, preferably one who has studied with a master

---

[3]Ravi Shankar, the renowned sitar player from India, gives a beautiful description of the ancient master–student relationship in his book *My Music, My Life* (New York: Simon and Schuster, 1968), p. 11ff. and p. 43ff.

player. Choose a local teacher who is experienced in both teaching and playing so that he can be of great practical help to you. Be prepared to pay enough so that you can go to a fine instructor right from the beginning of your studies. That way you avoid learning the fundamentals badly from an unskillful teacher. It is usually difficult to unlearn such bad habits. Remember to ask with whom the teacher studied. Most good teachers have studied with at least one master guitarist.

To learn the most from a fine teacher, it is important to be respectful and receptive. Be alert and learn to imitate quickly what the teacher does. Do not be in a big hurry. Give yourself plenty of time—it may take some years—to absorb his approach to music and the guitar. Do not be afraid that you will lose your own personality if you imitate a master player or your local teacher during your studies with him. Quite to the contrary, you will tend to learn more quickly and you will gain a foundation for developing your own unique approach to the guitar. No one can perfectly imitate another player anyway. Ask good questions and apply yourself diligently to your teacher's suggestions. Above all, avoid arguing with him and you will learn more. You may not agree with everything he does, but do not waste energy by dwelling on such things. There will always be plenty of time to play just the way you want. Be sure to enjoy your teacher and the whole learning process. When it ceases to be enjoyable and fruitful, then it is time to reevaluate the situation and either change yourself or find a new teacher.

Learning from Concerts

One of the best ways to learn how to play is by attending as many concerts as possible. It is good to see how different players—especially the best ones—actually perform. Normally you will do well to sit right in the front row of the concert hall because then you can see and hear everything the player is doing. However, depending on the player and the acoustics of the hall, it is sometimes better to sit farther back. In any case, the student should become a sharp observer of every detail of playing and musical interpretation. Listen to the player's tone; see if he looks at ease while he plays; does he make distracting movements?; see how he makes the strokes and how he moves his left hand; listen to the way he deals with rhythm; does he have a strong rhythmic pulse?; see if he is able to make his melodies sing out clearly over a soft accompaniment; open yourself to the feeling of the music that comes through—is it convincing?; does the playing move you deeply?; is the player trying to impress you with his technique or is he more concerned with the overall musical effect?; what does this particular player do best? There are many things that players do—both good and bad—that you can observe and learn from. Imitate the good and forget the bad.

Learning from Recordings

An important learning resource is the phonograph record or cassette tape. For a relatively small investment, the guitarist can have recordings of the best players of our time for private study. If you cannot take lessons from a master player, at least you can study his records or tapes. Naturally the player should not become slavishly dependent on recordings for all his technical and interpretive ideas. However, for beginning and even advanced players, recordings can be very useful learning tools. Advanced players usually will do better to work out their own interpretations and fingerings first and then refer to a recording later. But the beginning player should feel no compunction about listening very carefully to the interpretation of a master player and then imitating every nuance as exactly as possible. Even though you may later change your mind about how to play the piece, you can learn an enormous amount in this way.

Just as in listening to a live performance, it is good to listen to every little detail of a recording. Having the score in hand as you do this is helpful so that you can make notations about the fingerings and interpretation. In the listening process you should be able to pick up such things as: the emotional feeling of the piece and each passage, the quality of the tone, where the performer places slurs, whether he is playing staccato or legato on certain notes, whether he is bringing out the melody clearly, what notes are being accented, whether he is playing rest or free strokes, how he handles tempo changes, where he arpeggiates chords, where he adds or deletes notes, and so on. With some experience, you should even be able to tell what strings the notes are being played on. Many of these details are difficult to discern when the record is going at 33⅓ rpm. But, if you slow it down to 16⅔ rpm (which makes the pitch an octave lower), it is usually much easier to hear such details as slurs, rest strokes, and tempo changes. It helps to turn down the bass and bring up the treble so that the sound at the slow speed is not so muddy. The same slowing down effect can be achieved by taping the record on a dual-speed tape recorder at fast speed and playing it back at slow speed. In order to hear one passage over and over, you can put the music on a tape recorder that has the capability of being switched between playback and rewind very quickly. Most of the currently available cassette recorders have that feature.

Maestro Segovia

Andrés Segovia is an example of a master musician who has served as an inspiring model for many players during their guitar student days. I have been fortunate to have seen many of his concerts and to have attended two master classes he gave: one in 1968 in Santiago de Compostela in northern Spain and one in Los Angeles in 1981. In both classes his presence was very powerful. When he walked into the classes—which included well-known professional players—there was a potent electricity in the room. Everyone became very quiet. It was as if some royal personage had arrived—such is the dignity and presence of Segovia. It is this personal dignity that has rubbed off on his serious students and made them into finer persons as well as finer musicians. Segovia's presence and his masterful playing have helped to give the guitar its present place as a respectable concert instrument throughout the world. In any case, it was uplifting just to be in the same room with this great artist.

How does Segovia teach? Here are some observations from my experience in Santiago and Los Angeles and from seeing films of his classes. He does not spend an excessive amount of time talking and he does not dwell much on technical matters. He expects that students who come to him have already mastered technique. He tends to focus right on the soul of the music, that is, the emotional and spiritual interpretation of it. Segovia's teaching is anything but dry or academic. He prefers to teach by example. When he wants a student to change the way he is playing a passage, he will pick up the guitar and demonstrate the way he thinks it should be played. Then the student is encouraged to imitate that approach. Like other fine artists, Segovia frequently will sing along with the music as the student plays. When he has a suggestion on phrasing, tempo, or dynamics, he will stop the student and *sing* the passage the way he would like it. He emphasizes strongly the idea of making the guitar sing like a human voice. At the class in Los Angeles, he said to one player that he should sing *"en mente"* ("in the mind") when he plays for others and sing out loud when he practices at home. Characteristically, Segovia jokes about his own singing voice, although he is quite skillful with sol-fa. He says in his quaint English "I am not the seenger!"

Segovia spices up his teaching by telling first-hand stories about composers and players he has known. He also likes to use vivid, sometimes amusing imagery or a well-turned phrase to illustrate some point he wants to make to a student. For example, in Santiago de Compostela he was helping a student with the interpretation of the *Fandanguillo* by Turina. He felt that the student was playing the dark, velvety melody in the middle of the piece too loudly and harshly. So he told the student that he was playing this part as if he were shouting at a pretty girl "¡Qué bonita eres!" ("How pretty you are!"). Segovia said this in a gruff voice which both made the point clear and brought a laugh from the class. I doubt if that guitarist will ever forget the delicacy with which he should play that passage. To another student who was playing a piece by Granados with technical perfection but without the appropriate feeling, Segovia said, "You must be something more than perfect!" In other words, if the player wants to be an artist, he cannot get by with mere technical perfection; he must also be able to express the emotion proper to the music.

Segovia is a gentleman in the old-fashioned sense of the word. He is normally courteous and patient with his students. He usually lets them play all the way through their pieces and then makes suggestions. He has definite preferences in both music and interpretation, but he does make some allowances for different ways of interpreting a piece. Occasionally, when he disagrees with a student's approach, he will give the student a strong opinion about it. In any case, he tends to be generous to his students and praises them when he feels they have done well. If a student seems to have exceptional talent, he will do everything to encourage him.

The picture of Segovia that emerges from my experiences is one of a sensitive, humorous, highly conscious and poetical man who loves life, people, and music very dearly. Above all, it is the intangible quality of feeling that comes from Segovia's love of life and music that enlivens and inspires his students. His success as a teacher has been amply demonstrated by the success of his students, many of whom are now famous. Some of the more well-known are: Alirio Diaz, John Williams, Oscar Ghiglia, José Tomás, Christopher Parkening, George Sakellariou, and Michael Lorimer. At some point in their careers, they all have learned by apprenticing themselves to Segovia by attending his classes as well as by studying his recordings and musical editions. Of course, they have developed distinctive styles of their own, but all of them gained a great deal of knowledge and inspiration from Maestro Segovia. Alirio Diaz, the well-known Venezuelan guitarist, among others, has spoken of the tremendous value of being in Segovia's presence and imitating his way of playing. This direct experience allows the player to absorb Segovia's feelings and ideas about musical interpretation in a very effective way.[4]

Segovia's unique, natural style of playing is an excellent model for the guitarist to study. Seeing and hearing him live is best, but if that is not possible, then his many recordings can serve as inspiring examples of refined musical expression. It is also useful to study his transcriptions, editions, and technical exercises. Even if you do not agree with all of his interpretations and transcriptions, the musicality, sincerity, and loving care with which he approaches every piece—indeed, every passage—is very striking and deserves your attention. Segovia's best live performances and recordings tend to make the listener forget about the mechanics of playing and draw one's attention magnetically to the beauty of the music and its delicate inner meaning. The player is reminded of what Segovia means when he says to "study music more than the guitar."

Most guitarists will agree that Segovia is a great master, but everyone will naturally have his own preference for a particular player or teacher. So choose the master or teacher you admire and use him as a model for your

[4]George Clinton, *Andrés Segovia* (London: Musical New Services, 1978), p. 59.

approach to the instrument. The best way is to study with one player for a length of time. Of course there is nothing wrong with studying with more than one master player—just so long as you do not become confused by hearing too many conflicting opinions. The intelligent player can learn something from everyone, including his peers.

MASTER PRACTICE STRATEGIES

Now let's look at some of the highly effective practice methods used by fine players. If you apply these methods intelligently, you can make your own practice sessions more productive. Keep the following eight points in mind.

1. Set Goals and Priorities
2. Do One Thing at a Time
3. Break Down the Problem
4. Slow is Fast
5. Repeat Until It Feels Natural
6. Set Up a Regular Practice Schedule
7. Take Breaks
8. Do It Now

Set Specific Goals

The goal-directed approach of the best players is your most useful study tool. In order to get concrete results, you must have concrete goals in mind. First, it is good to define your overall guitar goals. Then define the smaller goals you want to achieve today and in the near future. You will get the most from your practice sessions if you ask yourself in very specific terms, "What do I want from today's session?" Aim directly at the particular details of your playing that really need work.

For the best short-term results, *set small goals that can be actualized in one or two practice sessions.* Even if you only work out the fingering of one awkward left-hand change or make one phrase sparkle, you will have accomplished something definite by the end of a session. As a check for yourself, it is good to ask yourself after each practice session, "What specific goals have I achieved today?" If you cannot see some definite results, you probably need to rethink your practice approach and set goals that are more concrete and easier to achieve.

To make your guitar goals really clear, it helps to put them down on paper. Try making several lists. Write out your long-term guitar goals—say, for the next five years; then intermediate-term—for the next six months to a year; then short-term—for today's study session and the next few weeks. Be sure to make your lists concrete; for example, "Work on accurately planting the right-hand fingers in Villa-Lobos *Etude No. 1*" or "Memorize the Agustin Barrios piece *La Catedral* by the end of June" or "Work out the chord changes in bars 7 and 8 of Tárrega's *Estudio Brillante* today." Writing your three lists in a notebook or on 3 × 5 cards is an interesting exercise because you have to make decisions. You may find that you do not know exactly what you want. If your guitar study goals are not clear, then at least make some tentative choices so that you will have some direction for your work. Remember that you can always change your goals later if they are not what you want.

To keep your goals in mind, it is good to put them on the wall of your practice room or in some other obvious place. Then you can have the pleasure of crossing off those items that you achieve. Every month or so it is a good idea to go through your lists and see if your goals are in line with your current thinking. Update your lists if necessary. Do not be overly concerned if you do not accomplish all your goals exactly on time. Projects almost always take longer than you think. However, do try to stick to your deadlines and avoid procrastination.

Set Priorities

Once you have decided on your practice goals, the next step is to set priorities. Now you have some idea of what you want, at least tentatively, but what comes first in your practice goals? What do you want to accomplish right now and which things do you want to postpone? Take a good look at your three lists and pare each of them down to a few items that you really want. Rewrite your lists so that the items are in the order of importance, with the most important one at the top. Time management experts often recommend putting your goals into priority categories such as "A" for the most important goals, "B" for the next most important, and "C" for the least important. To make this concrete, you can put an A, B, or C in front of each goal on your daily list according to your evaluation. This can also be done with the long-term lists. The object is to do all the "A" items first, then the "B's," and if there is any time left over, the "C's." Remember to focus on the "A's" since most of the real value is going to come from doing them. The famous 80–20 rule can be helpful here. According to this rule, if you have a list of ten items to do, two of them, that is, 20 percent, will be most worthwhile and will yield 80 percent of the value of the list. These two items should be your "A's." The other eight items (80 percent) will yield only 20 percent of the value and should be your "B's" and "C's."

The natural approach to the question of guitar priorities is to aim at the highest first: Work on music that you want to play. Thus the primary items on your long-term goal list will be pieces that you want to learn. With the music as the first priority, everything else should relate to it. All the scales, coordination exercises, and bar chords that you have on your daily goal list are only for the purpose of making beautiful music. This may be obvious, but many guitarists are not very clear on this point and get lost in hours of fruitless technical exercises instead of working on music. Technical study is very important, but not without relation to the music. Even the so-called pure technical exercises can be approached musically, that is, with good rhythm, balance of melody and accompaniment, beautiful tone quality, good legato, and so on.

Normally your study priority will be to work on music you like, but your daily, weekly, and monthly priorities will shift according to need. When you first begin to play the guitar, you will usually need to spend more time on basic technical exercises rather than on pieces—although pieces will help you learn technique as well. When you are more advanced, normally your high priority will be on pieces and low priority on exercises, except where specifically needed.

Do One Thing at a Time

At this juncture, it is good to recall the value of concentration during your practice sessions (see Chapter 3). Try not to scatter your attention by working on ten things at once. Concentrate on one important task at a time. Then you will have *quality* of practice, not just quantity. Also keep in mind that merely "going through" your practice routine for hours at a time is a waste. Fernando Sor warns against this kind of approach in his method book, saying "Hold reason for much and routine for nothing."[5] Just because you "played through" an hour of scales, an hour of arpeggios, and an hour of pieces does not mean you have done much constructive work. However, if you *think carefully* about what you are doing and concentrate on one detail at a time, you can accomplish much more in one hour than in three. The following section suggests specific ways of doing one thing at a time.

Break Down the Problem

The process of guitar learning is similar to digesting food. If you want to get the maximum value from your food, you naturally want to chew it up well so that your body can digest it properly. However, if you are in too much of a hurry and swallow your food whole, it usually results in indigestion. In the same way, in your work on the guitar, if you break down your musical and technical problems into bite-size pieces, then your mind and fingers can assimilate the material easily and effectively. Concentration is easy when you focus on one small thing at a time. On the other hand, if you are too eager and

[5]Fernando Sor, *Method for the Spanish Guitar*, trans. A. Merrick, Da Capo Press Reprint Series (New York: Da Capo Press, 1971), p. 48.

you swallow your music whole, you will get musical indigestion, which leads to frustration and mistakes.

The bite-size approach makes the guitar-learning process enjoyable because you are always working on a problem so small that you can solve it in a very short time. If you have a series of twenty chords in a piece, it is easy to learn them. Just learn one chord at a time and work on the connections between the chords one at a time. Do not listen to people who keep telling you how difficult it is to learn to play the guitar! You can learn anything in small bits.

This bite-size approach may seem to be an obvious one since everyone uses it to a certain extent. However, most players do not break down their musical and technical problems far enough. For example, one common student approach is to play a phrase (or an entire piece) all the way through from the beginning to the end every time instead of going directly to the particular measures or beats that really need work. Many student hours are wasted in going over parts of a piece that they already can play and not doing enough on the parts that really need work. Now let's look at some specific examples of how to break down guitar problems.

Work on Each Hand Separately   Many players realize that it is helpful to work on problem passages only a few beats or measures at a time. However, many do not realize that technical problems can often be broken down to a more manageable size by practicing the right- and left-hand parts separately as pianists do. For example, let us take Sor's Study in B minor, Op. 35, No. 22 (No. 5 in Segovia's edition), which is based on a series of arpeggiated chords. You can work on the left-hand movements by playing the chords in blocks instead of arpeggiating them. The original piece (Figure 7–1) is like this:

Figure 7–1   Original passage from Fernando Sor, Op. 35, No. 22

But you can play it as shown in Figure 7–2.

Figure 7–2   Block chord arrangement of Figure 7–1 for left hand

In the second way of playing, it is easier to learn the left-hand part because you can see the simple chord forms that underlie the complex
arpeggiations and the melody. Moreover, you do not have the extra burden
of having to think about complicated right-hand movements. You can also
apply the staccato Play–Relax technique here to save left-hand energy while
you learn the correct movements. Plant the right-hand fingers on each chord,
play it, and then quickly release the pressure on the left-hand fingers, thus
cutting the value of the chords short. (See Chapter 5, "Play–Relax for
Chords.") When the left-hand movements have been learned, then you can
work on making them legato.

Now you can take the right-hand part of Sor's study and practice it without using the left hand at all. You simply play the right-hand part on the same
strings that are actually called for in the piece, but you play it all on open
strings as in Figure 7–3.

Figure 7–3   Right-hand part of Figure 7–1 without left-hand fingering

This procedure makes pieces sound rather odd, but it is worthwhile as a practice technique because it allows you to work out the right-hand fingering
without the confusion of using the left hand at the same time.

Another Bite-Size Approach   As you can see, the essence of the bite-size
approach is to make things simple. A favorite simplifying trick of experienced
players is to leave out the ornaments and ornamental notes in their pieces
when they are first learning them. This approach reduces the number of
things you have to think about and makes learning the basic rhythmic structure of a piece much easier. When a piece has many ornaments, they sometimes make it difficult for the student to see where the beat is. In any case,
when the basic structure is learned, then the ornaments can be put in. This
tactic can be particularly helpful in pieces with many ornaments and signs
written in the score, such as the Prelude or Allemande from Bach's *Lute Suite
III* or Tárrega's *Mazurka in G.* Ornamental notes that are not indicated by special notations or signs can also be temporarily deleted. This approach makes
learning the left-hand parts much easier in pieces such as the Andante Religioso from *La Catedral* by Barrios. In bars 14 (Figure 7–4a) and 20 (Figure 7–4b)
of that piece, for example, the quick fill-in notes (in brackets) can be omitted
until the player is comfortable with the surrounding chords.

Figure 7–4 (A): **Omission of ornamental notes: Agustin Barrios,** *La Catedral*
(B): **Omission of ornamental notes: Agustin Barrios,** *La Catedral*

Excerpts from *La Catedral* by A. Barrios Mangoré, ed. Jesús Benites R., © 1977 by Zen-On Music Co. Ltd., Tokyo, Japan. Used by permission.

An even more useful tactic is to omit temporarily the sixteenth-note part of the beat wherever there are repeated chords in dotted eighth-sixteenth (♪♪) patterns. The technique is especially helpful in the Andante Religioso in the awkward sequence of chords from the second beat of bar 12 to the first beat of bar 19. Instead of playing the sixteenth notes as written (Figure 7–5a), the player simply leaves them out (Figure 7–5b).

Figure 7–5 (A): **Ornamental sixteenth notes: Agustin Barrios,** *La Catedral*
(B): **Same passage as 7–5A without ornamental sixteenth notes**

Excerpts from *La Catedral* by A. Barrios Mangoré, ed. Jesús Benites R., © 1977 by Zen-On Music Co. Ltd., Tokyo, Japan. Used by permission.

When the player omits these sixteenth-note chords, he will have a much easier time practicing the transitions between the chords because he will not have to make such quick, abrupt chord changes. Later, when the player has become proficient at making the changes, the sixteenth-note chords can be reinstated and played with relative ease.

The technique of breaking big problems into small ones is very powerful and will make a tremendous impact on how much you get from your practice sessions. Keep in mind that *every* musical or technical problem in your pieces can be broken down into small, digestible parts. You can solve any problem by just taking care of those small parts. Of course you must never entirely forget the overall musical conception of a piece so that you can fit all of the small parts together into a coherent whole. Remember the forest when you are dealing with the trees.

Slow Is Fast

Everyone naturally wants to play his pieces up to tempo immediately and make them sound like a finished product—a laudable desire. However, if you approach the music in too much of a hurry, it seldom leads to a beautiful result. It is fine to sight read a piece at tempo when you first obtain the music in order to get the overall picture of it. But once you have the overall musical idea, it is most productive to spend whatever time is necessary working out the difficulties slowly and carefully before you try to play the piece at tempo again. Unfortunately, most guitar students tend to practice everything too fast—perhaps in an unconscious attempt to keep pace with the hurried tempo of modern life. The problem is that, when you practice too fast, the coordination breaks down between your mental conception of the music and the physical execution of it. If your fingers are trying to move too fast and your eyes are trying to see too many notes at a time, it causes confusion and makes it difficult to concentrate on precise mind–body coordination. Thus many mistakes are made. The player often learns these mistakes all too well!

One of the best ways to promote good mind–body coordination and avoid practicing mistakes is to slow down your practice tempos considerably. Some of the best musicians spend as much as half of their practice time working at very slow tempos. How slow is slow? The most common advice given by professionals is *to slow down so much that you do not make mistakes.* That may mean slowing down your practice tempos to one-half, one-quarter, or even one-eighth of the desired performance tempo. Even one-eighth of the tempo may not be slow enough—particularly for certain parts of your piece. Use the metronome to help you slow down in a precise way. It is interesting that many guitar students simply do not realize how fast they are practicing. At their lessons, when they are asked to slow down, they frequently do not slow down at all or only a very little bit. When students actually do slow down at their lessons—which they often forget to do at home—they are usually struck by the fact that they do not make mistakes. A revealing experience!

When you practice a piece at one-quarter or one-eighth of the performance tempo, you may find that it seems very slow—so slow that there is too much time between clicks of the metronome, making it difficult to feel exactly where the beat is. In such a case, the best course is to *subdivide* the beat. That means that you divide each beat into two or more parts. For example, in $\frac{4}{4}$ time, suppose that you have the metronome beating quarter notes at 40 per minute. You find that this tempo is good because you do not make mistakes, but there seems to be so much time between beats that you are not sure when the next beat is coming. So you subdivide and, instead of counting each quarter note as one beat, you cut the beat in half and count each eighth note as one beat. The metronome would be set to beat eighth notes at 80 (the speed of the piece remains exactly the same as when you were counting quarters at 40). Thus you would have eight counts to a bar instead of four, making it easier to play at a very slow tempo and still keep track of the beats.

There is an important element of slow practice that is worth mentioning here. It is actually *peaceful* to play very slowly and carefully. It has a calming influence on your mind. This is how music can be truly relaxing and uplifting. It is not good to play the guitar with the same frantic approach that many of us use in everyday life. Also it should be clear that, if you want to play for other people, it is much better for them and for you if you bring a peaceful attitude from the practice room with you. It is not good to bring stress and strain.

Finally, *slow is really fast*, that is, you will learn much better and more quickly if you take your time to digest and assimilate everything very well. This idea also applies to the actual development of speed in playing—such as playing fast scales or arpeggios. First you achieve the precise coordination of finger movements in slow motion and eventually it will be easy to do everything at high speed. This is another application of the principle of balancing the opposites, that is, in order to do something well, you must first learn to do its opposite. To go fast, you must learn to go slow.

Repeat Until It Feels Natural

As everyone knows, repetition is a vital part of learning the guitar or anything else. However, repetition must not be mindless; it must be intelligent. Thus, whatever you repeat over and over again—that is, what you *program* your mind and fingers to do—should be carefully thought out beforehand. You do not want to repeat an ineffective or unmusical fingering 100 times! It is a tremendous waste of time and energy.

Due to lack of awareness, guitar students often practice their mistakes. One student worked very hard on his pieces—*Prelude No. 5* by Villa-Lobos, for example. He learned a good portion of the piece quite well, but there were always some spots that went awry. He would make the same stumbles in the same places each time he would play the *Prelude*, thus indicating that he had very effectively *practiced* those stumbles. Once he started to pay more attention to the mistakes he was practicing repeatedly, he got rid of them and made much better progress. Thus you must learn to heed the saying of the masters, "You play what you practice," and be careful what you repeat. Repetition is definitely a double-edged sword. Since your subconscious mind is neutral, it will learn whatever you put into it repeatedly—good material or mistakes. Make sure that it is not mistakes.

The violinist Suzuki has some strong ideas about repetition. He feels that, once good fingerings and a good interpretation have been found, you should never give up in your attempt to learn to play a passage or a piece. You should practice a passage or a piece as many times as necessary to master it, that is, until it feels completely natural. That may mean as many as 10,000 times! Nothing should be regarded as impossible. This thinking corresponds closely with what the master players actually do. Segovia has said that he may work for weeks on a single passage, "burnishing it until it sparkles." Of course, repetitive practice must not be unconscious. It is good to remain open to the possibility that you may discover a new and better way of playing a passage during the process of repeating it. Repetition should not negate your imagination.

Set Up a Regular Practice Schedule

If you want to make steady progress with the guitar, it works best to have a regular practice time. Most musicians will tell you that it is good to practice every day, preferably at the same time (or times) and for the same length of time. For example, the serious amateur player might practice two hours a day from 7 to 9 P.M., or possibly break up the two hours and do one in the morning and one in the evening. Or, if you are aiming at a professional career, you might try Segovia's practice schedule. He practices five hours a day, but he divides up the time and does different things during each segment. In the morning, he practices for two and one-half hours, divided up into two one-and-one-quarter-hour segments with a break between. Then he stops for a midday lunch and rest period. In the afternoon, he works another two and one-half hours, broken up the same way as in the morning.

Not everyone works well on a regular schedule. Some advanced players do best by setting the length of their practice sessions according to how they feel. The professional players who practice more irregularly emphasize that, in order to practice in such a way, you should have an established technique and really know how to be efficient with your time. Otherwise you will not make much headway. In general, a regular practice schedule is best, particularly for beginners so that they establish good habits quickly.

The discipline of regular practice is very healthy. Your mind and fingers get used to the idea of working on music at certain times every day and thus playing starts to come more naturally and easily. You actually develop a musical rhythm in your practice schedule. This rhythm will carry you along so you will not have to work so hard for results. For that reason it is good not to miss your study sessions. If you cannot practice the normal amount of time for some reason, pick up the guitar for at least ten or fifteen minutes and work on some small detail. That way you will tend to maintain the good habit of regular practice. Regular lessons—typically once a week—also tend to encourage regular practice habits.

One great benefit of regular practice is that it makes playing such an integral part of your life—like speaking your own language—that you will become more and more comfortable with it when you play for other people. For this reason it is good to have your guitar and music in an easily accessible place where you can pick it up and play it without much fussing around. Thus playing will eventually become a perfectly natural way of expressing yourself to others.

Just exactly how you structure your practice time is an individual matter. But, however you do it, it is best to approach it with some kind of plan. You need not be too rigid in how you divide up the time for different aspects of playing. Many players recommend some daily practice on the basic types of exercises such as scales, arpeggios, slurs, and bar chords in order to maintain and improve your technique. Just remember to spend time on whatever really needs work: technique, sight reading, theory, interpretation. If you are an intermediate student and have two hours to practice, you might arrange your time by spending the first hour improving your technique—twenty minutes on scales, twenty minutes on arpeggios, ten minutes on slurs, and ten minutes on bar chords—and the second hour on sight reading (fifteen minutes) and pieces (forty-five minutes).

Take Breaks

People learn best if they do not study for excessively long periods at one time. Some of the most successful guitarists practice in short, concentrated sessions and take frequent breaks. Sometimes short study periods are all that the busy concert artist gets! In any case, it is usually easier to digest a technical exercise or a musical passage if you work on it intensively for fifteen to twenty minutes and then take a break and go on to something else. Then you can come back to the problem later and work on it for another short period. This is a better approach than hammering away at the same thing for hours without rest.

You will waste a great deal of time by practicing one thing too much or by practicing too much at one sitting because your mind and fingers get very fatigued. Your mind will wander and you will start practicing mistakes. Remember to use the "stop-and-let-go" technique discussed in Chapter 2 if your hands get tired—even if you have only been playing for a minute. Your hands will last longer if you give them many micro-breaks. This is another offshoot of the Play–Relax idea discussed in Chapter 5.

When practicing, give yourself a short rest at least once an hour—preferably more often—so that you remain fresh and receptive to learning new material. During these breaks it is good to "disengage" yourself from practicing—stand up, stretch, walk around, get some water, sit with eyes closed. The violinist Yehudi Menuhin suggests to his students that they lie down flat or, better yet, lie down with their feet propped up in order to get good blood circulation to the brain. These breaks—even very short ones—are important not only because they give you a rest, but also because they give your mind a chance to settle down and connect with your subconscious which will supply you with solutions to your musical problems. After about two hours of practice, take a good, long break before starting again.

The length of practice time for the guitarist, as we have mentioned, depends on the individual. There is no best fixed amount of time. What really counts is the *quality* of the practice time, not the *quantity*. Neither the aspiring concert guitarist nor the amateur should over-practice. Most full-time guitarists seldom do more than four hours of concentrated study each day, while the amateurs usually do an hour or two. (Younger children usually study only from fifteen minutes to half an hour.) Both types of players should take frequent breaks.

Do It Now

> *If you have an idea, do it. . . . We should get so that it is second nature to put our thoughts into actions.*
>
> Shinichi Suzuki[6]

Getting to work *today* is the way the great guitarists approach music. All the power to accomplish anything is in the present. Do not put off working toward your goals until tomorrow. Start working on them *now* and you will make quick progress. It is certainly important to spend time thinking about your goals and what you want from music and the guitar, but it is equally important to start actualizing these goals in a concrete way as soon as you have formulated them with reasonable clarity. Keep your big goals in mind, but work every day on the small goals that will help you accomplish the big ones. *Do it now.*

SUMMARY

A significant step on the path to guitar mastery is learning how to learn. There are many valuable things that can be learned by studying books about the guitar and figuring out problems for yourself. However, the fastest, most

[6]Suzuki, *Nurtured By Love*, pp. 98–99.

effective, most enjoyable way to learn is by imitation of the best players. The natural process of imitative learning is the most successful model of learning that we have. When we were children consider how easily and joyfully we learned to speak our own language—merely by imitating others.

Beginning and intermediate guitarists should learn as much as possible by closely studying and imitating the best players. Of course the advanced player is expected to avoid excessive imitation and should develop his own independent style. In general, the imitative approach helps the student to avoid bad habits and tends to inspire him with the actual sound and feeling of the music. The student's interest may actually be stultified if he spends too much time studying only the dry printed notes of exercises and pieces. This is not to belittle the study of the notes, but rather to suggest that too much "note playing" and too little inspiration from hearing good players dulls the musical mind.

Perhaps the most important thing to learn about the guitar learning process is to *enjoy* it as much as possible. Always keep in mind that music involves work, but *pleasurable work,* not stress and strain. Contact with a fine player will remind you of the enjoyment that is possible with the guitar because his enthusiasm will be contagious.

We have emphasized the imitative, intuitive part of the learning process in our discussion, but, like the finest players, you should also use your intellect to make your studies progress more quickly. Using your intellect is just as natural as using your imitative and intuitive abilities. The intellect can help you plan and organize your practice strategies in such ways as: setting goals and priorities, working on one thing at a time, analyzing and breaking down problems, and arranging a good practice schedule. The intelligent guitarist will blend his imitative, intuitive qualities with intellectual discrimination to produce the best results from his daily study. In short, he will apply both his heart and his mind to the guitar. The next two chapters discuss further applications of your intellect and intuition to the guitar learning process.

8.

Mind Over Fingers (I)

visualization for guitarists

It is in the mind that the musical decisions are
made. The physical movements must evolve
naturally . . . "Let it happen!" is the cue.

Claude Kenneson, *A Cellist's Guide*

No barriers, no masses of matter, however
enormous, can withstand the powers of the
mind; the remotest corners yield to them; all
things succumb; the very heaven itself
is laid open.

Marcus Manilius, Roman author, 40 B.C.

THE POWER OF THE MIND

Because of a lack of time for actual practice at the keyboard, the great pianist Artur Rubinstein once had to learn an entire concerto just by studying the score on the train from Paris to Madrid. He "practiced" the piece in his mind and then played the piece successfully in a recital. This mental practice approach proved to be very useful during Rubinstein's career. He has certainly not been alone in using the mental approach. Another pianist, Artur Schnabel, who was famous for his Beethoven interpretations, actually detested physical practice at the piano and preferred sitting quietly and practicing in his head. There is even a story about the virtuoso violinist and guitarist Paganini that suggests he also practiced mentally. A man was determined to find out Paganini's secrets of success and so, for a period of time, he followed the master wherever he went. The man would always arrange to have a hotel room next door to Paganini so he could hear how he practiced. However, much to the man's chagrin, he heard nothing! Paganini apparently did not always practice with the violin in hand.

Many of the great musicians both past and present have used this powerful "mind over fingers" method of working. The basic idea is that, *if you can think it clearly in your mind, you can play it with your fingers.* Well-known contemporary guitarists such as Leo Brouwer use this approach as an adjunct to other practice methods to obtain better results for their playing. Any guitarist can benefit by applying this approach. One of the most effective techniques of the mental approach is *visualization.*[1] In this chapter, you will see how visualization can be applied to smoothing out left-hand changes, strengthening your memory of a piece, interpreting a musical passage, increasing your scale velocity, and solving problems of counting. As you might imagine, these are not the only possible uses of the mental approach. As you may recall, in the sec-

[1]For a general introduction to this subject, see Adelaide Bry, *Visualization: Directing the Movies of Your Mind* (New York: Barnes & Noble, 1978).

tion on role playing in Chapter 2 we pointed out that you can change your style of performing for the better just by improving your mental picture of yourself. Using visualization to improve your self-image in this way is one of the most powerful applications of the mental approach. In Chapter 9, we discuss in detail how the mental approach can be used to help you study an entire piece. In Chapter 10, we explore how visualization can help you play better recitals and overcome stage fright.

Guitarists should not think that the mental approach is only for special people. It is for everyone because everyone has enormous mental potential. Many famous people have said that there are no limits to human mental potential and that whatever the mind of man can conceive, he can achieve. Unfortunately, much of our mental potential lies untapped. Psychologists say that most people are using only about 10 percent of it. Even Einstein thought that he was only using 25 percent. There are several reasons why so much potential lies fallow. The main reason is that people have too many stresses and impurities in their nervous systems and thus their minds and bodies cannot function at full capacity. In Chapter 2 we mentioned several mind and body techniques to help clear the system of such obstacles. These techniques, along with generally healthy living, will allow people to realize more of their mental potential.

Another reason why mental potential is often blocked is because of attitude. People often take the attitude that they are limited or untalented and give up too soon in their pursuits. Every would-be guitarist should realize that there is an excellent musician within him who is only waiting to be released. Everyone should take the attitude of Thomas Edison who said, "I refuse to recognize that there are impossibilities." Now, before we go to guitar applications of visualization, let's look at the visualization process itself.

HOW VISUALIZATION WORKS

In order to understand visualization, it is necessary to know something about how the mind works. The mind can be viewed as having two main divisions: the *conscious* and *subconscious*. The conscious mind, represented by the cerebral cortex, is the one that thinks and gives commands to the subconscious and the body. The subconscious mind and its ally the body, represented by the mid- and lower brain, attempt to carry out these commands. The subconscious mind and the body also carry out with amazing precision and intelligence all the vital functions such as breathing, digestion, elimination, and bodily repair—automatically.

The most important realization to make is that the subconscious mind, that part of the mind about which we know relatively little, is tremendously powerful and will try to do whatever the conscious mind asks of it. It is completely neutral. Thus, whatever we program into it will be actualized just as surely as instructions programmed into a computer will be executed. If the input is positive, the results tend to be positive and vice versa. Of course repetition of the input has a powerful effect; the more an idea is repeated, the more likely it is that the idea will bear fruit. As a negative example, if you keep telling yourself that you are going to make mistakes when you perform, then you will tend to make mistakes. As a positive example, if you practice a piece many times with correct fingerings, then you will tend to perform the piece correctly. Thus, success or failure in your playing depends on what your conscious mind puts into your subconscious and is not just the work of chance. As a man thinks, so he is.

That the mind and body, conscious and subconscious, are intimately connected is not just a fanciful idea. It has been shown by numerous scientific studies that what happens in the mind affects the body and vice versa. The physiologist Edmund Jacobson pointed out some years ago that the mere imagining of such physical activities as running causes minute but measurable contractions in the muscles that are used in actual running.[2] More recent studies show clearly that for every mental state there is a physiological correlate. This phenomenon is called the *psychophysiological principle*.[3] The connection between mind and body is the basis of the power of visualization. For all practical purposes, the body and subconscious can tell little difference between a real experience and one vividly imagined in the conscious mind. Thus, such things as mental guitar practice can have much the same effect as actual physical practice. In fact, experiments have shown that this is the case.

In order for the visualization process to work effectively, it is crucial that the mind should *cooperate* with the body and subconscious. Unfortunately, as we have seen in Chapter 2, the conscious mind often gets in the way of the subconscious and the body. As Aldous Huxley says:

> Malfunctioning and strain tend to appear whenever the conscious "I" interferes with instinctively acquired habits of proper use, either by trying too hard to do well, or by feeling unduly anxious about possible mistakes. In the building up of any psycho-physical skill the conscious "I" must give orders, but not too many orders— must supervise the forming of right habits of proper functioning, but without fuss and in a modest, self-denying way.[4]

Thus, in the learning of a skill such as guitar playing, the mind needs to learn when to give directions to the subconscious and the fingers and when to let them find their own way. The mind needs to know when to "let it happen."

[2]Edmund Jacobson, *Progressive Relaxation* (Chicago: University of Chicago Press, 1942), p. 254.

[3]Harold Bloomfield, *TM: Discovering Inner Energy and Overcoming Stress* (New York: Delacorte Press, 1975), p. 38.

[4]Aldous Huxley, *The Art of Seeing* (New York: Harper and Brothers, 1942), p. 38.

VISUALIZATION FOR THE GUITAR

The Technique

Now we can consider some practical applications of visualization to the guitar. Here are a few guidelines that will help you get the most from the visualization process:

1. Calm the mind and body.
2. Be specific about your goals.
3. Visualize one thing at a time.
4. Find a quiet place.
5. Persist until you get results.
6. Let it happen.

It is good to relax and calm your mind before you start a guitar visualization session. Your visualizations will not be clear if the body is tense or if the mind is filled with turbulent thoughts. When you feel that your mind is settled, decide on definite goals that you want to achieve with the visualization process. Be sure to ask yourself what you want from the process in specific terms because the subconscious mind tends to become confused when your goals are vague. You can prevent confusion by focusing on just one thing at a time. It is also good to do your visualization in quiet surroundings.

In the actual visualization process, create a vivid, detailed image, sound, or feeling of your desired goal in your mind. It may be the image of your fingers on the fingerboard, the pitches of a melody, or the emotional feeling of a particular passage. Visualization can be done with eyes open or closed depending on your goal. Eyes closed tends to make it easier to concentrate because there are no external visual distractions.

As many people have discovered, the visualization technique is quite powerful. However, for it to be most effective, a certain amount of persistence and repetition of each visualization project (for example, a piece) is necessary. Finally, do not try too hard to do the visualization process. It is important to focus on the particular "mental picturing" you are doing, but forcing the mind only creates stress. Do the process in an easy way and do not be anxious about the results. Just let the process and the results happen naturally. Now let's go on to the specifics.

Visualization for Left-Hand Movements

A powerful way of practicing smooth connections for the left hand is through visualization of finger movements. The basic idea of guitar fingerboard visualization is to have a clear mental image of where your fingers are going to land at the end of a movement. The following procedure is a visualization technique for chord changes in passages or pieces that you know by heart. Since this technique combines mental and physical processes, it should be practiced with the guitar in hand.

Now let's look at an example of how the technique is used. In this case, suppose you want to move from one chord to another. The first step is to play the initial chord and then stop. Leave the fingers in place but relax the tension on them. The next step is to look at the place on the fingerboard where the next chord will be and picture in your mind as clearly as possible what the new finger pattern will look like. Then, in a relaxed way, shape the fingers into the new pattern. Wherever possible, place the shaped fingers lightly on or very close to the respective strings on which they will be playing. The fingers will thus be ready to move as directly as possible to the notes they will play. The next step is to make the actual move. For greatest accuracy, move slowly and deliberately. To start with, you may want to keep your eyes open for this visualization exercise, but if your mental image is clear, you will be able to do it with your eyes closed.

Figure 8–1, an example from *El Testamen de N'amelia* arranged by Miguel Llobet, shows how visualization can be used to make a smooth position change.

Figure 8–1   Smooth position change: *El Testamen de N'amelia,* **arr. by Miguel Llobet**

First play the G melody note and the D bass and then stop. Relax the hand but leave the third finger on the G. Now look at the fingerboard and picture what the next chord pattern (G minor 7) will look like. See exactly where each finger will go. The third finger will slide up to the B♭, the second will go to the F, the fourth will be on the D, and the first will be on the G. Picture the entire movement in slow motion. Now, *before moving,* set up the fingers lightly on the appropriate strings so that they form the pattern of the next chord. The third finger is already in place, the second should be over the B string, the fourth over the G, and the first over the D. Now, maintaining the finger pattern and using the third finger as a guide finger (that is, letting it slide up lightly on top of the first string), move easily and naturally to the G minor 7 chord. After a few times of visualizing and making very slow movements, the position change should become both easy and accurate.

Once they have used this method to practice a series of chord changes, most players will find that they will not have to be so concerned about the exact way the fingers move from one position to the next. What is important is the clarity of the goal. If the goal, that is, the fingerboard pattern, is clear in one's mind, then the fingers will tend to find their own way in a perfectly secure and smooth manner. Relatively little conscious effort will be required.

Mental Practice of a Piece:
Inner Hearing, Seeing, Feeling

The previous visualization technique is very good for smoothing out individual left-hand movements *with* the guitar. However, when you use visualization to practice an entire piece—that is, a piece that you have mostly memorized—a slightly different approach *without* the guitar works better. This is a powerful approach that helps solidify your memory of the piece and gives you a way of working out your interpretation independent of the guitar.

It is usually easiest to start doing mental practice with eyes open looking at the score. If at all possible, this mental practice should be done in a quiet place where you will not be disturbed. Sit in a comfortable chair and relax the mind and body before starting. When you begin the mental practice, it is good to focus on one element of playing at a time, such as the sound of the melody or the visual appearance of the left-hand movements on the fingerboard. Start by trying to *hear* the melodic line clearly in your inner ear as you follow the notes on the page. If you come to a passage where you cannot hear it clearly in your head, sing it or pick up the guitar and play that part to clarify it. Then do a mental retake without guitar to make sure it is clear in your inner ear. Now do the same process for the other parts and see if you can hear all the parts together. Then try *seeing* the precise movements of the fingers on the fingerboard in your mind's eye while looking at the score. Now try to hear the sound and see the movements together.

If you know your piece well, you may want to go directly to practicing mentally with your eyes closed. This approach is similar to mental practice with the score but requires more concentration. It is the most powerful approach. You can start by closing your eyes and attempting to hear the sound of the piece. As above, see if you can hear the sound of the melodic line clearly. If you cannot, check the score and sing it or play it. Then close your eyes again, do a retake, and make sure the passage is clear in your inner hearing. Now try hearing the other parts separately. Finally, imagine the sound of the whole piece in your head. Make sure that every sound is perfectly clear in your mind.

Once the sound is clear, it is good to turn your attention to the finger movements. Sit comfortably, close your eyes, and turn on the "movie screen of your mind." Visualize in vivid detail the movements of the left- and right-hand fingers on every note of the piece. It is usually easiest to picture the left-hand movements, so it is best to start with that. See the fingers moving around the fingerboard in slow motion. See them from different angles. "Zoom" in on them. Feel the sensations of the movements. If any of the movement "scenes" are so fuzzy that you cannot see where the fingers go on the fingerboard, check them on the score and on the guitar. Then "reshoot" those scenes with eyes closed until they are clear on your mental screen. If you leave any fuzzy spots, they are just the ones that will come back to haunt you when you perform. Leave none of them undone. Now visualize the right-hand movements in a similar way. When you can hear the sound and see the movements, try visualizing the total act of playing the piece.

Another way of doing mental practice that works well for some people—the pianist Rubinstein used it—is to visualize as clearly as possible what the printed notes look like on the page and picture which fingers play each note. Whatever approach to mental practice is taken, for most players it is important to do it repeatedly to make it effective. The process will take more or fewer repetitions depending on the mental clarity of the individual.

Once the total piece can be *clearly* heard, seen, and felt in the mind, you will know it thoroughly. You will not have any fear of forgetting the piece when you play. Concert guitarist Sharon Isbin explains that she never performs a piece in public until she performs it in every detail in her mind.[5] Then she is sure that she knows the music. She also says that mental practice leads to better concentration when she is on stage. In a similar vein, concert pianist John Browning says that he does mental practice so that he knows every note of a piece and which finger plays it. Then he has "insurance" when he performs. This practice method requires considerable mental energy but it gives great self-confidence in performance. In the process of mental practice, do not be concerned if your mind wanders a bit. Just use the natural concentration technique to bring your attention gently back to your subject matter (see Chapter 3). After some experience you will find that concentrated mental practice, like any other habit, will become easier.

One of the most rewarding features of mental practice is that you will have great freedom to experiment with many different ways of interpreting your pieces. You will not be tied down to any particular way of playing the piece. In mental practice, your imagination is your only limitation. You can "conduct" the piece in any way you like, change tempo, use special effects, accent certain notes, and so on. You can do this until you find a satisfying interpretation. And you can always go back to your "mental practice room" at any time to experiment more.

Visualizing a Musical Passage

The pianist Alexandra Pierce remarks that

> a common way to learn a piece is to bumble in (read it through) and then bluster around (play it through, slowly, then faster,

---

[5]Ms. Isbin describes her technique of mental practice and other ideas she has about studying and performing in the article by Laura Koplewitz, "Sharon Isbin: Artist of the Classical Guitar," *Accent on Music*, 7, no. 5 (April 1982), 13ff.

many times, work on isolated technical problems, finger the "hard spots"), feeling that something will come of it in time.[6]

She then suggests that although a certain amount of repetitive busywork is necessary to learn a piece, there is an approach that can make the learning process work better. The basic idea, borrowed from the pianist Luigi Bonpensiere, is that if you can clearly conceive or visualize ("ideate" is Bonpensiere's expression) a passage in your mind, then learning it becomes much easier and quicker. Having that clear musical goal makes it definitely easier to find the appropriate technical means to play the passage.

An important feature of the visualization approach is that one does not try to control every physical movement of the fingers in order to play a passage. It is simply not possible to control all the complex aspects of a movement. However, as Bonpensiere and Huxley have pointed out, the conscious mind, in its anxiety not to make mistakes, often does try to control the movements and ends up making them more difficult. The fingers and subconscious mind work much better if the conscious mind does not interfere too much. There should be a healthy cooperation and coordination between mind and body. It is often the case that the mind needs to do little more than clearly visualize a passage and then *allow* the fingers to find the appropriate technique to play it.

The visualization process, as Bonpensiere describes it, is in three steps: *ideation* (gain clear conception of the passage), *volition* (ask the fingers to play it), and *release* (let the fingers play it without getting in their way). In short, *visualize and let it happen*. With some practice this process becomes automatic and effortless. According to Bonpensiere, the action of the fingers becomes very light "as if the limbs were becoming ethereal." In fact, this light quality of physical action is one of the characteristics of fine playing on any instrument.

To clarify the method of visualizing a passage for the guitar, it helps to alter slightly Bonpensiere's description of the process (which was intended for the piano) as follows:

1. Gain a clear mental image ("ideation") of the passage by a brief analysis of it. Determine which is the most important line. Look at the shape of that line (or lines). See where the beginnings, climaxes, and endings of the note groups (or phrases) are.
2. Sing or play the melodic line; clap or say the rhythm if it is not clear.
3. Feel the special character of the passage. Ask yourself if it is light or heavy, happy or sad, a dance or a song. Bring in any relevant historical information you have.

---

[6]Alexandra Pierce, "Ideation," *Piano Quarterly*, no. 90 (Summer 1975), 34. Dr. Pierce's article has been very helpful for this discussion.

4. Close the eyes and hear the passage in your head.
5. When the passage is clear in your mind, find a natural fingering that expresses your musical conception.
6. With the musical idea in mind, ask the fingers to play it ("volition") and then let the fingers play it without interference from the conscious "I" ("release").

Speaking as a pianist, Bonpensiere would say that the fifth step is unnecessary since, if your "ideation" of the passage is clear, the innate wisdom of the fingers would find just the right fingering. However, on the guitar the fingers need a fair amount of experience before they will naturally go to a good fingering since there are so many possible ways of playing a given passage. Thus it is best to experiment with fingerings that feel natural and sound good. When the fingers have had experience with many different patterns, then you will find that if you merely ask them to produce the sound you want—without trying to control how they do it—they will indeed discover good fingerings on their own.

This approach can be applied to the excerpt in Figure 8–2 from Robert Johnson's *Alman*.

Figure 8–2   Note groupings: Robert Johnson, *Alman*

First, gain a clear visual image of the shape of the melodic line. It may help to actually draw the shape of the line over the notes something like that shown in Figure 8–3.

Figure 8–3   Outline of the melody in Figure 8–2

The general shape of the line is an upward sweep to a peak on the high C in the third bar and then down to the end. The passage appears to fall into two main parts of two bars each (shown by the curved lines) which are made up of short rhythmic motives (shown by brackets). In the first two bars the tune moves through intermediate high points on C and D (bar one) to the climax on E (third beat of bar two); in the second two bars the melody moves right up the scale to the climax on C and then settles down on the G♯.

Such a visual image is helpful for learning the passage, but gaining a clear "sound image" is the most helpful. The best way to do that is to sing the melody without the guitar so that you can actually feel it in your body. If singing the tune is not so easy for you, then play it on the guitar and sing with it as well as you can. If the rhythm is not clear, put the guitar down and count it, then clap it, or say it on "la." Feel the rhythm by moving your body with it in whatever way strikes your fancy. To get the feeling of the passage, it helps to know that an alman was a moderately quick Elizabethan dance.

When the melody and rhythm are clear to you, put the guitar down and hear the passage in your mind. Imagine the passage moving from the beginning through smaller peaks to the first climax on E in the second bar and then moving up to the big climax on C in the third bar and finally relaxing on the G♯. Now, with the musical idea clearly in mind, pick up the guitar and ask the fingers to play the passage with the fingering suggested in Figure 8–4, but in this process do not try to control every movement of the fingers. Let the fingers find their own way as much as possible so that they have freedom to express the unique character of the music.

Figure 8–4 Fingering for the passage in Figure 8–2

You may be surprised at how readily the fingers find the notes and express the musical idea. You may also be surprised at the particular technique that the fingers find. The movements may be bigger or smaller than you expected and your fingers may be more comfortable with a slightly different fingering than the one suggested. There are many different ways that the fingers can play this passage and it is good not to inhibit the fingers too much so that slightly different and interesting ways of expression can be found each time the passage is played. In this way the interpretation of the passage will always have a certain freshness and spontaneity to it. This does not mean that there should be no discipline to the way you work out your fingerings but rather that there should be a certain amount of free play given to the fingers to keep yourself from becoming musically rigid. The fingers should be guided primarily by the musical idea.

If this visualization method of learning a passage does not seem to work for you immediately, then you probably do not have a clear musical conception of the passage and need to stop and rethink your conception. Or you may be trying to control the finger movements too much. After you have had some experience with this process, you should find that your fingers will be guided to musically expressive fingerings in an increasingly spontaneous way.

Remember that the visualization approach is just one way of learning a passage, albeit a very potent one. Advanced players usually get the most from it, although beginners may also find it useful. Keep in mind, as potent as visualization is, it does not entirely supplant the need for intelligent repetition and reasoned exploration of the various possible technical means for making a passage come out beautifully. Of course, the player must also explore the historical background and the emotional qualities of the music he plays. (The role of visualization and the mental approach in studying an entire piece will be discussed in more detail in Chapter 9.)

Visualization for Velocity

In Chapter 5 we showed how the Play-Relax technique can help you increase scale velocity. The visualization process can help improve it further. Through the use of the mind you will be able to transcend scale velocity limits again and again. Let's take an example. Suppose you can play a scale at four notes to a beat at 80 on the metronome, but cannot seem to get beyond that speed. You would like to play four notes to a beat at 100 so you can perform a favorite piece properly. How to go about it? Remember that, if you can conceive something clearly in your mind, you can do it. The method is to set the metronome at 100 (start slower if necessary) and then *think* the rhythm of four notes to a beat at that speed. Do this until your mental rhythm is going with the metronome. It helps to think the rhythm on one note with some simple syllables like "ti" and "ka"—depending on what you want. For example, if you want to play all four notes detached, like this ♩♩♩♩, with a slight emphasis on the first and third notes—a very common way of playing scales—then you would mentally think *tikatika* for each beat. If it is difficult to think the rhythm clearly in your head, then say the syllables out loud. Once you can *think or say* the rhythm clearly at a given speed, then you should be able to *play* it at that speed with the fingers without much difficulty.

Now play the scale or just a small part of it at your mental tempo. Trust that your fingers will be able to do it; do not think about it too much. You may not be able to play at the desired tempo immediately, but you will be surprised at how quickly your speed will increase. Once again you will see how powerful the visualization approach is. If you can think it, you can eventually do it. This technique combined with the Play-Relax approach will enable you to increase your scale velocity in a much shorter time than with conventional methods.

Visualization for Counting Problems

Guitarists, like other musicians, frequently have problems with counting out certain rhythms in their pieces. Unfortunately, many players think they can work out passages with counting problems by simply forcing their way through them enough times. More often than not, this "brute force" method results in learning the rhythm wrong. The visualization approach can help you solve such problems much more easily. Most often the difficulty lies in a complex rhythmic figure such as this one (Figure 8–5) from Fernando Sor's *Variations on a Theme of Paisiello*, Op. 16, measures 18–20.

Figure 8–5 Original passage from Fernando Sor, *Variations on a Theme of Paisiello*, Op. 16

Something like this figure (or worse!) may stop you in your tracks. Naturally you will want to be able to work it out as quickly as possible. If you mentally think out the figure before you try to play it, you should not have much trouble. *If you can count the rhythm in your head, it will be relatively easy to do it with the fingers*; however, if you cannot count it in your head, no amount of repetitive fingerwork will help you.

A good way to start the visualization process for the example in Figure 8–5 is to tap your foot on the eighth notes and count only the melodic line so that you know where all the beats are and how long each note should last. It helps to write out the counting over the notes as shown in Figure 8–6.

Figure 8–6 Melodic line of Figure 8–5 with counting

Next *think* or *say* the rhythm of the melodic line using a syllable such as "la" on a single note. Keep the eighth note pulse with your foot. The quintuplet (a five-note group) on beat three of bar two may be a sticky point. To get a proper feel for it, try tapping your foot and counting "1 2 3 4 5" evenly on each tap. That should make it easy to fit in the five notes on one beat in the example. Now, when you have worked out all the counting details, sing the melody line with the actual pitches if you can. If you do not sing well, do not be concerned. Just stick with saying "la" on one note. Once you can say or think the rhythm of the melodic line correctly, the remaining accompaniment parts should fall into place. If necessary, you can also count out and say the rhythm of the lower parts separately, as in Figure 8–7.

Figure 8–7   Lower parts of Figure 8–5 with counting

Then count the combined parts as in the first example, remembering that notes more or less vertically aligned over one another fall on the same count.

Now, with the clearly visualized rhythm in your head, play the passage and see how it comes out. Without a doubt it will be better than if you had blustered your way through it unconsciously. This process of visualizing rhythmically complex passages may seem involved at first, but with a little practice the entire process can be compressed into a short time.

SUMMARY

The intelligent player always seeks the techniques of practice that yield the best results with the least effort. Visualization is such a technique. This "mind over fingers" approach does require some mental concentration but little physical energy. All you need is to have a clear idea of the musical result you want. Then the fingers will tend to be guided naturally and automatically to the physical realization of that idea—provided that the conscious mind does not try too hard to control the process. Of course there are always some details of playing that resist automatic working out—and these require special attention, repetition, and careful analysis. However, much of that kind of drudgery can be avoided by doing more with your mind and less with your fingers.

When you apply visualization to guitar study for the first few times, you will find it a challenging task. However, it gives an exhilarating feeling of freedom and confidence when you can learn much of your music and technique independently of the guitar.

You have seen in this chapter that visualization can be helpful for practicing finger movements, increasing velocity, working out a musical passage, and improving memory and interpretation of an entire piece. Visualization also has other uses such as recital preparation as we shall see in Chapter 10. The subject of Chapter 9 is a systematic way of applying what you have learned about visualization and other techniques to the process of studying an entire piece.

Drawn by J. Goubaud.   Engraved by W. J. Baker.

F. Sor

9.

Mind Over Fingers (II)

visualizing and realizing
the musical meaning of a piece

Study music more than the guitar.

Andrés Segovia

THE MUSIC FIRST

The natural approach to the guitar would not be complete without bringing together the ideas of the preceding chapters to focus on the primary interest of most classical players: how to study a piece and express its musical meaning. In Chapter 8, we discovered some of the advantages of the mental approach to solving guitar problems. In this chapter, we will use that approach as the basis for studying an entire piece from the rough beginnings to the polished end result.

The essence of the mental approach is to form a clear overall conception of the sound, feeling, and structure of a piece *before* working out the details of fingering and interpretation. It is particularly important not to start repetitive practice or memorization before you have a good idea of what a piece is about. The procedure is similar to that of an architect who first mentally pictures the overall plan of a house, then draws it in rough form, fills in the details, and finally builds the structure. When you think before you start moving your fingers, you will obtain the best musical results in the least time. This "mind over fingers" approach is ultimately the most enjoyable because you focus mainly on the musical sound picture rather than on mere finger movements. After all, the compelling quality of the musical sound of a piece is normally what makes you want to play it, not the technique. The technique is just 'the means for expressing the music. Most importantly, only when focusing on the musical sound and its meaning can your playing have the magical effect of lifting everyone out of their ordinary selves into an exalted state. Thus it is good to keep your priorities straight and start with the musical meaning. Then see what technical means are necessary to realize that idea. In short, be a musician first and a guitarist second.

Least Action

If you start off with a clear idea of how you want a piece to sound, then the appropriate fingering and expression on the guitar will come with relatively little effort. It is definitely not good to wait until you have memorized a piece before you begin to think about the musical idea. That approach puts the cart before the horse. At the beginning of your study of a piece, it means that you will have difficulty finding logical fingerings. Further down the road, it means that you will have to waste time reworking those fingerings that do not express the musical idea that you have belatedly discovered. Of course, when you use the approach of "mind over fingers," it does not mean that you must cling rigidly to your initial idea of the piece. It is natural to revise and refine your idea as you study and play.

If you do not have at least some concept of the structure and meaning of a piece before you start to study it, you will have trouble making the piece sound coherent. The most common mistake is to approach the music in bits and pieces. That is, memorize small parts of the music at a time with emphasis on the mechanics of the fingering. This laborious "bits and pieces" approach most often results in patchwork—a kind of crazy-quilt in which the musical and technical pieces do not quite fit together. This approach is very inefficient. Even after you spend a good deal of time on this "brute force" attack on the music, the results may still be unmusical, that is, you may be able to play the piece mechanically but without any sense of musical form, emotional content, proper phrasing, balance of parts, and other elements of interpretation.

The Whole Is Greater
Than the Sum of the Parts

Because it saves time and energy, the great guitarists use the "mind over fingers" approach. Even more important, they use this approach because it allows them to express the *wholeness* of the music in a coherent way. Just as a house is more than a collection of bricks, a piece of music is more than a collection of notes. Thus the expression of a piece is incomplete without projecting its total structure and feeling. The mental approach is the best way to comprehend and express this musical wholeness. Of course the totality of the music is not something that can be understood completely by intellectual analysis. Intuition plays a vital role in grasping the wholeness because it can capture the vast world of subtle feelings and meanings that lie beyond words and analysis. As the cellist Pablo Casals said, "Intuition is the decisive element in both the composing and performing of music."[1] Nevertheless, analy-

---

[1] Pablo Casals, as told to Albert E. Kahn, *Joys and Sorrows* (New York: Simon & Schuster, 1970), p. 97.

sis can help to give your intuition an intelligent direction. The study plan in this chapter offers a way to use both intellect and intuition to encompass the wholeness of a piece of music and help you discover its meaning.

TWELVE STEPS OF STUDYING A PIECE

Now let's look at one possible sequence of steps you can use to gain a clear mental picture of a piece and then translate it into actual playing.[2] Naturally this is not the only way to learn a piece, but these steps are very practical and have been used in one form or another by many fine musicians. You may want to modify the steps to suit your individual approach, but the main idea of "music first, then technique" should be preserved. The twelve steps of studying a piece are:

I. Envisioning the Musical Idea
   1. Choose Music You Like
   2. Read the Score Mentally
   3. Absorb the Overall Sound, Style, and Inner Meaning
      a. Sight-read
      b. Listen to other players
      c. Listen to related nonguitar music
      d. Read background material
   4. Analyze the Music
      a. Analyze overall structure
      b. Study the texture and phrasing
         (Sing or play each voice; tap or clap rhythm)
      c. Make a preliminary interpretive analysis

II. Working Out the Technique
   5. Find Natural and Musical Fingerings
   6. Read Slowly with Metronome; Use Play–Relax Technique
   7. Polish Rough Spots; Purify the Sound
   8. Read at Tempo with and without Metronome

III. Bringing the Music to Life
   9. Memorize and Play at Tempo
   10. Practice Mentally; Use Feedback
   11. Refine the Interpretation
   12. Express the Wholeness of the Music; Let It Flow Through You

[2]This study plan was inspired by William Newman's Nine-Step Plan in his book *The Pianist's Problems* (New York: Harper and Row, 1974).

USING THE STEPS: AN EXAMPLE

To make our study plan more concrete, we will apply it to a minuet, Op. 2, No. 4 by Fernando Sor (1778–1839). This example will show how to use the plan for any piece you want to study. The original score of the minuet is shown in Figure 9–1. Figures 9–1 through 9–4 and particularly Figure 9–5 will help you follow the analysis. The twelve steps are explained in considerable detail here so that you have the effect of being with a teacher who guides you through all the intricacies of the piece. Imagine yourself taking a series of lessons on the piece and enjoy yourself as you do it.

I. ENVISIONING THE MUSICAL IDEA

1. Choose Music You Like

It is always best to choose music you like so that you will be able to play it with love and feeling and not become bored with it. It is not a good idea to choose a piece only because you think you will impress everyone by playing it. If you do that, you will often end up biting off more than you can chew and will find yourself disliking the piece. It is quite all right, however, to work on a piece that is very challenging to your abilities—as long as you like it. Do not listen to people who tell you that a piece is too difficult for you, even if it is the *Concierto de Aranjuez* by Rodrigo. Simply go right into it with the attitude that you will eventually learn the piece by quietly working on it as a long-term project. Take the "tortoise approach," in which you learn a little at a time and use the complex passages as exercises to improve your technique. In any case, you will always learn more when you like the piece you are playing. Of course it is a good idea to work on other less challenging pieces at the same time so that you can derive the satisfaction of being able to play something well in a short time.

Another consideration when you are choosing your music is that you probably will enjoy playing more if you become familiar with a variety of pieces. You may eventually learn to like almost every type of music in its own way. When you settle on a piece you like, it is good to look for the best edition. Your teacher or another guitarist can help you choose the best one. (For more on editions, see Chapter 11.)

2. Read the Score Mentally

This and the next two steps are very important in the mental approach. Using these steps, you will be able to master a piece much more easily because you will have the grand picture of the musical landscape right from the beginning. You can start to impress that picture on your mind by looking at the outstanding landmarks of the piece, such as the title, type of piece, style, tempo and expression marks, key signature, the shape of the melodic lines, the rhythm,

Figure 9–1 Fernando Sor, *Minuet,* Op. 2, No. 4

Tempo de Minuetto

the harmonic structure, and the overall architecture. (By "architecture" is meant the shape of the piece and how the parts of the piece relate to one another.) After some experience with the mental approach, you may even be able to get the sound and feeling of the piece by just looking at it, visualizing it, and hearing it in your "inner ear."

Now let's get a bird's eye view of the Sor piece. First, a look at the name. It is called *Tempo Di Minuetto*, which tells you that you are looking at a dance "in minuet time" and that there will probably be a strong rhythmic element. If you look up the minuet in a music dictionary you will find that during the classical–early romantic period in which Sor lived, it was a fairly quick, graceful dance in $\frac{3}{4}$ time. Of course not all minuets were danced; many were for listening. This one probably falls in the latter category.

Now a brief look at some other features. The key of the piece is clearly C. The lack of sharps or flats and the beginning and ending C chords are the primary clues. You might also notice some important harmonic ending points on G chords in measures 8 and 16. Another interesting feature is that the melodic phrases in the uppermost part are symmetrical: they are either four or eight bars long. The melodic movement has three upward sweeps with its highest point at the C in measure 23 just before the end. The overall architecture of the piece, at first look, seems to consist of two large sections, one eight bars and the other sixteen bars, separated by the repeat sign in measure 8.

Now that you have a general idea of how the piece looks, it is appropriate to hear how it sounds.

3. Absorb the Overall Sound, Style, and Inner Meaning

Sight-Read   There are several ways to impress the total sound of a piece on your mind. The first is through sight reading. (Sight-singing the melody is also good if you can do it.) That means reading through the entire piece a few times and not being concerned about making mistakes. It is ideal to be able to sight-read it right away and make it sound like a finished product. Depending on the complexity of the piece, that is entirely possible for a good sight-reader. However, even if you are not the greatest reader, it still is very useful to play through the piece as well as you can. If you have difficulty playing all the parts together, try playing just the main melodic line. You will get at least some idea of the overall flow of the music that way. Now let's go back to our example. The Sor minuet is not particularly difficult to sight-read for anyone who has had some experience with the guitar. However, it will be challenging to a beginner to play all the parts at once, so it is good to start off by following the suggestion to play just the main melody in the top part of the piece (the melody notes have their stems up.)

Listen to Others   The second way of absorbing the sound of a piece is to listen to a recording or hear the music live. If you are a beginning guitarist and do not sight-read very well, then listening to a recording of the piece made by a master guitarist or having someone play it for you (or tape-record it) is very helpful. In the case of the Sor minuet, there is certainly no harm in obtaining your "sound picture" from a good player you know. More experienced players can also benefit from hearing other guitarists, particularly the masters, although it is better for them to listen to performances or recordings *after* they have worked out their own ideas of the music. Whether you are a beginner or an advanced player, it is important to sit quietly when using a recording. Listen to it many times to hear all that is going on. Remember that it is good to analyze what you hear but be sure to open yourself to the emotional and intuitive aspects of the music as well.

Listen to Related Nonguitar Music   The third way of absorbing the overall sound picture is a very important one that is frequently neglected by guitarists, that is, listening to related nonguitar music of the same period from which the guitar music came. It is good to do this kind of listening because you will not completely understand a composer's music unless you know how it relates to the music of his time. Thus it is difficult to fully appreciate Sor's minuets and his other works if you do not know what was happening in the Viennese classical style of the late eighteenth and early nineteenth century. However, if you are familiar with some of the classical compositions of Haydn and Mozart, you will have a good feeling for the atmosphere Sor was creating with many of his works. Sor obviously admired both composers because, to a certain extent, he imitated their styles. He even arranged some of their music for guitar.[3]

Read Background Material   A further way of gaining feeling and understanding for the style of the music you play is to read about it. Spend part of your study time increasing your knowledge by using music dictionaries, music encyclopedias, music histories, and books on the guitar.[4] If you do not know what the Viennese classical style was, go look it up in a music encyclopedia. It is good to know something about that style since Sor and other guitar composers were influenced by it. You will not only find this research useful for the pieces you study but also very interesting. In the history books there are many colorful and telling stories of famous guitarists and other musicians that you will undoubtedly enjoy. Aside from the musical background of the pieces you play, it is also good to learn about the general cultural background in which the composer was living. Composers do not live in a vacuum and thus the science, philosophy, painting, architecture, sculpture, and literature of their times frequently have some influence on their work. Sor, for example, was living in the so-called "Age of Reason" and that influence

[3]Sor arranged part of Haydn's oratorio, *The Creation*. It appears in his *Method for the Spanish Guitar* (New York: Da Capo Press, 1971), p. xxviii. He also arranged or wrote variations on several of Mozart's works. See his Op. 9 and Op. 19.

[4]See the bibliography for both general music books and books on the guitar.

comes out strongly in the rational approach he takes in his *Method for the Spanish Guitar*.

So, what is the "sound picture" that emerges when you play the Sor piece and compare it with other music of his time? Naturally that is a subjective question and everyone will have his own feelings about it. The piece appears to be a light, graceful dance that suggests the atmosphere of elegant ladies and gentlemen in nineteenth-century salons. Resembling Sor's other minuets, it seems to have the same elegance and wit of minuets by Haydn and Mozart. Its three parts also suggest a classical string trio with violin, viola, and cello. This idea is plausible because Sor speaks in his method about making the guitar imitate other instruments.[5] See his Op. 6, No. 12 (Study No. 14, Segovia edition) for an example of a piece that suggests a classical string quartet.

4. Analyze the Music

Whereas the previous steps have emphasized the more intuitive, holistic approach to a piece, this step emphasizes the intellectual approach through a careful analysis of the score. In this step we deal with three aspects of a piece: analysis of overall structure, study of the texture and phrasing, and a preliminary interpretive analysis. Now we will continue to apply the study plan to the Sor minuet. As we analyze the piece, some initial suggestions will be made about how you might interpret it.

One thing to keep in mind is that a piece can be analyzed in different ways. The analysis here uses one possible approach that can be of help to you. To understand this approach it will be useful for you to have some knowledge of music theory because some of its terminology will be used. For an explanation of theoretical terms, refer to the *Harvard Dictionary of Music*, 2nd edition, by Willi Apel (Cambridge: Harvard University Press, 1969). Even if you do not know much theory, you will easily be able to understand the analysis because much of it is presented in the simple terms of tension and relaxation. In any case, when you do your own analysis and interpretation of a piece, make sure that it corresponds to the way you hear and feel it. Trust your *ear* and your *intuition* to be the final judges of how you should understand and play the piece.

Analyze the Overall Structure   First, let's consider the formal and harmonic structure of the Sor minuet more closely. An analysis of these two elements of the piece will give you important clues about how you might interpret it. For that reason it is good to look at the piece and discover the number of sections, the beginnings and endings of motives and phrases, the structural harmonies and how each element is related to the others.

[5]Sor, *Method for the Spanish Guitar*, pp. 16–18, 36.

You may already have some idea about the form and harmony from your mental reading of the score in Step 2. The harmony of the piece is relatively simple and never truly leaves the key of C. In Figure 9–5 the harmonic structure is outlined in traditional Roman numeral notation under the chords. The piece starts on the tonic (I) harmony of C and moves to a *cadence* (a point of relative harmonic relaxation) on the dominant G (V) in bar 8. The next eight bars move from the minor dominant (v) to the supertonic D minor (ii) in bar 10, to C (I) in bar 12 and then cadence on the dominant (V7/V-V) in bar 16. In the last eight bars the piece returns to the tonic (I), goes through several temporary dominants, and finally cadences on C (V7-I).

On a closer look at the form of the piece, it seems to be in three parts. The first eight bars is a *statement* of the main theme, the second eight bars appears to be a *digression* to somewhat contrasting material, and the last eight bars is a *restatement* of the original theme in varied form. This idea is confirmed by the harmonic structure with its clear ending cadences in bars 8, 16, and 24. Now we can use the traditional labels of music analysis and say that the first section (bars 1 to 8) is the A section; the second section (bars 9 to 16) with its different but related material is the B section; and, finally, the third section (bars 17 to 24) with its variation on the first 8 bars, is the A' ("A prime") section. Thus, when you include the repeat signs, the piece is in typical minuet form (||:A: || :BA: ||).[6]

The organization of most music can be viewed as a *hierarchy*, that is, it can be understood as having different levels from lowest to highest. On the lowest level of the structure we deal with the individual notes and on the highest level, with the work as a whole. The two highest structural levels of the Sor minuet can be represented as in the diagram in Figure 9–2.

Figure 9–2   Partial hierarchy diagram of Sor *Minuet*

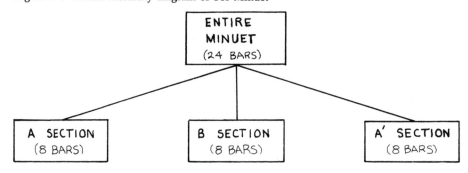

In order to understand the overall structure of the minuet more clearly, let's look at it in terms of the opposite tendencies of tension and relaxation. In Chapter 4 it has already been shown that the understanding of how to bal-

---

[6]For more analysis of this type of musical form, see Douglass Green, *Form in Tonal Music: An Introduction to Analysis* (New York: Holt, Rinehart and Winston, Inc.), p. 75.

ance tension and relaxation is the basis of an effortless guitar technique. The idea of tension and relaxation can also be applied to musical analysis. Music, after all, is made up of alternating waves of rhythmic, melodic, and harmonic tension and relaxation. The tension-producing elements make the music move toward climactic goals. Other elements relax the tension and lead to goals of repose. The basic stuff of music—the waves of tension and relaxation—always remains the same, but the many ways in which these waves can be created and combined lead to an unbounded variety of musical expression.

The following table gives a general idea of how musical tension and relaxation are produced:

Rhythmic Tension	Rhythmic Relaxation
a. unexpected accents	a. regular accents
b. counter-rhythms	b. simple rhythms
c. more notes per beat	c. fewer notes per beat
d. irregular rhythm	d. flowing rhythm
e. sudden stops	e. gradual slowing down

Melodic Tension	Melodic Relaxation
a. movement from high to low	a. movement from high to low
b. accented dissonances	b. unaccented dissonances
c. disjunct movement	c. conjunct movement
d. nonscale tones	d. scale tones
e. movement away from tonic	e. movement toward tonic

Harmonic Tension	Harmonic Relaxation
a. dominant harmonies (V, V7, etc.)	a. tonic harmonies (I, III, VI)
b. accented nonharmonic tones	b. unaccented nonharmonic tones
c. chromatically altered chords	c. diatonic chords
d. chromatic chord progression	d. diatonic chord progression
e. modulations to other keys	e. returning to tonic key
f. dissonant chords	f. consonant chords

Knowing these relationships of tension and relaxation will help you determine the beginnings, climaxes, and endings of the various parts of a piece. It is very instructive to play and/or listen to a piece carefully and make a subjective graph of what you feel are the major points of tension and relaxation. You really do not need to know all the terminology used in music theory to do this analysis. If you are sensitive enough, you will be able to come up with a reasonably accurate picture of the musical form—such as the A B A' structure of the Sor minuet—which will help you with your interpretation. The graph in Figure 9–3 shows one possible curve for the melodic and harmonic tension of the piece.

Study the Texture and Phrasing First let's look at the texture of the Sor piece. An important part of the texture of any piece is the number of parts or "voices." Most pieces have one or more voices. Even arpeggiated pieces such

Figure 9–3 Tension Graph of the Sor *Minuet*

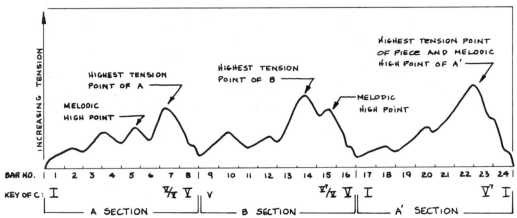

as Bach's *Prelude in D Minor* from *12 Little Preludes* (originally for keyboard), which do not appear to have different parts, actually do.[7]

In the Sor minuet, the number of voices is quite clear. There are three that are consistent all through the piece. You can label them as you would actual voices in a choir or you can think in terms of a string trio. In this case, it would be soprano (violin) on top, tenor (viola) in the middle, and bass (cello) on the bottom. For example, on the first beat of the first bar the soprano has a C, the tenor has an E, and the bass has a low C. The three voices or parts of the piece are semi-contrapuntal in nature, that is, they are somewhat independent of each other, particularly the soprano and bass. The middle part is more dependent, often going in parallel with the upper or lower part. In considering the *balance of parts,* that is, the relative weight given to each part in the piece, the soprano is the most important. Thus, in order to place it clearly in the foreground, it should generally be played louder than the other parts, although the bass sometimes vies for attention with its strong step-wise movements up or down.

When you study other pieces, you will often find that the voices are not as consistent as in the Sor minuet. They drop in and out in a "free-voiced" texture. Examples of this texture can be found in the Bach solo violin music transcribed for guitar, such as the Bourrée from *Partita No. 1.* Free-voiced texture suits the guitar quite well. Strictly-voiced texture, however, is difficult to finger when you have more than three parts that run consistently through an entire work. In a free-voiced piece, which is common in the guitar literature, the number of voices at any given point may vary from one to six. Usually,

---

[7]See Gerald Warfield, *Layer Analysis: A Primer of Elementary Tonal Structures* (New York: David McKay, 1976), p. 17ff.

however, there are at least two parts—soprano and bass—that are present throughout the piece and that hold everything together.

Now let's define the meaning of *phrasing* and related ideas, since they are important in analysis and interpretation. Phrasing in the broadest sense is the artistic shaping of a piece of music so that its inner meaning and emotion are revealed. Phrasing in this sense includes the expressive devices of *dynamics* (gradations of loud and soft), *articulation* (staccato and legato), *accents* (emphasizing certain notes), *tone color* (variations in the way a note is played), and *tempo variations* (changes in speed). These means of expression are used to set off one melodic group from another, to emphasize certain notes, and to give a feeling of movement toward musical goals.

In its more restricted sense, musical phrasing consists of dividing up melodic lines by the use of greater or lesser pauses into smaller groups of notes, that is, periods, phrases, and subphrases. (The latter are sometimes called *motives*, particularly when they are short note groups that assume structural importance in a piece.) One useful definition of a musical phrase is " . . .the shortest passage of music which, having reached a point of relative repose, has expressed a more or less complete thought."[8] These phrases or groups of notes have their approximate parallels in the sentences, phrases, and words of spoken and written language. Thus the good musician, like the good actor, "punctuates" the beginnings and endings of note groups and sections with pauses of varying lengths and other devices, thereby making the musical structure clear to his listeners. Naturally every performer will have his own unique idea about how the phrasing should be done. However it is done, there should be some logic to it.

Now you can use the visualization technique from Chapter 8 to get a clear idea of the phrasing of each of the three voices of the Sor piece, particularly the soprano or top voice. (See "Visualizing a Musical Passage," Chapter 8.) Visually follow each part as it wends its way through the musical landscape. Notice its particular shape, its beginnings and endings, its peaks and valleys, and how it blends with the other parts. Then sing and/or play each voice a number of times to hear its actual sound, tapping or clapping the rhythm as you go. Try to sense the emotional character of each phrase. After each phrase, close your eyes and hear it in your head. Then let the fingers find a simple provisional fingering for the passage. The fingering can be made more definite later. If the rhythmic figures are not clear to you, then work them out in your head carefully before playing them. (See "Visualization for Counting Problems" in Chapter 8.)

In order to clarify the structure of any piece you are studying, it is good to think through your ideas of phrasing and then pencil them in using arched lines or whatever notation suits you. In Figure 9–5 you can see how the arched lines mark phrases and brackets mark the subphrases.

[8]Green, *Form in Tonal Music*, p. 7.

Interpretive Analysis   At this point you can apply the idea of tension and relaxation in more detail to analyze your piece more closely. This analysis should help give you some ideas about the character of the piece. Once you have discovered the expressive character of the music, you can work on interpreting it with the various musical and technical devices available.

Now let's continue our analysis of the Sor minuet. As we go along, we will make some initial suggestions about how you might use phrasing, dynamics, and other expressive means to interpret the piece. In Step 11 we will discuss refinements of the interpretation. Refer to the original score of the piece (Figure 9–1), the score with phrasing and harmonic analysis (Figure 9–5), the tension graph (Figure 9–3), and the diagram in Figure 9–4, which is an expansion of the hierarchical structure diagram that we created in Figure 9–2, to help you follow this discussion.

Figure 9–4   Complete hierarchy diagram of Sor *Minuet*

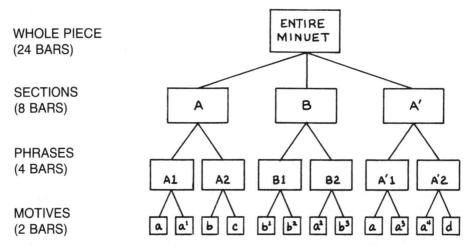

The hierarchical structure of most pieces consists of different levels of parts. The highest level is the whole piece—twenty-four bars, in this case. The next level down consists of the large sections—three sections of eight bars each in the minuet. One more level down and you find the phrases that make up the sections. In the Sor piece there are six four-bar phrases. Then comes the level of the motives that make up the phrases. In the minuet these are two bar units. Finally, at the lowest level, come the individual notes. The diagram in Figure 9–4 shows the levels of the minuet from the entire twenty-four bars down to the two-bar motives that are the basic structural elements of the piece.

For this particular piece, it is not necessary to depict the individual notes in the diagram because they do not form important structural patterns by themselves. The advantage of this diagram is that it gives the idea that all the

Figure 9–5 Sor *Minuet,* Op. 2, No. 4 with Phrasing and Analysis

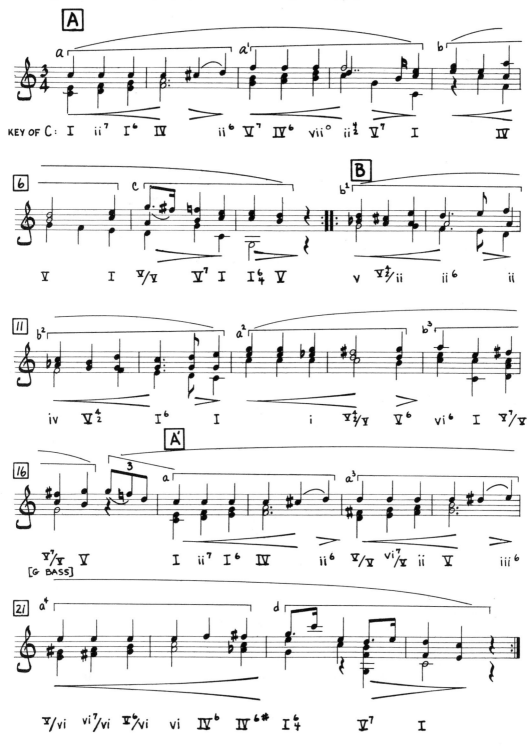

parts of the piece are interrelated and form a consistent whole—something like an upside-down tree with branches of increasing fineness growing from a central trunk.

Now let's delve into the details of the analysis. Remember to keep the overall shape of the minuet in mind as we go through the particulars. For our analysis we will focus mainly on the soprano part because it would be the part most emphasized in performance. The upper part in the first eight bars of the piece—the "A" section—is divided into two symmetrical four-bar phrases, A1 and A2 (see Figure 9–4 and Figure 9–5). Each of the phrases is in turn divided into two-bar subphrases or motives. A1 has the related motives *a* and *a1* while A2 has *b* and *c*, which are different. Notice that the tension elements in each of the two phrases directs the flow of the music toward goals or high points, the first on the half-note F in bar 4 and the second on the G in bar 7, the highest tension point of the first eight bars—although not the highest note.

The first phrase starts off with a C in the melody with a C chord supporting it. The C is the restful home base or root of the piece from which it branches out at various points and to which it always returns. As we shall see, the other notes and chords relate to this home base in terms of greater or lesser tension. Part of the tension arises as the notes move away from the home base. There is relatively little tension in the first bar since the restful note C is repeated three times. The small amount of tension in the first bar is created by the upward movement of the two lower parts. In the second measure, more tension is introduced because of the accent created by the slur on the C♯ on the ordinarily weak second beat. The tension is released somewhat as the C♯ resolves to the D, thus ending the first subphrase or "*a*" motive. In performance the increase and decrease of tension here can be brought out by a *crescendo* (increase of volume) starting at the beginning of the piece, continuing to the C♯ in the second bar, and then changing to a slight *decrescendo* (decrease of volume) to the D. Crescendo is indicated by ⬥⬥ and decrescendo by ⬥⬥ on the score.

Even though the first two bars appear to be a complete unit, it is clear that the first phrase is not finished there since the D minor chord at that point does not give a solid feeling of restfulness. Moreover, the bass line does not stop moving upward until bar 4. In fact, the soprano melody, as it repeats the first four notes of bar 1 at a higher pitch level, continues to increase in tension up to the half-note F in the fourth bar. That F, which is part of a dissonant D minor 7 chord (7th in bass), is the highest tension point of the first four-bar phrase. The tension is finally resolved on the third beat of the bar as the F moves to a clear resting place on the E of the tonic chord. Thus the first phrase comes to an end.

To bring out the dynamic shape of bars 3 and 4 in performance, it is appropriate to have another crescendo and decrescendo. The crescendo can be started at the beginning of bar 3 and continued to the peak of the tension on the F in bar 4. From there a graceful decrescendo can be made to the E. To achieve a sense of overall movement to the peak of the phrase, it is good to have the second crescendo start at a slightly higher level of volume than the first one in bars 1 and 2. The effect will be like two small waves within the movement of a larger one that crests in bar 4.

Notice that, if you sing the first four bars, it can be easily done in one breath. When you sing it, you can also physically feel the ebb and flow of tension and relaxation that we are discussing. Vocally, the C♯ in the second bar feels tense because it is a chromatic note and because of the accent created by the slur on the weak second beat. Then, in contrast, the D feels more relaxed. The F's in bars 3 and 4 feel tighter because the pitch is higher and thus require more energy to sing them. When you arrive at the E on the last beat of bar 4, you will normally feel a sense of physical release. This is because you have arrived at the natural end of your first breath, which corresponds with the end of the first phrase. The feeling of release is enhanced by the lessening of tension caused by moving down a half-step from the F to a note of the tonic chord. After bar 4 it will feel quite natural to pause very slightly and take a breath before going into the next phrase. Thus you can see that some of your ideas about the form and phrasing of the piece can be derived from your breathing patterns and by how tight or loose your voice feels when you sing it.

After the slight break between phrases, we launch into the second four-bar phrase (A2). This phrase consists of two different two-bar motives, *b* and *c*. The soprano melody now moves up to the A on the third beat of bar 5, generating some tension. Although the A is the highest note of the phrase, it is not the highest tension point since it falls on a weak beat and has a mild F harmony. Therefore it should not be overemphasized. However, since the A is the highest note, it is nice to bring it out a bit with a small crescendo and a slight lengthening (*tenuto*). The melody turns down in bar 6 and ends up on a relatively restful E; a slight decrescendo is appropriate here. In bar 6 the bass line makes a steady descent and helps to carry us into the next measure.

The highest tension point of the phrase is on the G on the first beat of measure 7. The tension here is created mainly by the dissonance of the G against the D chord beneath it. The other part of the tension is created by the *secondary dominant* nature of the D chord. This name is used for a chord that is the dominant of any chord of the scale other than the tonic. Dominant and secondary dominant chords tend to be tension-producing because they contain the leading tone of the chord they precede. Here the D chord is the dominant of the dominant ("V of V" in Figure 9–5). The F♯ leading tone helps to generate tension. This note tends to push the music toward the resolution on the F in the G7 chord. In any case, you can bring out the high tension point by accenting the G. From that point it is natural to make a decrescendo to the E on the third beat of bar 7. Now you can bring out the last tension point before the end of the phrase by slightly accenting the E in the somewhat dissonant chord at the beginning of bar 8. Such chords, where a dissonance falls on the beat, are sometimes called *appoggiatura* chords. Then the melody should be allowed to relax to the final D in the G chord. The tension built up in the first eight bars has been largely released as you land on the G chord. However, there is still some tension remaining because you have not yet returned to the home base C. Refer to the tension graph (Figure 9–3) for a visual picture of the musical wave activity in the piece up to this point.

The next eight bars, the B section, is a contrast to the A section since new melodic and harmonic materials are introduced. The B section is the digression in the overall design of statement–digression–restatement. There are chromatic alterations of the notes and new rhythmic figures. The new material gives this section some tension because it is not quite certain where it will lead. However, the B section is clearly related to the A section in both structure and melodic material. As in A, the structure is made up of two four-bar phrases—bars 9–12 and bars 13–16—each of which has two subphrases or motives. The first phrase, B1, contains the motives *b1* and *b2*; the second, B2, includes motives *a2* and *b3*. The relation of the melodic materials will be apparent as we proceed.

To start off the new section, Sor makes a low-tension transition from a G major chord in bar 8 to a G minor chord in bar 9. Bars 9–10 consist of a motive, *b1*, whose shape has apparently been derived from motive *b* in bars 5–6. Some tension is created here by stating this brief motive in D minor harmony. The high point of the phrase in bars 9–12 is on the dotted eighth D in bar 10. There is a definite feeling of having arrived at a goal on that D because it is a long note and comes in a rhythmically important place. The sense of movement to the D minor chord can be enhanced by slightly accenting the C♯ in bar 9 and making a small crescendo to the first beat of bar 10. A relaxing decrescendo at the end of the motive (on the E and F in the melody) will round it off. Bars 11–12 repeat the motive of 9–10 at a lower, less tense pitch level in tonic C harmony. The dynamic shape of the second presentation of the motive, *b2*, is the same as that of the first. It can be played at a somewhat softer level as an echo. This four-bar phrase then ends on a restful C chord.

After a very slight breath, the next phrase moves us into a higher tension area with a variation on the *a* motive from bar 1. The highest tension point of the phrase and of the entire B section comes on the F♯ half-note on the first beat of bar 14. It is natural to have a strong crescendo to that point and a strong accent on the D7 chord on that beat. The tension of the D7 (V_2^4 of V) is then resolved on the G chord on the third beat. Thus there should be a decrescendo here. Sor himself made this point clear with his original dynamic marking of $\Longrightarrow$ over the two chords. The first should be loud and the second soft. Bars 15–16 are relatively low tension. Even though the A in bar 15 is the highest note in the B section, it is not the highest tension point in the phrase. In comparison with the D7 chord under the F♯ in 14, the simple, nondissonant A minor chord under the A sounds mild. Still, since it is the highest note, it could be played with a slight tenuto. The phrase is then finished by a graceful curve down from the A and then up through an appoggiatura chord (V⁷/V with G bass) to the final G on the second beat in bar 16. Thus the four-measure phrase and the B section are rounded off with a cadence on the dominant chord. At this point it is good to have another pause before starting the last section since the piece has finished its digression and should have a chance to catch its breath, so to speak.

The last eight-bar A′ section is a restatement of the original motivic material but with variations. This section can be viewed as two four-bar phrases with two-bar motives or as one eight-bar phrase, also with two-bar motives. The latter idea is shown in Figure 9–5. Whichever way you look at it, there is a strong upward movement from the triplet upbeat on the last beat of bar 16 all the way to the climax of the piece in bar 23. An overall crescendo to the climax along with smaller crescendos and decrescendos in each presentation of the motive will give a feeling of considerable energy moving toward the final high point of the piece. The dynamic marks in Figure 9–5 should make this idea clear.

Sor begins the A′ section in bars 17–18 by repeating the *a* motive of bars 1–2 exactly. In bars 19–20 and 21–22 he repeats that same motive at higher pitch levels (*a3* and *a4*), using secondary dominants with their strong leading tones to give a greater feeling of tension and movement toward the final goal. There is a V of V (D) on the first beat in bar 19 which creates tension that moves the music to a brief resolution on the G chord on the first beat of bar 20. Similarly on the first beat of bar 21 there is a V of vi chord (E) which produces further tension that is briefly resolved on the A minor chord in bar 22. The tension becomes greatest at the IV6♯ chord (a so-called Italian sixth chord) on the last beat of bar 22 since that chord has two chromatic tones that are only a half-step away from two tones in the climactic chord. The relatively dissonant IV6♯ chord is the force that carries us up to the climax of the minuet in bar 23 on the G. The leap to the ornamental high C, the highest pitch in the piece, gives a witty sparkle to the climax. Now the energy built up in the piece has been largely spent and the melodic line descends gracefully to a charming dissonance on the penultimate note (an appoggiatura) and finally returns to the restful home base of C with which the piece started.

Thus you can see how to analyze and understand a piece in the simple terms of tension and relaxation. All the special terms of music theory that we have used are descriptions of the various tension and relaxation elements in a musical composition. In this analysis, we have made suggestions about phrasing and dynamics that can help you bring out the tension and relaxation when performing the piece. Naturally there are more possible interpretive nuances, but we will save them until Step 11. Now that you have a good picture of the structure of the piece it is time to work out the technical details in the next four steps of the study plan.

II. WORKING OUT THE TECHNIQUE

5. Find Natural and Musical Fingerings

Before you do any fingering, be sure to work out a clear mental concept of the music using the above (or similar) steps of visualizing a piece. The fingering for both hands, but particularly for the left hand, should be based on the expression and phrasing that you have visualized. When you practice the piece, allow the fingers to discover the correct movements as much as possible. Let them find the *simplest,* most natural way to play each phrase. The simplest possible fingerings that express your concept of the sound are best because then the music can flow effortlessly and you will not feel stress and strain while playing. The simplest ones are not always the most obvious; you may have to help the fingers with some careful planning. You may need to try several different fingerings until you find the one that works best. Occasionally, you will find some passages that seem impossible to finger in a flowing way. Just remember that nothing is impossible and that there is usually a relatively uncomplicated way waiting to be discovered—or at least a way that will work with persistent practice.

Now let's look at one possible fingering for the Sor minuet that is not particularly difficult and yet gives a good musical result. Refer to Figure 9–6 for the fingering examples. The concept of the fingering used here is based on the idea that the minuet is a light, airy creation and therefore best played with the bright, clear sound of the notes on open strings and in lower positions. Naturally you may have some of your own ideas about the concept of the piece and the fingering, which is fine. Keep in mind that the fingering presented here is not to be taken dogmatically, but rather as only one possible way of doing it. You are welcome to change it. There are many ways to play a piece and make it sound beautiful.

Figure 9–6 Sor *Minuet* with Fingering

Figure 9–6 *(Con't.)*

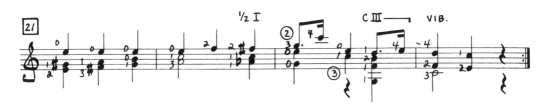

One useful principle in choosing fingerings is that, where possible, it is best not to change the tone color in the middle of a motive or phrase. In that way the integrity and unity of the motive or phrase is maintained. In the first two measures, it seemed best to keep the first finger on the C so that the left hand would be stable and the tone color of the two-bar motive would stay the same by playing on the same string. That is the reason for the long stretch on the second beat of the first measure. This is not the easiest fingering, but it is the fingering that gives the best musical result. It is easier for short or inflexible fingers to play that chord with the third finger on D on the fifth, first finger on F on the fourth, and the C on the third string taken with the fourth finger. However, when you change the string in the middle of the motive, you lose the unity of tone color that helps to hold the motive together.

The choice of fingering in the second bar, although it may seem unusual, is logical in terms of the music. The F and A are supposed to sound for three beats in the two lower voices, therefore it is best to leave the second and third fingers where they are and move the first finger to produce the C♯ and slur with the fourth finger to the D. Moving on to measures 7 and 8, it is nicest to keep the tone color of the phrase the same by playing it all on the E string except for the last D. However, for the sake of making a smooth transition from the C chord on the third beat of the seventh bar to the appoggiatura chord on the first beat of the eighth bar, it seems better to play the upper notes of the C chord on the second and third strings. As an experiment, you might look for a smooth alternative fingering that will keep the melody on the first string up to the D. There are several possibilities that may work.

In the first chord of bar 9, it is best to use the fourth finger on the G because then it can be sustained easily for two beats and it is in place for the chord on the third beat.

In bar 16 the fingering was chosen to minimize left-hand effort and help make good connections. It is easiest to play the triplet figure on the third beat with the fourth finger on the G and D instead of the third for several reasons. First, the fourth finger was already on the G from the second beat; second, the two-fret distance taken with the first and fourth fingers is much easier than with the first and third because the fingers do not have to stretch; third, playing the D with the fourth finger leaves the third finger free so that it can connect easily to the low C in bar 17. The intelligent player will do well to take every opportunity such as this one to keep the left hand compact and relaxed.

On the A minor chord in bar 22, the A is taken with the third finger so that the second finger is free to play the F on the second beat. Then the second finger can shift easily up to the F♯ on the third beat. Since the first finger can be free before the shift, the small bar is easy to make. In measure 23, after trying a number of different ideas, it was decided to play the C chord with the G on the second string. Sor himself indicates this kind of fingering in some of his pieces, such as Op. 8, No. 3. Other fingerings work well also, but this one flows very nicely. To make the fingering work, it is necessary to prepare the third finger by letting it hover right over the second string while you are still holding the small bar on the third beat of measure 22. Then, when you are ready to shift, it is an easy matter to let the third finger glide—noiselessly—up the second string to the G at the eighth fret. The high C follows without difficulty because it can be played with the fourth finger at the same fret on the first string. Then, in order to keep the tone color bright and make the connection easy, the E on the second beat is played open and the C is taken on the third string.

In the last measure, the fingering may seem awkward at first, but it is the only feasible way the passage can be played in exactly the way Sor wrote it. The little finger on the second string E in bar 23 connects nicely with the D in bar 24. The third finger goes to the C and the second finger is somewhat awkwardly squashed onto the F. Then, on the next beat, the second finger moves easily to the E while the first finger goes to its final resting place on the C. The important element here is that the third finger remains on the low C so that it continues to sound when the resolution of the appoggiatura comes on the second beat. This produces the feminine ending (soft resolution on a weak beat) that Sor intended. Of course it is possible to play the last measure by leaving the bar at the third fret for the appoggiatura and then stretching to play the E and C with the fourth finger on the fifth string and the second finger on the third string. However, this fingering cuts off the low C and diminishes the effect of the resolution of the appoggiatura.

This concludes our brief discussion of fingering for this piece. The main idea in doing your own fingering is to experiment with several alternatives and decide which one is both the most economical and most musical. Remember that there are always several possible ways you can play a given piece or passage, so be imaginative. The great guitarists are always coming up with fresh ideas about how to interpret the music they play and thus they are always discovering new fingerings. There is no need to be stuck in only one way of playing a passage.

6. Read Slowly With Metronome; Use the Play–Relax Technique

Read Slowly with Metronome This is an important and frequently neglected step that should be repeated a number of times so that every aspect of the music can be clearly understood. As we mentioned in previous chapters, slow practice gives your mind and fingers a chance to form good habits because it is easier to avoid mistakes at slow speed. Playing with the metronome will do several things for you. First, if you are having any rhythmic problems of rushing or dragging, you will become acutely aware of them. It is difficult to fool the metronome. Second, the metronome will help you establish a regular rhythmic pulse for the piece that will be the foundation for playing the piece more freely without the metronome. Third, counting with the metronome is a good tool to check your understanding of the rhythm. For these reasons many good players recommend the metronome.

For the Sor piece it is good to start with the metronome at a very slow tempo, say ♩ = 44. For most people such a slow pace is difficult to keep steady because there is so much time between beats. It is usually better to use the eighth note as your counting unit and set it at 88. At this point in your study of the piece, take care to stay with the metronome as exactly as possible. Precision in rhythm makes playing much easier. Later, that rhythmic precision will make the music much more appealing to both you and your audience.

Use the Play–Relax Technique The Play–Relax practice method discussed in Chapter 5 is an excellent way of securing the coordination between the two hands and the exact rhythmic placement of the notes on the beats. It has the further advantage of allowing you to practice all the basic movements of the piece without wearing out your left hand. When working with the Play–Relax approach, remember to plant the right-hand fingers wherever possible and release the tension at about the same time as the strokes are made. Also release the pressure on the left-hand fingers between the notes. The Play–Relax approach can be applied very successfully to the Sor minuet as shown in Figure 9–7.

Figure 9–7 Passage from Sor *Minuet* showing Play–Relax practice technique

P R P R P R etc.

It is best to do this exercise with the metronome set at ♪ = 88 as previously suggested so that you are aware of the silences between the notes. Be sure to relax the hands quickly and deeply during those silences.

7. Polish Rough Spots; Purify the Sound

Diamonds and other gems are very attractive, especially when they are beautifully cut and polished. Few people are impressed by rough stones. The same applies to the performance of a guitar piece. To really bring out all the value of a piece requires that you polish it thoroughly until all the roughness is gone and it scintillates like a fine gem. The main idea is to eliminate all the unwanted sounds and irregularities so that only the pure essence of the music remains.

Polish Rough Spots   After you have worked on a piece for a short time, you normally will find that large sections of it go very easily. However, there are always some sticky spots that cause you to slow down or stumble. The efficient approach here is not to spend too much time practicing what you already can play well, but rather to clearly identify the rough spots and work on them until they shine like the rest of the piece. You can make such passages stand out by bracketing or circling them on the music lightly in pencil. It is a good idea to mark not only the specific rough spots but also to include a bar or two before and a bar or two after so that you learn to connect the rough spots with the rest of the piece. Then work through those spots very carefully, checking everything including the musical idea (are you bringing it out the way you wanted to?), right- and left-hand fingerings (do they flow easily?), rhythm (are you counting it correctly?). As suggested in Chapter 2, it is helpful to memorize these short problem passages so that you can focus on the finger movements rather than on the printed music. The method of breaking down the problem (Chapter 7) and left-hand visualization (Chapter 8) can also be very helpful for polishing the rough spots. When you have worked out the musical idea and the fingering, repeat the passage slowly and carefully in rhythm until you have implanted it perfectly in your mind and fingers. One rule of thumb is that if you can play the passage at tempo without mistakes seven times in a row, you know it well.

Purify the Sound   An important part of polishing a piece is to purify it by damping unwanted sounds. (See "Damping" in Chapter 6.) Let's look at some examples from the Sor piece. On the third beat of the first measure, when the E on the fourth string is sounded, it sets the octave harmonic on the sixth string in sympathetic vibration. This does not matter—until you play the F chord on the next beat. At that point, if you listen, you will hear an undesirable minor second interval between the E harmonic on the sixth string and the F bass note on the fourth string. So, to clean up the sound, you can place the right-hand thumb on the sixth string right after playing the F chord. There are several other places where you will find such unwanted harmonics or bass notes that should be damped. Your ear will tell you where they are.

In the majority of cases, it is important to clarify the beginnings and endings of phrases by cutting out sounds that overlap from one phrase to the next. In the last measure of the first four-bar phrase in the Sor minuet, the C chord on the third beat generates a fair amount of sound, including a harmonic on the sixth string. In order to prevent that sound from clouding over the beginning of the second phrase, you can damp the unwanted notes of the chord by laying the right-hand thumb across strings 6, 5, 4, and 3 just before playing the E and G on the first beat of the fifth measure. This procedure requires alteration of the hand position somewhat, but the improvement in musical clarity is worth it. The effect will be to make the ending of the first phrase clear and make the beginning of the second phrase stand out in relief. Needless to say, this damping idea can be applied very effectively to the junction points between the other phrases in the piece. We will discuss the silences created at the junction points in more detail in the twelfth step of the study plan.

8. Read at Tempo With and Without the Metronome

After all the rough spots have been smoothed out, you should be ready to work the piece up to tempo. It is good to continue to read the piece from the music for a time, since many students get away from the music too soon and memorize it incorrectly. It is still useful to work with the metronome at this point because it will keep the rhythmic pulse steady. If you increase the speed a bit at a time, it will also give you a clear-cut way of keeping track of your progress in working the piece up to performance tempo. However, it is not always good to try to increase the tempo. Go back to slow, deliberate practice part of the time so that the precision of the movements can be established. As soon as you can play the piece up to tempo with the metronome, spend a good part of your time working without it. Return to it periodically to check for rhythmic mistakes.

The tempo of the Sor piece, as with many pieces, can be varied some-what and still sound good. Since the classical minuet tended toward the light and quick side, the performance tempo here should not be too slow. $\downarrow$ = 100 is about the lower limit of tempo that avoids the feeling of dragging. $\downarrow$ = 120 is about the upper limit, which avoids the feeling of being rushed. Most players will find a performance tempo within that range that will feel appropriate and comfortable to them.

III. BRINGING THE MUSIC TO LIFE

9. Memorize and Play at Tempo

In the first part of these steps of learning a piece, you develop your basic con-cept of the music. In the second part, you work out the technical aspects of that musical concept. In this last part of the study plan, you internalize what you have done so far and then refine it into an integrated artistic creation.

When you have worked out the musical ideas and fingerings carefully, it is time to memorize the music. It is definitely good to memorize because it liberates you from having to look at the printed music all the time and thus allows you to concentrate on improving technique and musical expression. Take your time with the memorization process so that you learn the music right the first time. Unlearning your mistakes is not much fun.

Memorization of music need not be a difficult matter—provided that you do not work at it too hard. If you study the form, expression, and finger-ing of your piece thoroughly, you probably will memorize much of it without even trying. That is undoubtedly the least painful way to get the music into your head. If you do not obtain good results just by letting the music sink in as you study it, then there are other ways to make your memory of a piece secure.

One of the easiest ways to memorize is by using an adaptation of a yogic technique. The basic idea is that, once you have worked out the piece, you play the piece before you go to bed every night for a week or however long it takes to learn it. Do not consciously try to memorize the piece. Just play it once or twice at a comfortable tempo looking at the music. This approach works best if you play in precise rhythm. This effortless memorization method is much better than trying to force the music into your head. Playing the piece just before you go to bed is good because then there are no distract-ing activities between playing the music and going to sleep. Then, during the quiet of the night, the music will tend to settle into the long-term memory more easily. After you have done this process for a few days, check your memory during one of your regular practice sessions by playing as much of the music as possible without the score. You may find some spots in the music that are not clear in your mind; in that case, look at the score and play those spots a few times. Then play them several extra times at your nightly sessions.

Even if memorization comes easily, it is still a good idea to go over each part of the piece *consciously* and make sure that you know it well. The technique used by Suzuki for his young violin students is quite effective for improving memory. He has the students play through their pieces one melodic fragment at a time—usually one or two bars. After each fragment, the student stops completely in order to have time to recall and prepare for the next one. Of course the fragments should be coherent musical units such as the two-bar motives in the Sor minuet. You would start by thinking of the sound of the first two-bar fragment. Then play it. Following that, stop and think of the sound of the next two bars before you play them and so on through the piece.

Even after you have the piece well memorized, it is a good idea to play through it a number of times very slowly, so that you do not make mistakes. Do not rush into playing at full tempo before you can do it with relatively few errors. On the other hand, do not practice slowly forever, or you will never play at tempo! At some point, you simply have to speed up your playing. After you are able to play the piece at the desired tempo, it helps to be able to play the piece a few metronome marks higher than the actual tempo you want. This approach will give you a measure of insurance and confidence. After you have played at the faster tempo, you will find that the desired tempo will feel very comfortable. It may even seem slow in comparison. During this process, if you are making frequent mistakes, it is time to slow down and focus on the spots that are giving you trouble. You may discover that a fingering that you thought was excellent does not hold up very well at the performance tempo.

10. Practice Mentally; Use Feedback

Practice Mentally   The most powerful tool for memorization and refinement of the music is your mind. In particular, it is your ability to see, hear, and touch *mentally* that is most useful. Once you have studied your piece for some time, you can begin to rehearse it in your mind—without the guitar. This practice method was described in detail in Chapter 8. It is very rewarding to apply this method to the Sor minuet.

When the piece is clear in your mind from beginning to end, you can focus your mental practice on how you want to interpret the piece. You can experiment in your head with different ways of playing it, using different dynamics, tone colors, and tempo variations, and see what emotional feelings arise. You may find that some of the interpretive ideas that come from mental

practice will lead you to change your fingerings to reflect what you have imagined in your mind. You may be surprised at the never-ending fountain of
interpretive ideas you will find inside yourself.

When you are able to hear, see, and feel your piece clearly in your head,
you will be confident about your ability to remember it and play it for others.
You will not feel as though you have left anything undone. The piece will
really be yours. (If you feel that you want to give yourself a final trial-by-fire,
you might try writing out the piece from memory, but that is not usually necessary if you have done the mental practice well.)

Use Feedback   Even though the word *feedback* has not been mentioned
until now, it is a process that is vitally important for learning a piece and improving your playing. It is good to check on yourself and see if you are really
playing the music the way you think you are. This requires that you listen to
yourself with great care and sensitivity. Practicing with eyes closed and ears
open is immensely valuable. It is important to be honest with yourself in this
listening process. Frequently you will be absolutely convinced that you are
doing something perfectly well, such as bringing out the upper melodic line
in the Sor minuet, when, in fact, your listeners hear too much of the bass part.
It is easy to have a distorted perception of your playing because (1) you are
physically very close to the guitar, so the instrument sounds different to you
than to your audience; and (2) you have become accustomed to hearing yourself play in a certain way, mistaken as it may be, and so you do not recognize
any error.

For these reasons, it is good both to listen carefully to yourself while
practicing and to have other people listen and give their opinions about your
playing. It will give you a more objective view of what you are doing. Constructive comments from teachers, friends, and relatives are valuable and
should be carefully heeded.

The tape recorder is also a very valuable source of feedback—and probably the least biased! Every serious guitarist should invest in at least a small
cassette tape recorder so that he can see his playing "in the mirror," so to
speak. This may be a dreary prospect for some players, but it need not be.
When you feel that you know a piece reasonably well, do not be afraid—just
sit down with your tape recorder and play. Then give yourself your own guitar lesson by listening to yourself and noting or writing down all the things
you would like to correct or change. Refer to the score as you are listening and
tap your foot to check on your rhythm. Then work on the changes and record
yourself again to see if you have achieved the desired results. During the recording and listening process, be indifferent to any negative thoughts you
might have about your playing. Focus on what is already good about it and
what you can do to improve it. Aim at the ideal of having your actual playing
reflect the beauty of your musical conception.

11. Refine the Interpretation

> *When I hear one of my fine students wait for me*
> *to tell him how a passage should be played, I say*
> *to him, "You have the sacred fire, there, inside*
> *yourself. Don't wait for me to provide it."*[9]
>
> Andrés Segovia

In your study of a piece, you will undoubtedly come up with various ideas and intuitions about how to refine the expression of its inner meaning. Although it is not always possible, or even desirable, to specify exactly what refinements you want to express, you may find that penciling your ideas into the score will clarify your thinking about the music. In Step 4 of this plan we already explored to some extent how phrasing, accentuation, and dynamics can help bring out the expressive character of the music. Now we can consider further ideas to make your interpretation of a piece a more artistic one. We will take another look at phrasing and consider some of the refinements we have not yet discussed that include the use of alterations of tempo (*tempo rubato*), legato and staccato articulation, rolling of chords, tone color, and vibrato. The way you use these means of expression in a given piece should be a natural outgrowth of the musical ideas you have discovered in the process of working through Steps 2, 3, and 4 of the study plan.

The best way to understand these expressive resources is to apply them to a specific piece. So, let's look at the Sor minuet again and see what refinements we can make in the interpretation.

Phrasing   First, let's consider the phrasing in more detail. An important point is to make sure that each phrase has a sense of movement toward a *goal* and is not just moving along aimlessly. In the first four bars, for example, the phrase has a definite direction to it if you aim at the half-note F in bar four as your goal. When you start off, have that note in mind as your first significant destination and when you actually play the note, give it relatively more volume and accent than the previous notes so that it will be clear to your listeners that you have arrived at a climactic point. Be careful, however, not to play the note too hard or it will sound out of place. The intensity of the melody should increase *gradually* over the first three bars, peaking on the F in the fourth bar and then settling down on the E. With respect to refinement here, be sure to play the E somewhat more softly than the F, but not so softly that

---

[9]Andrés Segovia, quoted in notes by Alan Rich on the album *Segovia On Stage*, Decca Record DL 710140. Decca Records, A Division of MCA Inc., New York, N.Y.

you cannot hear it. Then check to see if you are making a very slight, but clear break between the E and the start of the next phrase.

In the process of checking over each phrase, see if you are playing the melodic line at a consistent volume level. It is the sure mark of an amateur if you are playing some of the melody notes so softly that they cannot be heard. At these points the alert listener may wonder for a moment what happened to the melody.

Tempo Rubato   In order to help separate one phrase from the next in a piece, thus allowing the music to "breathe" and making the musical structure clear, you can use a tempo alteration called *tempo rubato*. This term translates literally as "stolen time." It means that the tempo is varied, more or less, according to what the expression of the music requires. In *strict rubato*, it means that you steal time from one part of the music and make it up somewhere else so that the basic rhythmic pulse is not disturbed. In *free rubato*, the stolen time is never given back! Before you try to use tempo rubato in a piece, remember that you should be able to play the piece in strict time. Otherwise you will have no steady rhythmic base from which you can make meaningful rubato deviations.

You can use a strict tempo rubato in order to make a small breathing space between the first two phrases of the Sor minuet. You can do this type of rubato by making a slight delay in the entrance of the G melody note on the first beat of bar 5. However, do not stop the steady pulse of the rhythm. Simply steal some time from the C chord by starting a bit late, thus making it shorter. But then come in exactly on the second beat. This idea can be used to good effect elsewhere in the minuet as well as in other pieces you play.

Tempo rubato can be applied in another way in several places in the minuet. In bar 2 the C♯ has a nice emotional effect if it is accented and played slightly longer than written. In order to keep the rhythm straight in that measure, it is necessary to cut the D a bit short. Then you should arrive exactly on time on the first beat of the third bar. You can practice keeping the rhythm straight, and yet still be able to do the rubato on the C♯, by having the metronome click on the first beat of each of the first two measures. In that way you can be somewhat free with the rhythm of the notes within the bar, but still arrive at the beginning of the next bar in strict time.

The idea of rhythmic freedom within the bar can be applied to other parts of the minuet. For example, in the appoggiatura on the first beat of bar 16, the F♯ has more poignant feeling if its value is slightly longer than a quarter note. To obtain this effect, the G on the second beat needs to be shortened. At that point it is also good to put in a slight break between the G on the second beat and the triplet on the third beat to separate the phrases. The triplet serves as an upbeat to the final eight bars. The break should not take up much time and it is good to rush the triplet slightly so that you do not arrive very late at bar 17. Some players may wish to do a free rubato in bar 16 with a longer break between the second and third beats. That is fine, but the break should not be excessively long. Discover for yourself other places where you might use rubato in the Sor piece. The examples here should give you a good idea of how to go about it. In any case, the tempo rubato effect is a natural form of musical expression that can be used in other pieces you play—with care and discrimination, of course. A general rule of thumb is that most dance music requires a strict rubato, whereas other pieces may or may not allow the use of the free rubato, depending on their character.

Articulation How shall we use legato and staccato articulation in the minuet? (If you are not sure about the meaning of articulation, review the section on "Legato and Staccato" in Chapter 6.) Sor does not provide many indications. He has marked only a few slurs in measures 2, 7, 16, 18, and 20. There are no signs to tell us what to use in the rest of the piece. Here you must exercise your own judgment. Since the melody has a certain singing quality, it seems appropriate to play the piece more legato than staccato for the most part. However, since the piece is also a lively dance, it is good not to overdo the legato or the minuet will lose its rhythmic incisiveness. You can compromise and obtain both the song and the dance qualities by using *detaché* articulation, which means playing each note for most of its value but still articulating a small space between the notes. In the first bar, for example, the left-hand fingers should remain on each chord for almost the full quarter note value with only slightly noticeable breaks between the chords. As we discussed in Chapters 5 and 6 and Step 7 of this study plan, it works well to plant the right-hand fingers on each chord before playing it, but just a short time before, so that the previous chord will not sound too staccato. The singing effect of the piece will be better served if you are careful to connect most of the notes of the soprano melody rather closely. It is fine for the lower parts to be a bit more staccato than the melody since that will give more clarity to the rhythm.

Although most of the melody seems to sound best played in *detaché* style (leaning toward legato), a more staccato articulation in selected places can lend the piece an air of liveliness and wit. For example, in measure 7, the C chord on the third beat can be played staccato (approximately an eighth note instead of a quarter) to create a sense of lightness and a bit of tension just before the cadence on G. The same staccato device can be used on the D7 chord on the last beat of measure 15. A most striking and delightful staccato effect can be achieved at the climax of the piece in bar 23. There, if you play the chord on the first beat as a sprightly eighth note (instead of a dotted eighth) the climax will sparkle like a jewel in the sunlight. To obtain the staccato, damp the notes that are ringing by laying the thumb across the bass strings and planting the ring finger on the first string—which prepares for playing the high C. A similar but less brilliant echo of that effect may be obtained by staccato playing of the G7 chord on the third beat of the same bar.

Rolling Chords The effect of the staccato "surprise" in bar 23 will be heightened if you *roll* the chord on the first beat. Rolling a chord usually means playing its notes from bass to treble in more or less quick succession according to the effect you want. *Arpeggiation* is another term for rolling chords. (For a way to practice rolls, see Figure 3–4.) The highest treble note of a rolled chord generally receives an accent, partly because it is the last to be struck and partly because it is often the melody note. Thus the player purposefully hits the note more forcefully than the others. In this particular case, however, the player should accent the G on the second string as much as possible because that is where the melody is. When done well, the accentuation created by the roll in bar 23 sets the high point of the whole piece in strong relief and helps make it come alive.

It is naturally not good to roll every chord in the minuet (or in any other piece, for that matter) or it will not have much effect. There will be no contrast between rolling and not rolling. Let's look at how such a contrast can be used to convey the feeling of movement in the first four-bar phrase of the minuet. Play the chords in the first bar without rolling them and then roll the chord on the first beat of the second bar. Then play the chords in the third bar straight and roll the first chord in bar 4. You should notice a feeling of expectation and tension in the nonrolled chords and then a feeling of release when you play the rolled ones. It is easy to see that this device can be very useful to accent high points and dissonances. It can thus help to outline the crescendos and decrescendos in the phrases that were discovered in Step 4.

Another place for a chord roll is on the first beat of measure 7 to bring out the spicy dissonance there. The same can be done with the appoggiatura chord on the first beat of bar 8.

Rolling the A minor chord with *p i m* on the first beat of bar 15 is a natural way to bring out the high A, which is the highest melody note of the B section. For the best effect, arpeggiate the chord quickly, accenting the A somewhat. Now you can experiment on your own with rolling and nonrolling to express your musical ideas in this piece and others.

Vibrato Vibrato is yet another guitaristic nuance that can be used to highlight and intensify the emotional feeling of important melodic notes or even entire chords in a piece. Like other musical effects, it should always be woven into the musical fabric in a natural way. Vibrato is particularly effective when done in combination with the chord rolling just mentioned. One such spot where that can be done is on the high point of the B section in bar 15 on the first beat. First roll the chord as previously described and then do a standard vibrato (do not overdo it!) on the chord with emphasis on the A. This gives a warm shimmering quality to that note and takes the dryness out of the interpretation. It is fine to hold the A for a bit longer than its value. Places where vibrato might be used are marked with "vib." in Figure 9–5.

Tone Color   The various tone colors of the guitar are a rich resource of expressive refinement. (See the discussion of tone color in Chapter 6.) There is more than one way to use color in the Sor piece, but do not overdo it because the minuet is a short piece and contrast can be achieved by other expressive means, such as dynamics and articulation. Also, the color effects should sound natural to the music.

It actually sounds fine to play the entire piece with the full-bodied sound of the guitar at the right edge of the soundhole. However, to make the piece more interesting, you might try using a nasal, oboe-like color about an inch from the bridge in the B section in bars 9–12. Another nice color can be obtained in bars 13–16 by changing the left-hand fingering so that most of the notes are played on strings 2, 3, and 4 instead of strings 1, 2, and 3. Be sure to keep most of the melody notes on the second string so that there is no awkward change in color in the middle of the phrase. Then, if you play with the right hand over the middle of the soundhole, the passage will sound something like French horns.

There are many details such as these in any piece and each one should receive some attention so that your performance will be polished. Of course, not every refinement will occur to you before you perform the piece for the first time. In fact, you will probably continue to discover additional refinements to the piece as you play it over a period of time. In any case, it is good to polish it as much as possible for the first performance so that it will be satisfying to you and your audience.

12. Express the Music in its Wholeness and Let It Flow Through You

In this final step of studying a piece, you bring together your overall musical concept and all the various individual threads you have been working with, weaving them into an integrated musical tapestry. In other words, the whole now must become greater than the sum of the parts. It is difficult to say exactly when this will happen, because no one can force it to come about. All you can do is set up the conditions and let it happen. The setting up is done by studying the piece with great care, integrating it into your consciousness, and finally, letting go of your concern with technical matters so that you can concentrate on the musical meaning. Then the piece can become a complete work of art.

Time to Ripen   Even though you may be able to learn a piece in a short time, it is important to give it plenty of time to mature. For a complex, profound piece, the maturing time may be considerable. In any case, whether the piece is short or long, simple or complex, shallow or deep, take time to become intimate with it before playing it in public.

Hierarchy of Dynamics Certain aspects of creating an integrated interpretation of a piece seem to elude deliberate working out; however, there are elements that can be worked on consciously. One such element is the hierarchy of values in the piece. We have already discussed the *structural* hierarchy of the Sor minuet in Step 4 and showed it in pictorial form in Figure 9–4. Now let's consider the *dynamic* hierarchy. Such a hierarchy suggests that there can be higher and lower dynamic levels in the piece that reflect the relative significance of the different parts. So, if you have some overall conception of what parts are more important than others, it will be appropriate to let the dynamics conform to that idea.

Let's apply one possible hierarchy of dynamics to the various parts of the minuet. According to our analysis of the piece (see Steps 1–4), there are two climactic points in the first eight bars, one on the F in bar four and one on the G on the first beat of bar seven. Since the second one seems to be the goal of the eight-bar section, in our hierarchy we would give it more dynamic emphasis than the first.

In the second eight-bar section, although the highest note is the A in bar 15, the highest tension point seems to be the F♯ in bar 14 and therefore it should receive the strongest dynamic emphasis. That high point on the F♯ seems to have more tension than the high point in the first section.

In the final eight-bar section in measure 23 on the first beat we have the climax of the entire piece. It comes after a powerful build-up in the previous six measures. In the dynamic hierarchy it should be the strongest point. If the high point of the first section is *mezzo forte* and the one in the second section is *forte*, then the big climax in bar 23 should logically be the loudest, that is, *double* forte. However, since the dynamic range of the guitar is somewhat limited, it is good to strengthen the impression of double forte by accentuating the notes on the first beat and holding them slightly longer than written. With the help of the dynamic hierarchy we have just described, you can create a clear idea of the overall structure of the piece for yourself and your listeners. The relative levels of the dynamics indicate where the principal goal of the piece is and how the other goals relate to it. Thus dynamics are an important way of projecting the wholeness of the piece and showing the relationship of its parts.

The Meaning of Silence

> *Hearing juncture is as if the piece were poured into a mold of living silence. The result is, in a manner of speaking, two pieces. One piece is the sound . . . shaped by . . . the silences; the other piece is the silence shaped by the sounds.*[10]
>
> Alexandra Pierce

[10]Alexandra Pierce, "Juncture," *In Theory Only*, Journal of Michigan Music Theory Society, 3, no. 6 (September 1977), 28.

Besides dynamics, there are other elements of your playing that you can consciously work out so they fit into the piece as a whole. One of the most important, and yet most neglected, of these elements is to allow silences or breathing places in the music. From the pregnant stillness before a piece begins through the pauses within the piece to the restful quietness at the end, well-played music is filled with silences. Music cannot really exist without silence to create the boundaries of its sounds. Without silence no one would know where a note or phrase began or ended. Thus the wholeness of a piece of music cannot be fully realized by a performer until he balances the sound with its opposite. All the fine players have a keen awareness of the power of silence and use it in their interpretations to great advantage.

Silences are the best way to clarify the structural hierarchy of a piece. When properly placed, they bring alive the structure "tree" in Figure 9–4. You can use a greater or lesser silence before a piece begins to dramatize the first notes. Within the piece, the relative lengths of the silences between the parts should reflect the hierarchical level of the parts: Smaller parts such as single notes and motives will have shorter silences between them, whereas larger parts such as phrases and sections will have longer silences.

Alexandra Pierce points out that the silent points in our breathing are analogous to the silences between musical events. She calls those silent points *junctures.*[11] In breathing there are junctures or still points between inhalation and exhalation and between exhalation and inhalation. If you pay close attention to your breathing, you will notice a clear difference between the two. The juncture or stillness between inhaling and exhaling is very brief and the two phases "run on" into each other. However, the juncture between exhaling and inhaling is longer and more distinct. The first type of "run on" juncture in breathing is the kind of brief silence that a performer can discover between the individual notes or motives. The second type, the longer juncture, can be found in the relatively greater silences between phrases and sections.

In order to understand the value of the musical silences we are discussing, it is good to become acutely aware of the silences between events in your own behavior. We have already mentioned breathing, but there are countless other opportunities to see how silences alternate with activities. A general characteristic of our life is that it is filled with smaller and greater cycles of rest and activity, silence and sound. Recall, for example, the alternation of playing and resting in the Play–Relax technique in Chapter 5. Or notice in your social conversations that there are pauses between words and sentences. Notice the sometimes awkward gaps when no one seems to have anything to say. People often become anxious about these gaps and try to bridge them with such things as throat-clearing and other gestures. However, there is nothing wrong with these spaces. It is actually more enjoyable not to have to talk constantly.

[11]Ibid., p. 24.

After you become aware of the still moments in your daily activities, you will appreciate the silences in music much more. You will find that music is much more appealing with silences in appropriate places. It can be quite unsettling or tiring to listen to an overly "busy" performance that has no quiet spaces. The listener is dragged along by the "busy" performer who finishes one phrase only to charge into the next one without allowing enough breathing space between the two.

Let's look at how you can incorporate silences into the Sor minuet. It is most important for you to experience the silences or junctures at all levels of the piece. Refer to Figure 9–5 for this discussion. First, it helps to exaggerate the experience of silence. Try playing through the piece but stop completely for ten to fifteen seconds after each section—once after the eight-bar A section and once after the eight-bar B section. Now play through the piece several more times, first stopping after each four-bar phrase, then after each two-bar motive, and finally after each note (as in the Play–Relax exercise in Step 6). Take your time with this exercise. Relax and feel the silences.

Now try playing the whole piece through at tempo without the long stops in the above exercise but allowing the natural silent points to come out. Notice that the brief silences between the single notes and the slightly longer ones between the two-bar motives are like the "run on" junctures between inhaling and exhaling, whereas the ones between phrases and sections are like the longer junctures between exhaling and inhaling. The relative lengths of the silences set the different levels of the structural hierarchy in relief. Do not hurry over these silences. Allow them to become as clear to you as the notes themselves. You will soon notice that these silences are anything but dead spaces. They fairly quiver with potential energy and serve as gathering points for the energy of the musical idea that is coming next.

If the guitarist becomes aware of and experiments with these silences in his practice sessions, it will often be an exciting musical revelation. As Alexandra Pierce has said:

> . . . if I give my attention to the space, or moment in between phrases and allow its shape to form, I also unleash the expressiveness of the phrase itself.[12]

Thus the guitarist who wants to project the full musical meaning of his pieces will learn how to balance the great variety of sounds he makes with an equally great variety of silences.

These examples show how you can consciously integrate certain elements of your interpretation of a piece into a whole. There is naturally more than one way to do that and still be artistically convincing. Music is filled with ambiguities and thus allows different interpretations. However, keep in mind

[12]Ibid., p. 24.

that there is always a certain range of reasonability and good taste within which the responsible artist will stay. It is best to stay away from extremes of all kinds in your interpretations of the music. Look instead for a naturally balanced approach.

Of course it is impossible to analyze and consciously work out every detail of your interpretation. If you try to do that, your playing will generally sound affected and unnatural. At a certain point you must let go of any attempt to *control* the interpretation and let the music flow through you. Let it express itself. This will not always happen when you want it to, but if you set up the proper conditions, it will tend to happen more often. When it does happen, you will know it. The music will flow effortlessly and you will simply be a channel through which it will pass. You will *witness* it and enjoy it more than you could ever imagine.

SUMMARY

The foregoing has been a rather detailed discussion of how to study a piece and bring out its inner meaning because many guitarists have not had much exposure to the musical concepts in this chapter. It was important to make these ideas clear with many examples from an actual piece. The twelve steps emphasize the value of gaining a clear musical idea of the piece from the very beginning. "Music first" is the basic rule. When you have the musical idea in your mind, it is much easier to work out the details of the actual playing in a natural way. It is also much more enjoyable because you can see how everything that you are working out technically fits into your overall musical concept. When you have worked out the details thoroughly, then just *let the music happen* in order to express its full essence.

After you have successfully studied a number of pieces using the twelve-step plan (or a facsimile thereof) and you can play them reasonably well in the practice room, you will undoubtedly have some desire to play for other people. You may just want to perform for friends on an amateur basis or, if you are more ambitious, you may want to play recitals for large groups of people on a professional basis. The desire to play for others is perfectly natural and it should be fulfilled. Chapter 10 deals with ways to help you meet the challenges and opportunities of playing for others.

10.

Sharing Your Enjoyment of Music

the delight of playing recitals

An artist prepares for weeks, months and years . . . but lives only for moments. Moments, then, that have no sense of time. Moments that never will come back in the same way. They might be called moments of grace if listeners can take part in them. But as one may not force things which one has to be grateful for, the adventure remains; part of it consists of the hope for integration of the many moments of beauty into a larger whole, giving them coherence and bringing them to their logical end.

Gustav Leonhardt, harpsichordist

PLAYING FOR OTHERS

Multiplying Musical Enjoyment

When they start to play, most guitarists do it solely for their own personal enjoyment. Usually there is no strong intention to play for others when the guitarist feels incompetent on the instrument. However, after the player learns some pieces and has some fluency in the language of the guitar, he begins to enjoy himself and thinks that it might not be so bad to play for other people. He may want to perform just for fun or he may like it so much that he wants to make a profession of it. In any event, when the guitarist is enjoying the music he plays, it is a perfectly natural tendency to want to share that enjoyment. Moreover, there is a tremendous value in sharing that most musicians experience at least occasionally. The value is that the enjoyment of playing for others is greater than just sitting and playing for yourself. The enjoyment is multiplied when you play for groups of people. Obviously the effect is best when the player is in top shape and the playing goes well. Then everyone—including the player—feels uplifted and refreshed by the experience.

No one knows precisely how music creates such a powerful, uplifting effect in a group of people. However, one important factor seems to be a natural orderliness in music when it is well played. A particularly significant part of the orderliness of most music is a steady, but not necessarily metronomic, rhythmic pulse. When that pulse is present, the phenomenon of *entrainment* can take place. We already mentioned entrainment in Chapter 5 where it was defined as a "locking in" to the natural rhythm of the music being played. The result is effortless musical flow. Now, when you introduce your individual musical entrainment into a group, the possibility of group entrainment arises. What apparently happens is that, at certain times, everyone in the group "locks in" to the orderly musical pulse of your playing. Although no one has ever measured it, it seems likely that when group entrainment takes place, there would be some degree of synchronization (or harmonization) of everyone's brain waves. If true, that would give a scientific explanation of how a whole group of people can be totally enraptured by a musical performance. Be that as it may, with the onset of true entrainment, the entire group becomes focused on the music and acts—at least for a time—as one large, harmonious unit. This creates an exhilarating sense of mental and physical well-being for everyone.

Thus you can see that one function of playing for others is to make yourself and other people happier. But music should not just create superficial entertainment or show. As the contemporary German composer Stockhausen has said:

> When a musician walks on to the stage he should give that fabulous impression of a man who is doing a sacred service. In India, in Bali, when a group of musicians are performing, you don't feel they do it to entertain you. They do it as a holy service. They feel a need to make sounds, and these sounds are waves on which you ride to the eternal.[1]

Thus the musician has a very high function in society—that of bringing peace and harmony to an overstressed world. Listening to beautiful, well-performed music gives people a glimpse into a higher realm and gives them a spiritual lift. The beauty of the music takes them outside of themselves at least for a moment and thus helps them let go of their everyday problems. The orderliness of the music seems to create some orderliness in the listeners' consciousness. It makes them realize that there must be some deep level of order and harmony in the universe even though they ordinarily experience disorder on the surface. Thus people go away from a good concert better off than when they came.

As you can see, a musician can have a profound effect on his listeners. That effect can be good or bad, depending on the performer's state of being. In order to have a good influence on people, it is important that the musician practice, perform, and live everyday in a peaceful, harmonious manner. Otherwise he will not be playing his proper social role of spreading joy and upliftment.

The Recital Challenge:
Grow Musically and Personally

As a guitarist you have a marvelous opportunity to promote your personal and musical development when you prepare and play recitals. Your development will be furthered no matter whether you play for just a few friends or for

---

[1] Karl-Heinz Stockhausen, "Spiritual Dimensions," *Music and Musicians* (May 1971), 34.

a big audience, and no matter whether you intend to be an amateur or a professional. Whatever the case, recitals challenge you to really organize yourself, to put your mind and body in good shape, to develop the ability to be calm in the midst of performing (that is, to be dynamically relaxed), and to expand your emotional sensitivity by opening yourself up to others. The recital is an inspiration to do your absolute best. You should not dread it at all, but welcome it and use it as a means to grow.

Initially you may find public recitals, or even playing for friends, to be uncomfortable—in spite of knowing the music well. If that is the case, you will soon realize that just sitting and practicing is not enough to overcome the fear of playing for others. You will become aware of the need to develop your inner self as well. If you suffer in the recital situation, it is nature telling you to make some appropriate changes. For example, if you are nervous when performing, that suggests that you may need to do something to settle your mind and relax your body (see Chapter 2). If your concentration is not very good while playing, then you may profit by practicing the effortless concentration technique discussed in Chapter 3. If you have a heavy, dull feeling during a performance, you may find it necessary to eat lightly or not at all before you play.

The chief realization that eventually dawns on the guitarist who wants to play concerts is that the more he cooperates with the requirements of his body and environment, the more he will be successful in his music making. If you act in accordance with the natural principle of least action and the other principles in this book, you will find relatively little resistance to the fulfillment of your guitar-playing desires. Playing recitals will become an experience that is so enjoyable the player will want to repeat it often. Those magical moments in music that everyone talks about can become a living reality. Such moments make everyone realize that humanity has an enormous potential for happiness and achievement.

It should be plain that playing for others is worthwhile because it challenges you to reach beyond the small fraction of your potential that you normally use. It pushes you toward *full* potential. Take the opportunity to play for other people often—but also *learn* from each situation. Make each recital better than the last. Let your playing evolve to ever higher levels. Remember to aim for the ideal of uplifting and energizing yourself and your listeners so that everyone grows and benefits from your performance.

PREPARING FOR THE RECITAL

In this part of the chapter we look at some specific ways of mental and physical preparation for recitals. In the next part is a discussion of how you can best deal with the recital when you are right in the middle of it—a topic of no small interest. In the final section, we consider the attitude toward the recital after it is over and the challenge it presents. Now a look at what can be done *before* the recital.

Enjoy the Preparation

Enjoyment of what you are doing is undoubtedly the most important thing to remember when you are preparing a recital. If you enjoy your practice and playing, then that will be reflected at your recitals; if you do not enjoy it, that also will be reflected. In order to enjoy yourself the most and be successful, you need to be highly conscious of what you are doing. Even if you are just practicing some scales or arpeggios, be conscious of the sound and how the fingers feel. Being aware of what is happening *right now* in your playing will reap great rewards for your practice sessions and for your recitals.

Know Your Pieces Thoroughly

Needless to say, it is paramount that you know your recital material intimately in order to play it well. The pianist and writer William Newman says that one must be willing "to go the last mile" in one's preparation of a recital. All the fine artists emphasize the need to study all the details of a piece as well as the overall structure. Then you must *live* with the piece for some time, thinking about it, feeling it, playing it again and again until it reveals its "deeply hidden core," as the harpsichordist Wanda Landowska says. Then you can feel more confident of your ability to play the piece in a recital.

To truly know your recital pieces, it is good to do a thorough study of them as was outlined in Chapter 9. The knowledge gained from that process gives a solid musical and psychological foundation for your performances.

For the sake of good performance, it is of considerable importance that you be decisive and detailed in your fingerings. Once you determine the musical effect desired and find a good fingering to express it, then it is best to stick to that fingering. Of course you should remain flexible, and if a better, more expressive fingering comes to mind, you should be able to change. Just remember that it is usually best to avoid major changes when the recital is only a week or two away—unless you like living dangerously. Experiments with last-minute changes can result in great confusion when the moment of truth arrives.

One area that guitarists often neglect is detailed fingering for the right hand. Many guitarists do it slightly differently each time they play a piece and then they wonder why their fingers become tangled at recital time. The finer players tend to be very specific about right- and left-hand fingerings and frequently pencil them into the score. Some high-level players who know their music like an old friend may take more chances and change fingerings at the last minute (or even during the performance). This is because they like the freedom of expressing a phrase in different ways according to how they feel it. However, this approach is not recommended for beginning recitalists. It is better to be very decisive in the details of left- and right-hand fingering. It gives you self-confidence when you are on stage. You have the reassuring feeling that you have no "unfinished business" with respect to the details. You have "gone the last mile."

At this point remember that the method of mental practice (described in Chapter 8) can help you learn your pieces in detail. Spend at least some of your regular practice time sitting quietly without the guitar and practicing mentally. Play your pieces clearly in your "inner ear" and see the fingering clearly in your "inner eye." This method, although demanding of your concentration, is very powerful and will result in a feeling of real command over your pieces when you play them in recital.

Planning the Recital

People talk much about the value of planning in order to make any enterprise turn out successfully, but few do it in an organized manner. With respect to guitar recitals, those who do plan them carefully find it helpful. Planning ahead has the advantage of giving you peace of mind because, at an early stage of your preparation, you make most of your decisions about what you are going to play and in what order. Your mind is then free to work quietly on your pieces. Eleventh-hour decision making is avoided.

By far the two most important aspects of your program are playing pieces that you like and playing them only when you feel very comfortable with them. These may seem to be obvious points, but many guitarists are not conscious of them. You must enjoy and feel deeply about what you play or you will not be able to move others.

One of the first things to consider in your recital planning is whether you will play solo or ensemble music or a mixture of the two. The solo recital tends to be a higher pressure situation for most people, so it may be much more comfortable to start by playing some ensemble music. Guitar duets, trios, and quartets and guitar with voice are all very good for this purpose. Just knowing that someone else is up there with you helps greatly to overcome stage fright. Besides, you will discover that playing with the right partner is very enjoyable. After you have done some ensemble work you will probably feel easier about playing solos. On the other hand, you may feel like doing your "solo flight" right from the beginning. Whatever the case, just make sure you feel relatively comfortable with the recital situation before going into it. No one will enjoy hearing you play if you are not enjoying yourself. Your teacher and friends can give you some help in deciding whether you are ready for a recital—but ultimately the decision is yours.

Decide on the nature of your program well before the recital. Make it concrete by writing down the pieces you want to play, the order in which they will come, how long each piece lasts, how long the whole program will be, where an intermission should go, and how long it should be. The structure of the program should be carefully planned: it should be well orchestrated, like a good piece of music. It needs to have some kind of shape, some kind of logical progression. Transitions from one piece or part of the program to the next should be smooth. There should be "breathing room" and a feeling of spaciousness in the program. For example, it is not good to have many long, complex pieces in a row without the relief of lighter works. If you are playing a substantial work—such as an entire sonata—in the first half, you might start the program with a short group of two or more light pieces that you know well, then take a break before the sonata by going off stage for a minute or two in order to relax and breathe easily. That kind of break is what gives you a feeling of spaciousness and comfort in a program. It also gives the audience a chance to have a break and relax. No matter how you do it, there should be a balance between the different program elements—between playing and silence, fast and slow, light and heavy, long and short, popular and esoteric pieces. Balancing the relative lengths of each part of the program is also a significant factor.

If you examine programs of top concert guitarists, you will find considerable variety, but there is always some kind of logic to them. Some programs are arranged chronologically, from early to modern, to give a feeling of historical continuity. But other arrangements, based on affinities of certain pieces without regard to period, or on contrast, are also used to good effect. Programs are most commonly organized in sections—perhaps two or three in each half of a full-length program. Each section presents several pieces in some kind of coherent grouping, whether all in one style or all by one composer. One trend today is to present complete works instead of throwing together a piece from here, a piece from there. This "one dog from every village" approach is not always artistically satisfying. For that reason, some guitarists are now performing complete Bach suites, rather than just one or two pieces taken from different suites.

The first half of the program will often progress from lighter works in the beginning to a very substantial, climactic piece just before intermission. Nowadays it is usual for the weightiest pieces to appear in the first half of a concert because audience alertness is generally greatest at that time. It is usually wisest to have lighter fare in the second half. For the same reason, it is good to have the second half somewhat shorter than the first. Besides, if the second half is not so long, the audience will tend to want more. Better to leave them a bit hungry rather than trying to satiate them.

The program from a Segovia concert on page 236 is an example of a nicely balanced and spacious program. The order is not chronological but still it has a certain sense to it based on contrast and groupings of pieces from the same composer or era. The Sor pieces are relatively light in character and in technical difficulty—something to warm up on before the more demanding

---

A SAMPLE SEGOVIA PROGRAM

I

Two Studies	Fernando Sor
Theme and Variations in E minor	(1778–1839)
Sonata III	Manuel Ponce
Allegro moderato	(1886–1948)
Canción	
Allegro non troppo	

II

Two "Songs Without Words"	Felix Mendelssohn
	(1809–1847)
Eight Short Pieces	Robert Schumann
	(1810–1856)

Intermission

III

Suite Mystica	V. Acensio
Danse	Enrique Granados
	(1867–1916)
Romanza	F.M. Torroba
	(1891–1982)
Sevilla	Isaac Albéniz
	(1860–1909)

Sonata III by Ponce. Then there is a brief break, during which Segovia usually walks off stage for a few minutes. Then the first half concludes with some lighter pieces. Note that Segovia has grouped two Sor pieces together and contrasts them with the Ponce. Then, in Part II, he groups some pieces of the classical–romantic era together, which also contrasts with the Ponce.

Then comes the intermission and a decidedly Spanish second half, starting off with a contemplative modern suite. Then come three standards of the repertoire to finish off the program—the last being sure to please everyone. Segovia knows quite well, as most seasoned artists do, that the choice of the last piece is important because, if the concert ends well, then a favorable impression is left with the audience. Thus most artists select an upbeat, happy piece such as *Sevilla* with which to end. Much more could be said about programs, but it is best for guitarists to find out for themselves what makes a good program by studying the programs of famous artists—both guitarists and nonguitarists.[2]

Visualization and Dry Runs

There is nothing quite like jumping into the water to see how it actually feels. In the same way, there is nothing quite like trying out your recital program to find out how it actually goes. However, to make it easier, you can use a graduated, escalation approach to practicing your recitals. This approach consists of low to high pressure "dry runs" that simulate the real playing situation. The important thing is to do dry runs a number of times before the recital— with and without listeners—so that you feel completely comfortable with the musical material and the performance situation.

In line with the "mind over fingers" idea (see Chapters 8 and 9), you can use visualization as a powerful tool to do dry runs for your recitals. Probably the lowest pressure way to start is to practice your pieces mentally while lying down without picturing anyone listening to you. When that feels comfortable, try the same thing, but visualize some good friends listening. The next step is visualizing yourself playing the actual recital. It is possible to rehearse the recital in your mind in every aspect and become comfortable with it long before the actual recital. Thus, when the recital comes, it is not an unknown, fearful situation. You already know it well and are thoroughly prepared.

Here is a more detailed way to rehearse your playing situations in the "concert hall of your mind." It is most effective to see the situation in a positive light and to imagine it in *vivid detail* on your mental movie screen. You can start by sitting comfortably or lying down; then relax all the muscles of the body and close the eyes. After a minute or so of silence, mentally picture yourself picking up the guitar and walking into the place where you will play. See yourself walking in confidently, enjoying the presence of your audience. See all the details of the place: the people's faces, the lighting, the furnishings, the seat you will sit on. Feel the warm, friendly atmosphere. Realize that everyone has come to enjoy hearing you play well; realize that they are there to support you, not to undermine you. Picture yourself sitting with the guitar in an attractive, comfortable position. Feel the guitar in your hands as you begin to play. Imagine yourself playing your pieces—Bach, Sor, Ponce, or whatever you have chosen—and hearing how beautiful they sound. Hear every detail of the pieces. See yourself enjoying the music and the warm response of the audience. Feel yourself relaxing both during and after each piece. Picture yourself playing through the pieces without stopping. If mis-

---

[2]See articles on guitar recitals and programs by Michael Lorimer in *Guitar Player* magazine, August through December 1978.

takes come up, do not be concerned about them. Let them go. Hear the appreciative applause after you finish each piece and see yourself graciously acknowledging the applause. Remember that making music is more than just ego gratification; it has the ability to transport you and others to a higher, more enjoyable plane of consciousness. You can take people away from the problems of daily life and open up their minds to a magical world of sounds. When your program is finished, see yourself bowing gracefully and make your exit. Picture yourself having an enjoyable time when people come to talk to you after the program. Now, whenever you are ready, you can end the visualization. To avoid jangling your nerves, it is good to open the eyes slowly and not jump up too quickly from the relaxed state.

Although visualizations such as this are positive in orientation, you still may have some negative thoughts and physical tensions creeping in the back door. The way to handle the negative thoughts is simply to be *indifferent* to them. For example, if you start having queasy feelings in the stomach, sweaty palms, and thoughts of "I can't play, I'm no good" during the visualization, then do not pay attention to those negative thoughts and favor the positive ones. It is definitely best not to suppress or push out negative thoughts. That will merely strengthen them. Just be neutral toward them and they will tend to disappear.

If you have an overwhelming negative thought or some physical tension, then do not try to continue the visualization. Keep the eyes closed and allow your mind to do what it wants. In the case of a negative thought, your mind will often forget the thought and go to some physical sensation in the body, since every mental state or thought has a physiological correlate. When you do this, then the bodily sensation—usually some tension or ache—will take care of itself quickly. In the case of overt physical tension, simply let your mind go to the tense place with a thought of relaxation. In this natural way, the body and mind get rid of tensions that hinder your guitar performance.

Positive visualization of your recitals can help a great deal because what you visualize tends to structure what actually comes about. If the process is done a number of times before the performance, then all the difficulties can be removed. What will remain is a positive vision of the recital situation that will tend to fulfill itself in the performance. Of course you can go overboard with this "positive thinking" approach and lose your spontaneity, so avoid doing it too much.

For some, it may seem less threatening to sit and play their program in the practice room instead of trying to visualize the recital. Actually playing through the program (without stopping for mistakes) is, of course, one of the logical steps in your preparation. However, you must face the audience sooner or later and the visualization process prepares you for that.

Another way of simulating the concert situation is to play your program straight through for your tape recorder. Remember to keep going. Do not stop because of mistakes. The recorder may make you nervous at first—even more so than a person—because you know that it will quite objectively mirror your playing, both faults and good points. However, playing regularly with the recorder will not only help to get rid of your stage fright, but as we mentioned in Chapter 9, it will also be a fine source of feedback to help you improve your pieces. The tape recorder is a highly useful tool for the serious guitarist. For those who have access to them, videotaping facilities also afford an excellent source of feedback. In addition to hearing the music, you can see if your sitting position is good, if the fingering flows, or if you are making faces.

After audio- or videotaping by yourself, you can escalate and play for a small group of good friends, relatives, guitar students, or your teacher. It is good to set up your chair, footstool, and distance from the audience in a way similar to the ultimate recital situation in which you will play. It even helps if you play the practice recital at the same time as the actual one will be. Then play the program, enjoying each piece as it comes. *Remember not to apologize* for your playing either before or after you play a piece. Nobody wants to hear excuses. Negative thoughts about yourself in the form of apologies are not good. Remember that you are playing for everyone's enjoyment and upliftment. No one will care if you make a few mistakes as long as you do not become upset about them.

For very shy guitarists, an especially low pressure way of playing for your friends or others is to do it in a situation where their attention is not solely directed to you. For example, you might go to a party, take out your guitar, and start playing in a quiet corner where you think almost no one can hear you. This approach is very nonthreatening and you will not worry much about mistakes—mainly because everyone is talking so loudly that you cannot be heard! After you have played under these circumstances several times, you will notice an interesting development, that is, you will become disgusted with playing to deaf ears and party noise. As a result, you will probably start to play louder—even fiercely—in order to be heard. Some self-confidence usually comes of this. Eventually you will not be able to tolerate all the noise and distraction of playing at parties and you will want to play for quiet and attentive listeners. Thus, what we have just described is a "back door" approach to escalating the performance pressure that seems to help those who are particularly shy or nervous.

Another good preparatory step for a recital is to go to the hall where you will play to get the feel of it. The German composer Stockhausen thinks that it is best to be in the hall for twenty-four hours before the concert so that the atmosphere can be made positive and harmonious. In most cases, it would be difficult to follow Stockhausen's suggestion, but the idea is an important one since you can have some influence on how the recital hall feels to yourself and your audience. You can usually spend *some* time in the hall before playing there. If possible, it is good to go to the hall several days before the recital to see what it is like and play your program in it.

If you can, sit down quietly on stage and play some of your pieces. This procedure will make you feel more at home with the hall and its acoustics. If possible, have someone listen to you in different parts of the hall to see if you need to play louder, softer, quicker, or slower because of the acoustics. If the hall is too "live" and the reverberation time is long, then it is better to use somewhat slower tempos than normal to avoid the overlap of the guitar sound and the echoes; conversely, if the hall is "dead" and there is little re-verberation, then quicker tempos are more appropriate. You may want to relocate your sitting position in order to obtain the best sound projection to all parts of the hall. If available, an acoustic reflector or "shell" can be very help-ful to focus the soft sound of the classical guitar on the audience and prevent it from being lost—especially in a large or dead hall. Most acoustic reflectors consist of two or more moveable, upright panels that are placed edge-to-edge in a semi-circle at a short distance behind the guitarist. The position of the reflector should be adjusted for maximum projection of the guitar sound to-ward the audience.

Another way of increasing the guitar sound projection is to play with the right hand fairly close to the bridge to obtain your normal tone rather than over the soundhole. Of course you do not want to play too close to the bridge or your normal sound will be too metallic and there will be no room for tonal contrast. Exactly how close to the bridge you play is something you should experiment with until you are satisfied with the tone quality and projection of the sound. The advantage of playing nearer to the bridge is that it emphasizes the higher harmonics of the notes and these high sounds have a greater carry-ing power. Segovia and other artists do this, particularly in a big hall, since it allows the guitar to be heard throughout the audience—although one must still be very quiet to catch all the notes.

Of course it is possible to amplify the classical guitar in a concert situa-tion, but usually the process ends up ruining the quality of the sound. Nor-mally the sound will not need amplification, but if it does, it should be done with special equipment that reproduces the sound with as little distortion as possible.

Now, as you practice some of your pieces on stage, imagine how it will be when the hall is filled with people. See yourself playing well for them. Re-member that people soak up sound and thus you may have to play a bit louder at the actual recital than when the hall is empty.

If the recital hall and some friends are available you can escalate the re-cital simulation to nearly the real thing. Do not neglect to get feedback from both friends and the tape recorder. When you go through your program in the recital hall, practice energetic entrances and exits, taking graceful bows, acknowledging the audience and other such stage manners. Make it clear that you are really happy to be on stage. Give everyone the feeling that you are having a celebration. If you are not happy to be playing, then why are you there? All these considerations, plus some intangibles, constitute stage presence. It is a vital ingredient in your performances.

It should be clear that dry runs are a significant part of recital preparation and that it is good to take *every opportunity* to do them so that you are comfortable with the situation. If you have trouble finding people to listen to you, then see about playing at hospitals, convalescent homes, schools, and other such organizations. They usually welcome student performances. As a final suggestion, it is a good idea to start your practice recitals at least a week or two before the actual performance if you can because then you will have time to work on improvements without pressure.

Relax on the Day of the Recital

The best way to be comfortable on the day of the recital is to "be happy," as the Cuban guitarist Leo Brouwer says. He suggests spending most of the day of the recital by yourself, taking it easy, and avoiding arguments. In other words, he means stay away from what makes you nervous and do what makes you feel relaxed. What makes you feel relaxed? It is naturally different for everyone and there are many approaches to it. Some of the most useful ones have already been discussed in earlier chapters and thus will only be mentioned briefly here, but a few new approaches will be added to the repertoire as well.

Mind-Settling Techniques   The most fundamental approach to relaxation before a guitar concert is settling your mind. Various ways of doing it have been outlined in Chapter 2. Remember that if your mind is quiet, like the ocean without many waves, then concentration comes easily, you do not make mistakes, and the music flows effortlessly. On the other hand, if your mind is like a stormy sea, concentration is difficult, you make mistakes, and everyone suffers. So, if your mind is not as clear as you would like, you might want to do one of the quieting techniques—at least on the day of your recital.

Another way of settling your mind and giving you inspiration is to listen to quiet music you love. It may be a favorite guitar piece, a piece on another instrument, an orchestral work, or some meditative music from the Orient. Pachelbel's *Canon in D* is a perennial favorite to soothe the nerves. The exact piece you choose does not really matter, but it should have the effect of soothing and quieting rather than irritating and exciting.

Body Relaxation Techniques   The total body relaxation process (progressive relaxation) described in Chapter 2 is a good one to do before a concert because it is easy and takes so little time. Other good types of body relaxation (also discussed in Chapter 2) are: yoga postures and various kinds of physical exercise, such as walking, swimming, cycling, and running. Of these exercises, walking is one of the favorites of concert players. The rhythm of a leisurely walk seems to loosen up the body and put you into a tranquil state of mind.

The most direct way to relax is simple rest. If you are playing an evening recital, a long nap in the afternoon seems to be very beneficial. A well-known conductor takes a four-hour nap before each performance. He claims that the nap leaves him very fresh and alert. You may not need four hours; perhaps an hour will do very well if you are not tired. That extra rest does wonders for lessening tension and increasing alertness.

A good massage is an excellent way of releasing excess tensions from your body. Another famous symphony conductor regularly goes to a physical therapist for a thorough massage on the days of his concerts. Massage has the effect of taking your mind away from the concert and focusing it on the pleasant sensations in your body. It is best not to talk much during a massage. Just feel it, enjoy it, and forget everything else. After a good massage you should feel relaxed and ready to play.

Avoidance of Overpracticing   Excessive practice shortly before and on the day of a concert is a common mistake. It is just like cramming for an examination. It usually has the effect of wearing you out and making you nervous about your performance. It is generally much more relaxing to practice no more than about two hours on the day of the concert. Do some exercises, perhaps some polishing of fine details, run through the program once or twice, then forget about it and do something else. If you do not have the pieces worked out by now, "cramming" will more than likely make things worse. Concert players have tried the "cram approach" and the resulting performances tend to be shaky. So it is better to take it easy. Trust that the native intelligence of your body and subconscious mind knows exactly how to play your pieces.

Spacious Schedule   Aside from the avoidance of excess practicing, it is not good to have a lot of hectic activity on the day of your concert. Allow time to do something that is relaxing and energizing for you, such as walking, napping, or meditating. Make sure you have plenty of time to get to the concert hall without racing. Arrive there at least an hour early if you can so that you have time to become comfortable with the atmosphere. Remember that, as a guitarist/musician, you can serve the valuable social function of uplifting people by presenting music in a peaceful, harmonious way. It is very difficult to do that if you are nervous and harried.

Light Eating   As was discussed in Chapter 3, it is most relaxing for your mind and body if you do not eat too much at the meal just before a concert. In fact, it is best not to eat too much during the entire day of the concert. Light eating frees up energy for clear thinking and concentration on the music. Furthermore, if you feel at all nervous and you have a big meal in your stomach, you will surely have some digestive problems. To this it should be added that, just as it is not good to eat too much, it is also not good to eat too little. A young concert guitarist once made the mistake of eating only a sweet roll and a cup of coffee on the day of a concert. On top of that, he overpracticed during the day. At the recital that night he started off well, but his right-hand strokes gradually weakened and he started to make mistakes. Then his face turned chalk white. Finally he felt so bad that he could not go on. He excused himself and walked out. At that point he confessed that he had not eaten much and someone gave him the only source of protein around—a bag of salted peanuts! He ate them with gusto and was able to finish the concert reasonably well. Now he is careful to eat enough food on concert days (and he also avoids overpractice).

The moral here is clear: For good performances, practice moderation in all things.

In Sum   There are numerous ways to relax before a concert and each person can choose for himself whatever way seems best. Even if you think you are relaxed in concerts already and ask, "Why do I need to relax more?", you may find that some of the relaxation techniques described will make your playing even better. These techniques may release some hidden mental or physical tensions that will enable you to concentrate more perfectly and allow you to feel the full emotional depth of the music. There is almost always some improvement that can be made. For that reason, most of the fine guitarists practice some form of relaxation. In any case, it is good to be aware of the value of settling your mind and relaxing your body before playing for others. It is even better to do something about it. You will reap the rewards in your concerts.

ENJOYING THE RECITAL

Now, after a considerable amount of preparation you are ready for the recital. This is where "the scaffolding must come down and the building must stand by itself," as Segovia says. This is where you find out if you have prepared properly. If you have done it well, the recital will be a pleasure for everyone, like a rose with no thorns; if not, the pleasure may be mixed with some pain, like a rose with thorns. Whatever the case, it is best to play the recital with a cheerful attitude and do as well as you possibly can.

Appearance

Appearance is an important but frequently neglected aspect of concert playing. Remember that it is a reflection of what you think about yourself and your audience. If you are well-groomed and well-dressed, both you and the audience will feel good. The psychological impact of your appearance is very strong. If it is not so attractive, it will detract from the music. Some younger players do not realize this, and even though they play well, they sometimes alienate or distract their audiences by the sloppiness or bizarre quality of their dress. When in doubt, lean toward simple, elegant apparel rather than something flamboyant. It is not usually necessary to wear a formal gown or coat and tails. An attractive dress for women and coat and tie for men are appropriate for most occasions. Whatever you wear, make sure it is comfortable and does not inhibit your arm and hand movements.

Arrive Early

Now it is time to go to the recital hall, preferably without rushing. If you go an hour or more ahead of time, you will have plenty of time to set everything up: your seating (an adjustable, backless piano bench is a preferred type of seat), your footstool (make sure it will not slide around), the place where you will be when you are not on stage, the lighting arrangement, and tuning the guitar. Do not forget to check the acoustics briefly if you have not done so earlier. You need to know how loudly you must play in order to be heard. Remember that you may have to play somewhat louder when the hall is filled with people because they tend to soak up the sound. Now spend a bit of time playing on stage to make yourself comfortable in the hall.

Cold or Moist Hands?

Now that the hall has been set up, it is a good idea to discuss the problem of cold and/or sweaty hands since so many guitarists complain about it. Warm hands are obviously best because they tend to move more easily than cold ones. However, remember that one fine concert player said that he has played some of his best concerts with cold hands! Cold hands are not necessarily a good excuse for not playing well. There are several causes of cold hands: cold environment, lack of warm clothing, poor circulation, and nervous tension (which reduces circulation). You can do something about each of these problems. If it is a cold day, see to it that the concert hall thermostat is turned up high enough. If you think you might be cold at your concert, then put on a long-sleeved undershirt to keep the upper body warm. When the upper body and arms are warm, the hands usually are warm too. Another way to prevent cold hands is to wear gloves until it is time to play. If your circulation is generally poor, regular exercise, a lean diet, and relaxation are helpful.

The chief culprit in the case of cold hands is nervous tension, which generates muscular tension and thus reduced circulation. Mind-settling and deep relaxation techniques reduce nervous tension and alleviate the problem.

Some other hand-warming techniques are:

1. rubbing them together
2. massaging them thoroughly
3. holding them in warm water
4. putting them in your pockets
5. sitting on them
6. shaking them vigorously with loose wrists (fifty to one hundred times)
7. holding the arms and hands straight, but loose, and rotating them like two propellers (twenty-five to fifty times)

You can prevent cold or sweaty hands in several ways. It is important to keep the hands warm, clean, and dry. Then all the fingers will move easily: the left-hand fingers will not slip on the fingerboard, and the right-hand fingers will not stick to the strings. Therefore it is good to wash the hands in warm water and dry them thoroughly before playing. Some players find that a bit of talcum powder on the hands will help keep them dry. In cases of extremely sweaty hands the problem is often one of faulty diet. The player may not be eating well and the body may sweat profusely to rid itself of undesirable waste materials. In any case, during the performance it is good to have a clean handkerchief with you to wipe off your hands, the guitar neck, fingerboard, and strings.

What Do You Do
Just Before You Play?

Now that everything is set up and you have taken care of your hands, there should be some time left for you to just sit quietly and take it easy before you play. Sitting and doing nothing is usually most relaxing, although few are able to be completely still. Twiddling your thumbs or pacing around may make you feel better. There are other solutions. To alleviate nervousness, the pianist Artur Rubinstein often used to play a simple scale or some little melody while he was waiting to go on. If you feel a shade on the nervous side, do not fight it. You might do the Total Relaxation Technique described in Chapter 2 for a few minutes. Or you can close your eyes, take a few deep breaths, and then, for a short time, do the alternate nostril breathing exercise described in Chapter 3. Or simply lie down and rest for a few minutes.

The Moment of Truth

When the time to play comes, just pick up the guitar and walk out confidently with bold steps and upright posture—just as in your dry runs. Be sure to carry the guitar in a dignified manner. Stop to look at the audience. Smile and establish contact with the people. Enjoy being with the audience. Artur Rubinstein said that he liked to play his concerts to his wife or to some beautiful woman in the audience because that would inspire him and make his playing more personal. Now seat yourself in a graceful manner and take time to make yourself comfortable. Be sure to sit up straight and lean forward slightly so that you feel you are in charge of the situation. Check your tuning at this point—but *quietly*. Tuning is just a technical matter and should not obtrude. It can be quite disturbing to hear a player loudly trying to put his guitar in tune. Remember not to fool around too long with tuning or you will lose the attention of your audience. Be brief and business-like about it.

At this time you may want to take a bit of oil from your hair or from the side of your nose to lubricate your right-hand fingertips. For many players, this tactic greatly facilitates the right-hand technique, particularly for fast scales and arpeggios. Needless to say, this process should be done as subtly as possible.

Some performers enjoy saying a few words about the program before starting and/or between pieces. This idea is good if you do not speak too long. It usually has the effect of loosening up the player and warming up the audience. However, it is just fine to come out and play without any talk. Do whatever feels right to you.

Creating a Relaxed Beginning

It is important to give yourself and the audience a few moments to settle down before you play. If the performer is quiet and relaxed before beginning, then the audience will also tend to be quiet. That quietness gives the people a chance to get in tune with each other and the performer. With this quietness, it is easier for everyone to focus together on one thing. Then the uplifting experience of musical entrainment in the audience and performer is more likely to happen.

One way for you to settle down is to take a deep breath before you start. Many guitarists actually hold their breath before and during their playing and become rather tight. So remember to breathe! Then, to further settle your mind and body, you might try Leo Brouwer's approach. In this approach, you close the eyes and let the body relax for about thirty seconds before each piece or group of pieces. During this time, it is good to let your head drop forward slightly so that the neck relaxes and let your arms hang down freely. The right arm should hang naturally over the body of the guitar in such a way that it prevents the instrument from slipping off your lap.

If you do not want to use the Brouwer approach, you can achieve a similar effect by just sitting quietly and relaxing the muscles for about a minute before you play.

The Silence Before the Music

In Chapter 9 we discussed the great significance of silence in the interpretation of a piece. Here it is important to emphasize the value of the silence before beginning a concert. A silence at the beginning of a concert has two important functions: It allows you to relax and clear your mind and it also gives you time to set the atmosphere for the music to come. You can use a part of that silence to hear the first few bars of your piece in your inner ear so that you can establish its feeling and tempo. During the silence, it is also good to set up your fingers on the first notes. The finest artists have a keen appreciation of the power of silence before one begins a musical event. The harpsichordist Wanda Landowska says:

> How should one start to play? One has to concentrate and be entirely ready so that when the first note is struck, it comes as a continuation of a soliloquy already begun. Too often the value and importance of the start in playing is belittled. . . . This silence preceding a phrase . . . acts as a background upon which the motive is sketched and set into relief. [The silences] have a positive value equal to the notes themselves.[3]

It should now be clear that how you begin a concert is far from trivial. It is vital for you to create some silence for a few moments so that everyone can become quiet. The performer should not start until the audience is still. When you allow that silence, you create a certain drama that seizes the attention of the audience. When the audience is clearly focused on you and the music, you will have set the tone for the entire concert to go well.

Focus on the Sound and Inner Meaning

At this point it is worth recalling C.P.E. Bach's words about performing: "A musician cannot move others unless he too is moved." The emotion of the music is a vital part of its inner meaning and must be communicated when you play or the music will not have much impact. It may help to remember and project the excitement that you had about the music when you first started playing it.

While the projection of the emotional character of the music is of great importance, it must be added that, to be a truly fine performer, you must also maintain a certain detachment from your playing. Then your mind will stay clear and you will avoid the danger of losing sight of the musical structure or losing control of your technique at crucial moments. The famous Mozart piano interpreter Paul Badura-Skoda put it very well:

> It may sound a paradox, but the ideal interpretation should fulfill both these conditions. One plays with absolute conviction, yet somewhere inside there is a controlling function that must remain

unmoved; otherwise one's feelings overflow the banks laid down by the intellect and the result is amateurish.[4]

Now, as you start to play, you will find it helpful to use the natural concentration technique (see Chapter 3) to focus in a relaxed way on the main melodic line and the flow of feeling in the music. Do not be concerned about the fingering. You can put your full attention on only one thing at a time, so let the details take care of themselves. If your mind drifts away from the melodic line, bring it back gently. In this focusing process, do not lose sight of the overall picture of the music—beginnings and endings of sections, climactic points, mood changes, and so on. This process of focusing on the line with its emotion and yet retaining the vision of the whole piece will become easier with experience. Eventually you will develop what we described in Chapter 3 as dynamically relaxed concentration. Then the process will be truly easy.

In order to play most effectively and penetratingly, concentrate your energy only on the music and not on anything else. This applies particularly to excess showmanship. Putting on a big show of gestures distracts you and the audience from the inner meaning of the music. As Wanda Landowska puts it: ". . . it is in reducing and simplifying exterior gestures that one can intensify the expression."[5] Thus, while it is perfectly natural to move physically with the music and make some gestures—such as the sweep of the right hand when rolling a chord—it is good to keep them to a minimum. It is imperative to cut out unconscious movements such as loud foot tapping, ungainly scratching, face making, and the like.

Let Nature Do It

Once you have given the piece a strong starting impulse and have established a relaxed focus on the main melodic line, it is good to play with abandon. *Let your playing happen.* Let the natural intelligence of your subconscious mind and your body play the music through you. That does not mean that you should be sloppy, but rather that you should enjoy each musical moment as it comes without anticipating or trying to control things excessively. You have practiced and prepared well, so your subconscious mind and your fingers are thoroughly programmed to play the music. It is important to *allow* them to play beautifully. During the concert there is no need to try to "help them along" by giving all sorts of commands from your conscious mind. It is better to get that part of yourself out of the way and *not to think,* as some of the best players say. Just focus on the sound and feeling and let the fingers play. With

---

[4]Paul and Eva Badura-Skoda, *Interpreting Mozart on the Keyboard,* trans. Leo Black (New York: St. Martin's Press, 1962), pp. 1–2.
[5]Restout, *Landowska on Music,* p. 370.

this approach, effortless playing is most likely; in fact, the music will often seem to play itself.

What About Tightness?

At this point you may ask: "What can I do as an *immediate* help during a performance if I become tense in spite of all my preparation?" The method to use is the body awareness technique described in Chapter 3. First, slow down the tempo of your piece somewhat to quiet yourself down. (Most players speed up instead!) Then send a relaxation signal to wherever you feel tension. If either hand feels tight, just let it loosen up by shaking it during a pause in the music. Right-hand tightness is often caused by excess pressure of the right forearm on the guitar. If that is the case, relax that pressure. If you feel generally tight, you may discover that you have been holding your breath. The treatment is obvious! Take a deep breath. If the tension is very great, then walk off stage between pieces and do a relaxation technique for a minute or two.

Dealing with Mistakes

What about technical mistakes? Obviously the best thing is not to make any and to hold the idea that it is not necessary to make them. However, if you still have some imperfections in your playing or your concentration, some mistakes may pop up. How can you deal with them? The crucial point is your attitude toward them. If you make some mistakes, just let them go and keep on playing. If you concentrate on *rhythmic continuity and musical expression* the mistakes will hardly be noticed and they will not absorb much of your energy. But, if you get mad at yourself and make a face every time you make a mistake, you will only waste energy, get more tense, and alienate your audience. Remember that mistakes are in the past very quickly and every moment is a fresh opportunity to play well. Even the best concert artists make mistakes, but there is nothing left to do but go ahead and play the rest of the music beautifully as if the mistakes were never made. Whatever happens, keep your attention on the inner meaning of the music, not on the mistakes. A good point to remember is that most people want to see you doing well. People come to enjoy the overall flow and feeling of the music, not to count your mistakes.

If you play from memory, as most guitar soloists do, you naturally want to forget nothing. However, sometimes your concentration may flag or you may draw a blank for a moment. At those points it is best just to go on to the next familiar landmark in the music as if nothing has happened. If you have too many memory slips and the rhythmic flow of the piece is interrupted too much, then it may be best to start over again. If you have started over once or twice and still run into a memory block, then it is usually best just to laugh, drop that piece, and go on to the next one. Do not feel depressed about occasional memory problems since there is no concert artist who has not had them at various times in his career. Of course these things should not happen too often or you may have to look for other work! In any case, seek out ways to improve your concentration and memory.

The two main lessons about mistakes are (1) not to be attached to them while playing, and (2) to learn from them after the recital.

Intermission

Take advantage of the opportunity to unwind at the intermission. It is best to avoid talking much at this time except possibly to your teacher or coach who might have some suggestions on improving the second half of the concert. It is good just to get a drink of water and sit quietly for a few minutes. If you feel a bit nervous, you might do one of the relaxation techniques. When you go out to play the second half, remember to present yourself and play with the same energy with which you started the first half. Do not let the concert "sag" after the intermission.

Ending Graciously

When you have finished your last piece, no matter what your performance was like, stand up straight, look at the audience, smile, bow, and enjoy their applause. Let go of what you did when you were playing. Leave the audience with the feeling that you enjoyed yourself even though there may have been some imperfect moments.

The worst thing to do is to stalk off in self-disgust with a scowl on your face. That merely reinforces any negativity you might have and causes your listeners to leave with a sour taste in their mouths. One young guitarist at a master class recital walked off after his performance with obvious self-hatred because he made some mistakes. He did not even look at the audience and thus left an unpleasant feeling in the room. In strong contrast to the attitude of the first player was the way another young player handled his performance problems. The second player also made mistakes. He had a memory lapse and even started his piece over several times. He finally realized that he could not finish, so he stopped playing and just laughed! He stood up, smiled at the audience, took a nice bow, and walked off. Since he did not get angry with himself, everyone felt fine. In fact, everyone laughed with him, since many of them were guitarists and understood his difficulty. The second player's attitude of not being overshadowed by mistakes is definitely the better one.

Now back to the normal exit: After you have finished with your bow, do not linger too long before going off stage or the impression will not be one of modesty. If the audience calls you back, fine. It is better to come out again

than to overstay your welcome. If it seems appropriate, play one or more en-
cores.

When the applause is over, enjoy meeting your well-wishers and thank
them for coming. It is definitely not very gracious to apologize for your mistakes. Talk such things over later with your teacher, coach, or close friends.
Right after the concert it is better to have a good time seeing people and feeling the harmony you have generated with your music.

LEARNING FROM YOUR PERFORMANCE

Appraise Your Concert

Now that your concert has passed into the vaults of memory, it is a good idea
to appraise objectively how you played and see what can be improved for the
future. If the performance was not so good, then you will have a number of
things to work on—technical, musical, or personal matters or all three. What
is crucial is that you detach yourself from any negative feelings about your
concert and proceed to work on specific improvements. Do not waste your
time and energy feeling depressed about your mistakes. It is better just to
start working on your weak spots *now*.

Inner Growth and Inner Musical Meaning

Even if you played very well and feel quite good about it, there is always one
thing that can be perfected: your ability to bring out the inner meaning of the
music. You can improve in that area by doing whatever enhances your own
personal development and expands your awareness. Much of that simply
takes time. That means living with and getting familiar with yourself, your
music, your guitar, and your concerts. But your inner growth can also be ac-
celerated by practicing the self-development techniques presented in Chapter
2. These techniques help all aspects of your guitar playing because they expand the whole basis of yourself—your consciousness.

More Feedback

In order to make a really good appraisal of your performance, you should obtain feedback in various forms, just as you did for your practice concerts.
Again the tape recorder is a valuable tool that should not be neglected. Tape
record your concert, listen to the tape with care, and learn from it. Be sure to
get live opinions about your performance soon after the concert while memo-
ries are fresh. People can give you their impressions about intangibles that do

not come out in tape recordings. They can tell you if your stage presence was good and whether or not you appeared to be really enjoying yourself when you played. They can give you valuable opinions about the way you projected the style and inner message of the various pieces you played—which ones seemed natural and convincing, which ones not. Teacher and friends can also point out some of the technical strong and weak points that you might miss even if you listen to a tape of yourself.

Still Better Next Time

After you have collected all the feedback, use it! Start to work on those technical, personal, and musical points that will perfect you and your playing. Work on them in a quiet, deliberate way so that you create a good atmosphere in connection with the guitar. Remember to have a humble, open attitude that your playing can always be better, that you can serve the music better. When you have that open attitude, you will find that music will always be intensely interesting since you will be making new discoveries—a way of improving your tone, new ways of interpreting a piece or passage, a new emotional depth in Bach, or a spiritual experience in performing.

SUMMING UP

We have discussed recitals in some detail in this chapter. The observations and suggestions made should be useful to both amateur and professional players. Naturally there is much more that could be said about classical guitar performance, particularly for those who want to know how to make a career of it. However, such a discussion would provide enough material for another book. Moreover, others have already written excellent articles on guitar performance and concert careers.[6]

In any case, whether you are an amateur or a professional, playing the guitar for others can and should be an uplifting occasion. It can and should leave everyone better off than before they heard you play the music. That is the essence of performing. Your guitar playing has the capacity to help make the world a better place to live in, so it should be approached as a serious social function. Be sure to prepare yourself well in all ways before you perform. Be simple, natural, and direct when you play. Then you will be able to produce the marvelous musical effect of unifying and harmonizing yourself

---

[6]For more on concert guitar careers, see Alan Kozinn, "Classical Careers," *Guitar Player* 15, no. 9 (September 1981), 68.

and all the different people who hear you. Then you will fulfill the exalted exhortation in the ancient *Rig Veda* of India:

> *United be your purpose, harmonious be your*
> *feelings, collected be your mind, in the same way*
> *as all the various aspects of the universe exist in*
> *togetherness, wholeness.*[7]

Rig Veda X, 191, 2–4

---

[7]Excerpt from the last verse of the *Rig Veda*, trans. Maharishi Mahesh Yogi.

11.

Ensemble Playing and Other Topics

enjoy playing with others

This chapter touches on several subjects that will be of interest to the guitarist who wants to have a more complete knowledge of his instrument, including: ensemble playing, sight reading, repertoire, and improvisation.

ENSEMBLE PLAYING

Ensemble playing, that is, playing together with other musicians, is very good for the guitar soloist for several reasons. Ensemble playing is excellent training for your ear and for your overall musical sensitivity. For one thing, you learn to tune the guitar very carefully to the other instruments in the ensemble. Group playing also strengthens your rhythmic sense, because you cannot really play in a group without learning how to keep in time with the other players. You also learn the importance of balancing the different parts in a piece of music. In most places there is a musical hierarchy in which the various parts have different levels of prominence and function. Typically, at any given time only one part—usually the principal melodic line—is prominent and the other parts are there to accompany it. In good ensemble pieces, there is an enjoyable give and take between the parts, where one player has the principal part for a while and then it passes to another player. Each player must learn to listen closely to the other players' parts so that he can tell when to be in the foreground and when to be discreetly in the background. In short, the player in an ensemble must learn to relate his part to the whole musical structure in a harmonious way.

The skills developed in ensemble playing can be directly useful in solo pieces. The guitarist who has done ensemble work will tend to be more careful about tuning the guitar and keeping a steady rhythm. He will also be more conscious of the fact that most guitar solos have several parts that need to be balanced properly. He will realize that some parts should be in the foreground and others in the background. And he will be aware that the balance often changes and that an emphasized part may sometimes have to take a subordinate role. In sum, the soloist with ensemble experience will understand that all the parts of a solo piece must work together in a harmonious whole just as in an ensemble piece.

Ensemble playing is a good introduction to performing because you do not have to play by yourself. It is comforting to know that someone else is up there with you to share the responsibility of playing. It is good experience and just plain fun to play in any kind of ensemble that is available. Duets, trios, and quartets for guitars are very enjoyable. The repertoire for duets is quite large; that for trios and quartets is smaller but growing in quantity and quality. There is also a substantial quantity of music for guitar with voice and guitar with various other instruments. Some of this ensemble music is of high quality and some of it is just enjoyable to sight-read on a Sunday afternoon. The *Guitar Music Index* lists many ensemble pieces that are currently available.[1] If you cannot find enough ensemble music that you like, you might transcribe something that was written for other instruments. For example, there are a number of Debussy piano pieces that have yet to be transcribed that may fit well on two guitars. You will no doubt find numerous other pieces that transcribe well for a guitar ensemble.

Playing the guitar with other musicians is one of the most enjoyable activities in music. When things go well, there is something special that happens because you enter into perfect rhythm with the other players. The resulting enjoyment is greater than what you would have as an individual. It is much like the enjoyment of playing for a large number of people. The phenomenon of rhythm entrainment takes place in the group and the performance tends to go effortlessly. Everyone in the ensemble is moving as a unit to the same beat.

SIGHT-READING

Being able to read music well is certainly not all there is to being a good musician, but for serious classical guitarists it is an almost indispensable skill. Not all the great players are great readers, but they all have some proficiency in that area.

There are a number of reasons why it is useful to be a good sight-reader. First, it is simply a delight to have access to the rich literature of the guitar. You can buy or borrow just about any piece you want and play it. It will also help you become a *literate* musician who is really familiar with the music for his instrument. You can have the pleasure of playing through little-known

---

[1]The *Guitar Music Index* is published by Galliard Press, 1229 Waimanu Street, Honolulu, Hawaii 96814.

music and possibly finding some gems that no one else plays. Another great advantage of reading well is that you are able to learn pieces and discover good fingerings for them much more quickly because you do not have to struggle with the basic problem of finding the notes. Yet another consideration is that, if you want to be a professional musician, you may find that there are many jobs that require reading skill, such as playing in a recording studio. Finally, one of the best reasons to sight-read well is that it allows you to enjoy playing together with other musicians in ensembles.

There are many ways to improve your reading ability. An excellent approach is to simply go out and buy a large stack of pieces that you like—including complex pieces—and play through them. If your financial situation is not so strong, there are many inexpensive guitar anthologies for sight-reading.[2] You will find that it is very motivating to read through and become familiar with many pieces. It will not be boring. You might want to play through the easier pieces first in order to become more at home on the fingerboard. Then tackle the tougher ones. Do not be discouraged if you become tangled in black dots. Just take it a bit at a time and learn the notes as you go. The way to sight-read is to do it *every day* for a short time—about twenty minutes or so. It will not be long before you are going through many pieces with ease.

When you first learn to read or are going through a complex piece for the first time, it is best not to worry about the rhythm too much. Just find the notes in your own time. However, as soon as you have had some reading experience, you should develop the ability to *keep the rhythm going* and not stop every other beat for your mistakes. If you make a mistake, forget it and keep playing in rhythm. This ability to keep going—no matter what—is of vital importance for sight-reading, both for your solo playing and for playing in an ensemble. In that way, the rhythmic element of the music is made clear. To ensure that you keep to the beat, it is very helpful to practice sight-reading at least part of the time with the metronome. You can set it for whatever speed or subdivision of the beat you want. Start out very slowly so that the reading does not make you nervous and you can be reasonably accurate. If beating quarter notes is too fast, have the metronome beat the eighth notes. The metronome will carry you along and remind you where the beat is. Remember that, when you are reading, the important thing is to keep the rhythm going and not worry too much about making mistakes. Greater accuracy will come with time.

Consistent with the idea of "mind over fingers" that we have discussed earlier in the book, your goal in sight-reading should be to read for musical ideas (motives, phrases, periods, sections, overall structure, melodic shapes, emotional feelings), and not play unrelated individual notes. For that reason,

---

[2]The anthologies *The Renaissance Guitar, The Baroque Guitar,* and *The Classical Guitar,* edited by Frederick Noad (New York: Ariel Music Publications, 1974, 1976) are very good. There are numerous other inexpensive anthologies available.

it is good—even if you are a beginner—to look through the pieces you want to sight-read before you play. This process is virtually the same as the one we used in the twelve steps of studying a piece in Chapter 9. Look at the key signature, the tempo markings, the meter, and the total shape of the piece and determine, as much as possible, the phrasing you might want to use. That means you should check to see where the musical ideas or phrases begin and end; where their high and low points are. When you actually read the piece, use the speed-reading technique of attempting to take in at least a subphrase or a phrase at a time instead of single notes. That way you will have the joy of making real music. It is much like the pleasure of reading for ideas in a book, rather than just reading a bunch of individual words.

A good aid to improving your sight-reading is either to make or buy some flash cards for each note on the fingerboard.[3] Learning with flash cards is easy because you focus on just one note at a time. Each flash card should have a note in staff notation on one side and its name and location (or locations) on the other. You might include the string number on the note side of the card so that each card would refer to only one location of each note. To make the cards more graphic on the location side, you might include a diagram of the fingerboard with a dot on it to show where the note is.

Sight-reading is also made much easier if you have some knowledge of chords all over the fingerboard. There are numerous books on guitar chords and harmony that will give you the basic information on this subject. (See the bibliography for suggested titles.) You can also make or buy flash cards to learn chords in the same way as you can with individual notes.

If you like step-by-step note learning, you might find it best to go through one of the progressive method books now on the market. These methods will take you through the notes a few at a time in a painless way.[4]

REPERTOIRE

Repertoire has already been discussed to some extent in Chapters 9 and 10. One idea is worth repeating here: Play music you like. That is the only way you can enjoy yourself and give a convincing performance. However, play at least some unfamiliar music so that your musical horizons are not too restricted. Another point of great importance is that it is better to play a few pieces well than to play many badly. Do not be in a great rush to add new

---

[3]Guitar flash cards are available from *Guitar Notes*, P.O. Box 70, La Jolla, CA 92037.

[4]Some of the better-known modern methods in English are: *Solo Guitar Playing*, vols. I and II, by Frederick Noad (New York: Schirmer Books, 1976, 1977); *The Christopher Parkening Guitar Method*, vol. I, by Christopher Parkening (Chicago: Antigua Casa Sherry-Brener), 1972; and *Classic Guitar Technique*, vols. I and II, by Aaron Shearer (New York: Franco Colombo, Inc., 1963).

pieces to the ones you already play. Learn new pieces thoroughly before airing them in public. Frequent reviewing and perfecting of old pieces is also an important part of working on your repertoire.

Several catalogs of guitar music are presently available that can serve as repertoire information sources for the guitarist. Some of the catalogs, which are quite good, are put out periodically by various guitar stores to advertise their sheet music. The *Guitar Music Index* that we mentioned earlier lists all the guitar music available at the time of publication. At present, the *Index* is probably the best source of information for both solo and ensemble music for guitar. It includes information on composers, titles of pieces, publishers and publishers' agents, and the level of difficulty of each piece.

One area of repertoire development that guitarists often neglect is making sure that the editions they play are of high quality. Even in the case of original music written for the guitar there may be several editions available and the guitarist must make a choice. The best course is to find the original manuscript or the earliest possible edition of the music because that will usually be most accurate and closest to the intentions of the composer. Sometimes the interested guitarist may have to do a fair amount of detective work to uncover the best edition of a piece.

With respect to music written originally for the guitar, it is fortunate for the guitarist that there are now a number of good scholarly editions available and more are in the works. Now, for example, there is an excellent edition of the complete guitar works of Fernando Sor by the scholar Brian Jeffery.[5] Jeffery's edition contains the earliest known versions of Sor's works. There are also good editions of some of Giuliani's music by Thomas Heck.[6] In the realm of baroque guitar music, Robert Strizich has put out a fine scholarly edition of the complete guitar music of Robert de Visée.[7] Other good editions of baroque guitar music will be or are now available. At the present time there are also a good number of facsimile editions of various baroque and classical works for the guitarist who wants to look at the originals. Frederick Noad, for example, has put out collections of early editions of Carcassi, Giuliani, and Sor.[8]

In the case of guitar transcriptions, if you want to know what you are doing, check the transcription you are using against the original music. Make sure that the transcriber has remained faithful to the composer's idea. Even better, if you have the musical skills, is to make your own transcriptions. The best way to start doing this is to study a good transcriber's work very carefully and see what makes a transcription work. There are many good transcriptions

[5]Fernando Sor, *Complete Works for Guitar*, ed. Brian Jeffery (New York: Shattinger International Music Corp., 1977).

[6]Mauro Giuliani, *Oeuvres Choisies Pour Guitare*, ed. Thomas Heck (Paris: Heugel, 1973).

[7]Robert de Visée, *Oeuvres Completes Pour Guitare*, ed. Robert Strizich (Paris: Heugel, 1969).

[8]These three collections, edited by Frederick Noad, are published by Shattinger International Music Corp. (1976).

available by Andrés Segovia, Michael Lorimer, Oscar Ghiglia, José Tomás, John Williams, Julian Bream, Manuel Barrueco, and others. However, after you have made some transcriptions of your own, you may find that you are your favorite transcriber.

Familiarity with the guitar repertoire should be one of the serious guitarist's main concerns. That can be partially accomplished by collecting music and sight-reading through it as has been suggested, but it is also invaluable to establish a good private collection of guitar recordings—or at least take advantage of the recordings at local libraries. It is a good way of finding out what music you want to study. Listening to recordings of music on guitar-related instruments such as harpsichord and lute is also edifying.

One area of guitar repertoire that still has much potential is the lute and baroque guitar literature in tablature notation. The number of tablature pieces that can be played on the guitar without modification or with minimal arranging is enormous. Thus, for the early music enthusiast, it is essential to learn how to read tablature.[9] A good way of learning tablature—which is quite simple—is to find editions of tablature pieces which have both music and tablature and see how it works. Every kind of tablature is a bit different, but the basic idea of showing the player where to put his fingers by use of simple diagrams remains the same.

For information about the repertoire, it is good to consult guitar history books as well as some of the better Ph.D. theses on various guitar composers. Turnbull's *The Guitar from the Renaissance to the Present Day* is a good short history.[10] Frederic Grunfeld's *The Art and Times of the Guitar* is another good work, although it is short on musical examples.[11] The book on Sor's life by Brian Jeffery is of great interest, especially because it has a complete catalogue of Sor's works.[12] Among the Ph.D. theses, Thomas Heck wrote a good one on Giuliani that includes a catalog of Giuliani's works.[13] Richard Pinnell also wrote a very comprehensive thesis on the famed baroque guitarist Francesco Corbetta.[14]

---

[9]A general article on tablature appears in *The New Grove Dictionary of Music and Musicians,* ed. Stanley Sadie (London: Macmillan, 1980). James Tyler's book, *The Early Guitar* (London: Oxford University Press, 1980) is a good source of information about baroque guitar music and its tablature.

[10]Harvey Turnbull, *The Guitar from the Renaissance to the Present Day* (New York: Charles Scribner's Sons, 1974).

[11]Frederic Grunfeld, *The Art and Times of the Guitar* (New York: Macmillan and Co., 1969).

[12]Brian Jeffery, *Fernando Sor: Composer and Guitarist* (London: Tecla Editions, 1977).

[13]Thomas Heck, "The Birth of the Classic Guitar and Its Cultivation in Vienna, Reflected in the Career and Compositions of Mauro Giuliani" (Ph.D. Dissertation, Yale University, 1970), published by University Microfilms, Ann Arbor, Michigan. Copyright 1970.

[14]Richard Pinnell, "The Role of Francesco Corbetta (1615–1681) in the History of Music for Baroque Guitar, Including a Transcription of his Complete Works" (Ph.D. Dissertation, University of California, Los Angeles, 1976), published by University Microfilms, Ann Arbor, Michigan. Copyright 1976.

For more information about guitar repertoire and interpretation, there are several valuable periodicals. Three prominent ones are: *The Soundboard, Guitar Review,* and *Guitar and Lute.*[15]

IMPROVISATION

Classical guitarists are often overly attached to the idea of playing their music exactly according to the notes. As a result, their interpretations sound somewhat wooden and uninspired. They are playing "all of the notes and none of the music," as the saying goes. Although it is certainly important to respect the notes, one must always be aware of the music that is *between the notes.* One of the reasons for the rigidity among classical players is that they have never attempted to improvise and "let it happen." Making music spontaneously is a wonderful way to loosen up one's attitude toward performing and interpreting other people's music. In fact, the best classical performances of guitarists playing other people's music have a spontaneous, improvised quality about them, just as if the music had been composed on the spot. This gives the impression of really recreating the spirit of the music—all the emotions come out that could not possibly be included on the printed page.

The classical player can profit a great deal by learning at least a little about improvisation and putting it into practice. A good way to start is to play by ear an easy piece that you know. When you can do that, make up some simple variations on the piece. Another way of improvising is to play some simple chord changes into a tape recorder, play back the tape, and improvise some melodies that fit with those chords. Another perhaps more enjoyable way of doing the same thing is to have a guitar-playing friend play the chords while you create the melody lines. If you do not know where to start with improvisation, have someone show you a few ways of doing it.

A more subtle approach to improvisation is to spend some time sitting quietly with eyes closed in a receptive state and listen for the music that goes through your head. You may hear some familiar memorized tunes but you also may hear music that you have not heard anywhere else. If you like something you hear inside, pick up your guitar and see if you can play it and improvise on it. The deep, quiet levels of the mind are the source areas of many original musical ideas including the most profound inspirations of the great composers and improvisers.

Improvisation is a good preparation for playing in the styles of the Ren-

---

[15]*The Soundboard* is published quarterly by the Guitar Foundation of America, Box 5311, Garden Grove, CA 92645; *Guitar Review* is published irregularly by The Society of the Classic Guitar, 409 East 50th St., New York, NY 10022; and *Guitar and Lute* is published quarterly by Galliard Press, 1229 Waimanu St., Honolulu, Hawaii 96814.

aissance and the Baroque. In those times the performer improvised *as a matter of course*. If he did not he was considered "a very dull dog," as musicologist Thurston Dart once said. Of course it is necessary to develop a feeling for what kind of improvisation is appropriate for each type of early music. For that, Robert Donington's books *The Performer's Guide to Baroque Music* and *The Interpretation of Early Music* are invaluable.[16] There are also numerous articles in scholarly publications such as the *Lute Society Journal*[17] that give the early music enthusiast some ground to stand on.

Because musical performance is a mixture of order and chaos, discipline and freedom, it is good for the classical guitarist to make sure that he knows something about both aspects. He should not be too rigid in his approach to the music. Improvisation helps to remedy that. Improvisation not only gives you a sense of freedom, but also sharpens your ear. It puts you in the place of a composer and gives you the feeling of how composers come up with the ideas that make up the pieces you play. Best of all, with a little practice, it can be a very satisfying creative experience in itself and may lead you into the beautiful realm of composition.

SUMMARY

All of the knowledge and skills described in this chapter are directly or indirectly of use to the guitarist who wants to master his instrument. They broaden the vision of the player and help him see how the guitar fits into the mainstream of music. The playing of ensemble music is particularly valuable because it not only makes a better musician of the guitarist but also teaches him how to harmonize his personality with others. That is not a trivial skill because it will make the guitarist's life much better and more musical. Then he will have a good effect on everyone with whom he comes in contact.

[16]Robert Donington, *The Performer's Guide to Baroque Music* (London: Faber and Faber, 1973) and *The Interpretation of Early Music, New Version* (London: Faber and Faber, 1974).

[17]The *Journal of the Lute Society of America* is published annually by the Lute Society. Inquiries may be directed to Beedle White, 6 Lewis St., Lexington, VA 24450. Back issues can sometimes be found in university libraries.

12.

From the Guitar to the Self

> . . . music is a vessel, a vehicle which people can
> get tuned in to and discover their inner selves,
> discover what they have forgotten about
> themselves.

Karl-Heinz Stockhausen, *Spiritual Dimensions*

> Just as grains of sand take on orderly
> symmetrical patterns when laid on a flat
> vibrating surface, so, it seems to me, do the
> vibrations of music coordinate and reorder into
> harmonious symmetrical patterns all the
> elements of a human being's thoughts, emotions
> and physical make-up.

Yehudi Menuhin, *Violin and Viola*

THE FUNCTION OF MUSIC

Ancient Views

The ancient Greeks regarded the lyre, an early relative of the guitar, as a secret symbol of the human being.[1] The body of the lyre was supposed to represent the human form, the strings were said to be the nerves, and the musician was considered to be the spirit. In this analogy, if the human body and nervous system are in good condition, like a well-tuned lyre, then the spirit within will create harmony and fulfillment for the individual, but if the body and nervous system are in poor condition, like an untuned lyre, then whatever the spirit within tries to create comes out as discord and suffering for the individual. This view of the body as an instrument makes sense because modern physics tells us that all physical systems—gross matter, molecules, atoms, and subatomic particles—are vibrating at various frequencies. Since the brain and body are made up of such vibrating physical systems, it is reasonable to say that they can be in or out of tune like musical instruments. In fact, we use musical terms in our everyday speech that convey just that idea. "The relationship started off on a good note" and "She is really in tune with everyone" are common expressions. We are probably attracted to the guitar because it is a secret symbol of the musical nature of our minds and bodies. Perhaps unconsciously we want to learn how to tune and play the guitar well because somehow that will help us to "tune" and "play" ourselves well.

The Greek comparison of the human body to a musical instrument is complemented by their idea about the great power of music to affect human life for good or evil. The philosopher Pythagoras held that certain kinds of music played on the lyre could purify the soul of "irrational influences." He

[1]Manly P. Hall, *The Secret Teachings of All Ages* (Los Angeles: The Philosophical Research Society, 1972), pp. 81–83.

was said to be able to soothe emotional upsets such as rage and to cure various diseases by the playing of special pieces of music.[2] Like Pythagoras, Plato felt that music could influence people very strongly. In the *Timaeus* he says:

> . . . music too, in so far as it uses audible sound, was bestowed on us for the sake of harmony. And harmony, which has motions akin to the revolutions of the Soul within us, was given by the Muses to him who makes intelligent use of the arts, not as an aid to irrational pleasure, as is now supposed, but as an auxiliary to the inner revolution of the Soul, when it has lost its harmony, to assist in restoring it to order and concord with itself.[3]

Plato considered music of the utmost importance in education and felt that the kind of music to which people are exposed has a definite bearing on their character and actions. He believed that music ultimately has an effect on the quality of life of an entire nation. His idea was that people should be exposed to music that ennobles the mind rather than that which only gives pleasure to the senses. When the proper music is heard or played repeatedly, then that influence generates harmony and order in the individual, thus preparing him for the highest levels of personal and philosophical development. If improper music is heard or played over a period of time, it can actually cause a negative change in character. Other Greek and Oriental philosophers had similar views about the power of music.

Modern Views

A number of modern musicians, such as the violinist Yehudi Menuhin and composers Cyril Scott, Karl-Heinz Stockhausen, and Peter Hamel, agree with the ancient Greek notion that music has great power to affect human life.[4] These men believe that music can be used as a way of self-development because of its healing, purifying, and harmonizing properties. In this belief, not only can music help to cure problems, but it also can open up human

---

[2]Peter Hamel, *Through Music to the Self* (Boulder, Colo.: Shambhala Publications, 1978), p. 165.

[3]Plato, *Timaeus*, trans. R. G. Bury, Loeb Classical Library, vol. VII (Cambridge: Harvard University Press, 1961), p. 109.

[4]Yehudi Menuhin, *Violin and Viola* (New York: Schirmer Books, 1976), p. 21; Cyril Scott, *Music: Its Secret Influence Throughout the Ages* (New York: Samuel Weiser, 1958), p. 38ff; Karl-Heinz Stockhausen, "Spiritual Dimensions," *Music and Musicians* (May 1971), 33–34; Hamel, *Through Music to the Self*, pp. 1–4, 207–08; see also Ravi Shankar, *My Music, My Life* (New York: Simon & Schuster, 1968), p. 17. Shankar describes the exalted view that one can find the Creator through the study of music.

awareness to new and higher levels. The Japanese violinist and teacher Shinichi Suzuki points out the consciousness-raising factor in music:

> Bach, Mozart, Beethoven . . . live clearly and palpably in their music, and speak forcefully to us, refining us, and awakening in us the highest joy and emotion.[5]

What philosophers and musicians say about the strong influence of music on the human being is supported by personal experiences and a number of scientific studies. Not everyone will agree about the extent of the influence of music, but most will admit that music does have clearly noticeable effects on the psychology, physiology, and social life of human beings. Most people seem to use and even *need* music in their lives for various reasons. On the individual level, music is used for waking up, for going to sleep, for working, for dancing, for relaxation, for love, and for personal development. On the commercial level, music is deliberately utilized to induce people to buy more goods in stores or produce more goods in the workplace. On the governmental level, music is introduced to arouse patriotic fervor and even to prepare men for war. Each of these forms of music has its own characteristic effects— some energizing, some soothing, some sentimental, and some spiritually uplifting. Everyone is affected by music to some extent. There are many accounts of people who say that music has affected them so much that it has actually transformed their lives—often in a spiritual way. This kind of experience often happens while playing or listening to a particular piece of music by a particular composer. Certain pieces by J. S. Bach, for example, are said to bring about these spiritual transformations.

There have not been many scientific studies on the effects of music on people, but the ones that have been done suggest that the effects are significant. Research in England and the United States has shown that, in subjects listening to certain pieces of classical music, brain waves were produced in the alpha frequency range. This effect generally indicates a quiet, harmonious state of mind and body.[6] The subjects confirmed what the brain waves showed and said that the music made them feel relaxed. Other research from Europe has shown that either playing or listening to music of various kinds produces good therapeutic results for drug addiction, stuttering, schizophrenia, and other psychophysical problems.[7]

---

[5]From Shinichi Suzuki, *Nurtured By Love* (Smithtown, N.Y.: Exposition Press, 1969), p. 96. © Shinichi Suzuki. Reprinted by permission of Exposition Press, Inc., Smithtown, New York.

[6]Research presented on the *Nova* TV program called "Meditation and the Mind," produced by the BBC and WGBH in 1976.

[7]Hamel, *Through Music to the Self,* p. 166ff.

THE GUITAR AND PERSONAL DEVELOPMENT

The Way of the Guitar

The considerable power of music to heal, harmonize, and develop yourself can be experienced very well through the study of the guitar, a highly personal and multi-leveled instrument. However, when you first start to play the instrument, you usually do not think of it as a way of self-discovery. That aspect is hidden behind the veil of the external characteristics of the guitar. Normally you begin to play the guitar in innocence, so to speak. You simply love its sound and must play it. As you progress in your study, you start to realize, perhaps just dimly at first, that there is much more to the guitar than you suspected. You realize that in order to play well, not only do you have to master the external physical aspect of playing it, but you need to develop certain internal mental abilities such as concentration and remaining calm under pressure. Thus playing the guitar is not just a matter of learning notes and strokes, but also a matter of developing yourself personally, of "tuning up" your mind and body. In fact, the guitar and your personal development are so intimately interwoven that, without personal evolution, it is difficult to make progress on the guitar.

Sooner or later most guitarists give some thought to self-development, but often do not know what to do about it. There is a lack of emphasis on such things in the usual learning process. It is assumed that self-development either happens or it does not. However, the truth of the matter is that those personal abilities that will help you with your guitar playing can be consciously developed to a remarkable degree with the natural techniques described in previous chapters of this book.

Realizing Your Potential
with the Natural Approach

Many people start off playing the guitar without realizing the enormous potential of their minds and bodies. They usually have much too low an estimation of themselves. Students imagine that they have all sorts of limitations. They think that they will have difficulties learning to play. They think they will always be nervous and will never have the courage to play music for other people. However, if they use the natural approach, they will surpass these supposed limitations much more quickly than they ever thought possible. It is important for guitar students to realize that there is a very capable player within them who is just waiting to be let out. The ability to play is always there and it simply must be uncovered. The most interesting part of learning to play the guitar naturally is that its benefits start to spill over into other areas of life. If, for example, you have learned to play well for groups of people, either as an amateur or professional, you will tend to be more confident in other activities such as meeting and dealing with people or making speeches.

Since the study of the guitar is so closely bound up with your personal life, it is good to view the guitar as a means of self-development right from the beginning. What you learn from the guitar you can apply immediately to your personal life. The fundamental principle of the natural approach to the guitar—which also applies in everyday life—is to cooperate with nature rather than to fight it. In other words, let nature support your guitar playing and your daily activities. As we have discovered, one of the basic laws of nature is the principle of least action or "do less, accomplish more." Thus, if you use the minimum pressure necessary for the left-hand fingers to sound the notes on the guitar, then playing becomes relatively much easier. In the same way, if you do not grip the steering wheel of your car any more tightly than necessary, driving tends to become almost effortless.

All of the principles of natural guitar playing have implications for personal growth. If you apply the principle of increasing mind/body awareness to the guitar, it leads, among other things, to the realization that learning and playing are best if you simply focus in a nonattached way on what you are doing in the present moment rather than distract yourself with excessive self-criticism. That same insight can help you learn a new skill for your job more quickly or help you score better on a test at school. Applying the principle of dynamic relaxation to the guitar leads you to a balanced sitting position and a balance between playing and relaxing that makes playing much easier. The same principle can help you discover the value of balance in all aspects of your life. For example, if you have a balanced body posture and a balance between activity and rest, you will be healthier and more alert. The principle of "mind over fingers" and the technique of visualization can help the guitarist with everything from discovering the expression of a phrase to rehearsing mentally for a recital. Visualization has many practical applications in other areas of life. Golfers and tennis players use visualization very successfully to improve their playing and businessmen use the technique for practicing their sales presentations. Visualization can also be used to come up with creative solutions to problems of all kinds. In these examples, you can see a few of the ways in which the natural principles of guitar playing can be applied in daily life. You will no doubt find many other practical applications.

LOCATING THE BIG SELF

The Big and Small Selves

In the process of personal evolution through the study of the guitar the most interesting question is "What is the goal of this process?" At first, the guitarist may think in terms of limited goals such as being able to play a certain piece or being able to perform in front of an audience. To be sure, when these things are accomplished, the player will definitely feel some fulfillment. However, such experiences, satisfying as they may be, are apparently not the final goals because there is always a desire to play more difficult pieces or play for a larger audience or become better known. In short, once any limited goals are achieved, bigger goals replace them. The natural human desire is always for more. Where does this end? Apparently the process is not complete until infinite satisfaction is achieved. And it seems that such satisfaction cannot be found in the limited external world, but can only be located deep within ourselves.

The external world of limited goals and limited fulfillment is the world of what is often called the "conscious I" or "small self." It is called small because it tends to identify itself with the active, finite, ever-changing aspects of the body and mind. The small self says, "I am my body," "I am well-to-do (or poor)," "I am a good (or bad) guitarist." There is nothing wrong with having this limited part of ourselves because we need some boundaries and limitations to channel the flow of our energy in a concrete way. The discipline of studying the guitar, for example, is a set of boundaries to direct our energy and desire for self-expression in a specific way. Thus some boundaries or "rules" are good, but are they everything? Does operation only within the boundaries bring complete fulfillment?

The guitarist who studies himself and his playing with keen awareness will discover that there is something more than just the external activity and boundaries of the small self. The experience that is usually most revealing to the player is becoming aware of the silence, relaxation, and freedom between the notes and between the movements of the fingers. When the player practices the Play–Relax technique, becomes aware of the spaces or "junctures" in his interpretations (see Chapter 9, "The Meaning of Silence"), and realizes the possibilities for quietness, even in the dynamic act of performance, then he has taken a large step on the path of personal discovery. He realizes there is a silent but powerful counterpart to the active small self.

For both personal and musical progress, it is vital that we do not lose sight of the silent part of ourselves. We need to have a balance between the active and silent parts. The silent aspect of ourselves is often called the "big Self," although it has many other names. It does not really matter what it is called because the full experience of it cannot be captured in words. It is that subtle, hidden area of ourselves of which we are usually unaware because we mask it with the busy activities of daily life. The big Self is often described as the silent, unchanging basis of the individual's existence that can be found deep within. It is described as an unlimited source of creativity, intelligence, and happiness. This may sound very abstract and unreal but modern physics has discovered a striking parallel to this notion in the vacuum state of quantum field theory. According to that theory, the vacuum state of the quantum field is the silent, underlying source of all physical phenomena in the universe. It is a field of infinite potential energy. Fundamental particles arise from it and dissolve back into it in a continuous process of creation and destruction. The big Self seems to be analogous to the vacuum state described in physics—but on a personal level.

The reality of the big Self need not be taken on authority. To start to experience that hidden part of ourselves, all that is necessary is to become aware of the spaces between your activities. To get to know that quiet but powerful part of yourself in greater depth, you can spend some time in silence every day using a good mind-settling technique. When you experience deep quietness, you will find that it does not dull the mind or make you listless. Quite the contrary, the time spent in silence "doing nothing" is time well spent in terms of activity. In the deep rest that is experienced, you let go of stress and gain energy and creativity from contact with that unbounded inner part of yourself. Then you have more resources when you play the guitar or deal with the world in other ways. As you become aware of your inner self, guitar playing and daily life are experienced on a higher level. This more elevated state of life is called higher consciousness.

Higher Consciousness

A Definition　Higher consciousness means being acutely aware of what is happening in your existence. It means that your perceptions of reality are heightened and intensified. The level of one's consciousness is often compared to the amount of illumination put out by lights of varying size and intensity. When there is only a small light in a dark room, not much is seen. There may be many objects in the room that can only be seen dimly and the observer may mistake what he sees. He may see a snake when there is only a piece of rope. However, if the intensity of the light is increased, the objects are illuminated more fully and the observer can see more clearly. Thus it is with your consciousness. If you refine and clarify your mind and body, the light of consciousness will begin to grow and illuminate the hidden corners of your existence. At a higher level of consciousness, you can appreciate life more fully, especially in its more subtle aspects. At a higher level, you are also able to deal with life more successfully. What happens is that the previously hidden big Self starts to come out into daily activity. The best thing about becoming more conscious is that it is very fulfilling. It simply makes life more enjoyable.

Experiences of Higher Consciousness　Higher consciousness is very real and has been experienced not only by guitarists and other musicians but by people in every walk of life. Those who have had such experiences at one time or another do not necessarily identify them as experiences of "higher consciousness." However, they do tend to remember them vividly because they seem so much out of the ordinary. What is this "higher consciousness" like? We have already alluded to higher consciousness in Chapter 4 when we discussed dynamic relaxation, "flow," and "peak experiences." These experiences are associated with higher consciousness. Guitarists and other musicians describe such experiences as a unique state of mind and body at certain times when they are performing. They describe the state in glowing terms. They say they feel completely in tune with themselves, the music, and the environment. This feeling of being in tune with everything seems to be strongly connected with playing in perfect rhythm. The phenomenon of *entrainment* happens (see Chapters 5 and 10) and the performer's every thought, emotion, and action become at one with the pulse of the music. As we discussed in Chapter 10, when this happens to the performer, the audience often becomes entrained with the music also and an incredible amount of harmonious feeling and energy is generated. Everyone in the situation seems to be feeling and thinking as one coherent unit.

Players in such a heightened state of consciousness say they lose all fear and nervousness and feel perfectly relaxed even in the midst of a complex piece. This is true dynamic relaxation. Playing is on a much higher level than normal. The entire act of playing is accomplished with just the right amount of energy and it becomes "work without effort." The full, natural expression of the music flows out spontaneously. The player's hands tend to feel very light and ethereal and do not become fatigued. Another feature of the heightened state is that the player feels he can do no wrong. In fact, concentration is so good that he makes few or no mistakes. The player is perfectly focused on what is happening *now* in the music and is not distracted by thoughts of past or future. He is *unattached* to his playing.

Perhaps the most unique characteristic of a state of heightened consciousness is that the player feels he is not actually playing the music but rather that he is just a *vehicle* through which the music passes. Nature seems to be playing the music, not the player. Many guitarists and other musicians have said that they feel so uninvolved in the playing that they are just watching themselves play from outside their bodies. The player's consciousness seems, at least temporarily, to have outgrown the confines of his physical form. Such experiences of expanded consciousness are just tastes of what it is like when the small self or ego has really let go of its limitations and the big Self manifests itself in daily activity. Many people have had such mind-expanding experiences while involved in various activities. A story about the Russian dancer Nijinsky suggests that he must have had this experience frequently. Someone said to him, "It's a pity you can't see yourself dance." "Oh, but I do," he replied, "I'm outside myself watching and directing."[8] The feel-

---

[8]Sheila Ostrander and Lynn Schroeder, *Superlearning* (New York: Delacorte Press, 1979), p. 172.

ings accompanying this experience of "witnessing" one's actions are usually quiet joy and ecstasy.

The pianist André-Michel Schub, winner of the 1981 Van Cliburn competition, relates a "witnessing" experience he had during the competition. The experience came while he was playing the Tchaikovsky Concerto:

> There were times when I became curiously detached from my playing and I was able to observe and listen as though someone else were playing. And near the end of the last movement, that final big octave was almost like someone else's power and . . . strength. I must say that was enjoyable![9]

A professional guitarist described his experience of heightened consciousness as follows:

> (The two concerts) were superb, seemingly without technical inhibition and as if I were an open channel of expression for the emotional (and perhaps transcendental) energy. The audiences responded very enthusiastically and warmly.[10]

Another guitarist said that in one of his concerts he played the first half reasonably well, but it was nothing special. In the second half, something clicked with one set of pieces and he could do nothing wrong. He felt clearly that he himself was not playing, that something else was playing through him. He had the ecstatic experience of watching himself play from a slight distance and felt a delightful floating sensation. The remainder of the concert was a great success and the audience received it very well. Other guitarists have reported similar experiences of higher consciousness in their playing. It is a striking characteristic of these accounts that there is almost always a strongly positive audience response. Thus, higher states of consciousness are not merely subjective fantasies of some performers. They are noticed by both performers and audiences alike. Further, there are numerous accounts of other musicians who have had such experiences. The details of the accounts vary but the general experiences of effortless flow, joy, and "witnessing" one's playing always seem to be present.

The "Artless Art"

The experiences of witnessing and flow in guitar playing are similar to what the Zen archery master describes in the book *Zen in the Art of Archery*. The master says that when you know the art well, "It" (nature, the big Self, or

---

[9]Martin Bookspan, "André-Michel Schub: Thoughts on His Van Cliburn Victory," *Ovation* (October, 1981), 21.

[10]Personal account of a professional player as related to the author.

whatever you want to call it) shoots the arrow rather than the individual.[11] When "It" shoots the arrow, it never misses the bullseye, just as when "It" plays the guitar, it never misses a note. Both the archer and the guitarist must learn to "do just what needs to be done," then let go and let nature do the rest. This is what the Zen archery masters call the "artless art." It requires a considerable amount of discipline and study—that is the "art"—but the archer must learn the discipline so well that at a certain point he can forget it and let the art become "artless." The archer, like the guitarist, ultimately must let go of conscious control and let it happen. He must focus on what he is doing *now* and not worry about results. With that "artful" spontaneity and abandon in either archery or guitar playing, one will be most successful. One will also find that, when he has truly mastered the "artless art" in one of these disciplines, he also has one of the main skills needed to master his own self-development.

Self-Realization

Many experiences of higher consciousness are fleeting or temporary, although the impression they leave is so striking and enjoyable that they drive people on to try to recapture them. For the guitarist, such experiences, even if they happen only rarely, are often the impetus to keep on practicing for years in order to have them once again. How these experiences are generated is usually regarded as a mystery. However, if the natural approach is applied in a systematic way and the player achieves a balance of opposite tendencies, such experiences eventually become commonplace. Ultimately, when one acts totally in accordance with nature, when one is perfectly balanced, then the previously rare occurrences of higher states of consciousness become a permanent feature of daily life. This means that instead of experiencing only the small, limited part of ourselves, we always experience the big, unlimited part along with it no matter what the activities of the small self. When integration of the two selves is achieved, we can say that a distinctly higher level or state of consciousness has been reached. Such a state is called self-realization because the full extent of one's inner reality has been brought out into daily life. In such a state, every experience is joyful and fulfilling. The struggling aspect of life that one has in "normal" states of consciousness disappears. This state is also a state of real freedom in which the inner individual is no longer caught in the limitations and boundaries of his small external self. The individual is free in the present moment and is not attached to past or future. This self-realized state is the normal state. Everyone has the right to that state and the inherent ability to achieve it.

It must not be thought that a higher state of consciousness is far from everyday experience. It is nothing mystical or peculiar. In fact, you do not

[11]Eugen Herrigel, *Zen in the Art of Archery* (New York: Pantheon Books, 1953), pp. 85–88.

even need to believe in higher consciousness to experience its benefits. The benefits come in a gradual, evolutionary way as you pursue the natural, nonstressful approach to the guitar that we have described. Higher consciousness in connection with artistry on the guitar means such simple things as becoming aware of and fully appreciating the beauty of a single musical phrase. Higher consciousness can also be developed naturally in daily life. The refinement of the guitarist's self—or, we might say, the heightening of his consciousness—should be an everyday process and is a vital part of the development of musical artistry. The violinist Suzuki has put it well:

> The real essence of art turned out to be not something high up and far off. It was right inside my ordinary daily self. The very way one greets people and expresses oneself is art. If a musician wants to become a fine artist, he must first become a finer person . . . A work of art is the expression of a man's whole personality, sensibility and ability.[12]

Thus, if we want to become true musicians, we must make every aspect of our lives musical. We must develop a balance between the opposites of sound and silence, activity and rest, freedom and discipline. The quality of our daily lives can be as beautiful as a piece of music played well on the guitar. When our lives begin to have the effortless flow and natural rhythm of a fine musical performance, then it seems that, at least in a small way, we are making a contribution to the peace and harmony of the world. Thus, whether we are carrying out our normal everyday tasks or playing a concert of beautiful music on the guitar, we are, in effect, playing our part in the universal symphony. But it is not as if we are generating the harmony by our own efforts. Actually all we are doing is allowing the hidden music of life, which has always been there, to come through. As the poet said:

> *There's music in all things if men had ears,*
> *Their earth is but an echo of the spheres.*

---

[12]Suzuki, *Nurtured By Love*, p. 94. © Shinichi Suzuki. Reprinted by permission of Exposition Press, Inc., Smithtown, New York.

Bibliography

GUITAR BOOKS AND PERIODICALS

Guitar Player. GPI Publications, Box 28836, San Diego, CA 92128.

> A monthly magazine devoted to various guitar styles. There are usually some good articles on classical guitar each month. For several years (ca. 1976–1982) concert artist Michael Lorimer wrote excellent monthly columns on many different topics of interest to the classical guitarist.

Guitar and Lute. Galliard Press, 1229 Waimanu St., Honolulu, Hawaii 96814.

> An informative quarterly put out by the people who do the *Guitar Music Index*.

Guitar Review. The Society of the Classic Guitar, 409 E. 50th St., New York, NY 10022.

> A quarterly magazine with good articles, interviews, reviews, and illustrations.

The Soundboard. Guitar Foundation of America, Box 5311, Garden Grove, CA 92645.

> A quarterly magazine for classical guitarists.

ARAI, SHIRO, "The 'Pepe' Guitar Education System," *The Soundboard*, IX, no. 2 (Summer 1982).

Describes an approach to teaching the guitar to children that is similar to Shinichi Suzuki's famous violin teaching method.

CIMINO, BASIL and ROBERT LILIENFELD, *The Guitarist's Harmony*. New York: Franco Colombo Publications, 1965.

A beginning harmony textbook for guitarists who can read notes throughout the fingerboard. This book covers about two years of music theory and is best for players with some theory background.

CLINTON, GEORGE, *Andrés Segovia*. London: Musical New Services, 1978.

An enjoyable collection of photographs of Segovia with comments about him by famous guitarists and others who know him.

DUNCAN, CHARLES, *The Art of Classical Guitar Playing*. Princeton: Summy-Birchard Music, 1980.

This is an excellent book on both fundamental and fine points of classical guitar playing. It is based on careful observation of some of the best concert players and includes useful principles and examples taken from the guitar literature.

GRUNFELD, FREDERIC, *The Art and Times of the Guitar*. New York: Macmillan & Co., 1969.

An entertaining and informative history of the guitar. Replete with numerous photographs and lively anecdotes.

HECK, THOMAS, "The Birth of the Classic Guitar and Its Cultivation in Vienna, Reflected in the Career and Compositions of Mauro Giuliani (d. 1829)," Ph.D. Dissertation, Yale University, 1970. Ann Arbor, Michigan: University Microfilms, 1970.

A thorough discussion of Mauro Giuliani, his works, and the classical guitar in Vienna. Includes a catalog of Giuliani's works.

JEFFERY, BRIAN, *Fernando Sor: Composer and Guitarist*. London: Tecla Editions, 1977.

A well-researched and detailed biography of Sor. Contains a catalog of the complete works of Sor.

KOPLEWITZ, LAURA, "Sharon Isbin: Artist of the Classical Guitar," *Accent on Music*, 7, no. 5 (April 1982), 13ff.

In this interview Sharon Isbin describes her attitude and approach to the guitar. She tells about her technique of mentally practicing her pieces before playing them in a concert. She also tells how she uses meditation to calm her mind.

KOZINN, ALAN, "Classical Careers," *Guitar Player* 15, no. 9 (September 1981), 68.

A behind-the-scenes view about how careers are made in the world of concert classical guitar. The article is essential reading for anyone who wants to make his living playing concerts.

NOAD, FREDERICK, ed., *The Renaissance Guitar*. New York: Ariel Music Publications, 1974.

——, *The Baroque Guitar*. New York: Ariel Music Publications, 1974.

——, *The Classical Guitar*. New York: Ariel Music Publications, 1976.

Three anthologies of tastefully selected pieces.

——, *Solo Guitar Playing*, vols. I and II. New York: Schirmer Books, 1976, 1977.

An excellent, enjoyable classical guitar method. The first book has a nice set of duets and pieces for the beginner. The second book deals with different historical styles as well as advanced techniques.

PARKENING, CHRISTOPHER, *The Christopher Parkening Guitar Method*, vol. I. Chicago: Antigua Casa Sherry-Brener, 1972.

A good beginner's method with numerous photographs, drawings, and simple arrangements of well-known pieces.

PINNELL, RICHARD, "The Role of Francesco Corbetta (1615–1681) in the History of Music for Baroque Guitar, Including a Transcription of His Complete Works," Ph.D. Dissertation, U.C.L.A., 1976. U. Microfilms, 1976.

A discussion of an illustrious baroque guitarist and a transcription of his complete works into modern notation.

PUJOL, EMILIO, *Guitar School*, vols. I and II., ed. Brian Jeffery. Boston: Editions Orphée, 1982.

A comprehensive guitar method in Spanish and French with many useful exercises and pieces by a noted guitarist and musicologist. Volumes III and IV of this method are available in a Spanish-French edition from Ricordi Americana.

RICH, ALAN, *Segovia On Stage*. Album notes from Decca Record DL 710140, Decca Records, A Division of MCA Inc., New York, N.Y.

These notes contain some thought-provoking comments by Segovia about where musical inspiration comes from.

SCHNEIDER, JOHN, *The Contemporary Guitar*. Berkeley: University of California Press, 1981.

A guide for the guitarist who wants to play and understand the new music.

SEGOVIA, ANDRÉS, *Diatonic Major and Minor Scales*. Washington, D.C.: Columbia Music, 1953.

Standard scales for the classical guitarist. Knowing these scale fingerings (along with alternate ones) is fundamental to playing well. These scales can be used in many imaginative ways to improve technique and musicianship.

SEGOVIA, ANDRÉS, *Segovia: An Autobiography of the Years 1893–1920*, trans. W. F. O'Brien. New York: Macmillan Publishing Co., 1976.

Segovia's account of his early years and the development of his love affair with the guitar. His book is filled with poetic language and colorful anecdotes about the progress of his concert career.

SHEARER, AARON, *Classic Guitar Technique*, vols. I and II. New York: Franco Colombo, Inc., 1963.

A progressive classical guitar method with many useful exercises and ideas.

SHERROD, RONALD J., *Discovering the Art of Guitar Fingering*. Sherman Oaks, CA.: Alfred Publishing Co., 1980.

A thoughtful study guide with numerous examples and photographs to help the guitarist through the thicket of guitar fingering.

———, *Guitar Master Class*. Melville, N.Y.: Belwin-Mills Publishing Corp., 1980.

An interesting collection of favorite studies and exercises from well-known guitarists. The student can find an exercise for just about any problem here.

SOR, FERNANDO, *Complete Works for Guitar*, ed. Brian Jeffery. New York: Shattinger International Music Corp., 1977.

An excellent edition of the earliest known versions of Sor's works. This edition is a valuable one for the guitarist's library.

———, *Method for the Spanish Guitar*, trans. A. Merrick, Da Capo Press Music Reprint Series. New York: Da Capo Press, 1971.

A fine treatise on guitar playing by one of the leading guitar performers and composers of the nineteenth century. Although some of Sor's technical ideas are no longer used, much of his advice still holds good. His maxims (p. 48) are superb and to the point.

STRIZICH, ROBERT, "A Spanish Guitar Tutor: Ruiz de Ribayaz's Luz Y Norte Musical (1677)," *Journal of the Lute Society of America*, VII (1974), 68ff.

This article, although it focuses on Ribayaz, gives an idea of the performance practice of the Spanish baroque guitarists. The information about ornamentation and special baroque guitar effects is particularly interesting.

SUMMERFIELD, MAURICE J., *The Classical Guitar: Its Evolution and Its Players Since 1800.* Gateshead, England: Ashley Mark Publishing Co., 1982.

Includes guitar history, biographies of players, photographs, information on books and records.

TURNBULL, HARVEY, *The Guitar from the Renaissance to the Present Day.* New York: Charles Scribner's Sons, 1974.

A concise history of classical guitar. A bit brief, but a good overview.

TYLER, JAMES, *The Early Guitar: A History and a Handbook.* London: Oxford University Press, 1980.

Covers the history of the four- and five-course guitar and gives information on tuning, tablature, and technique on these instruments.

DE VISÉE, ROBERT, *Oeuvres Complètes Pour Guitare*, ed. Robert Strizich. Paris: Heugel, 1969.

The complete unarranged works of Visée put into modern guitar notation with all original ornaments. The modern guitarist can now see more closely what Visée actually wrote instead of looking at the music through an arranger's colored glasses.

OTHER MUSIC BOOKS AND PERIODICALS

Journal of the Lute Society of America. The Lute Society of America, 6 Lewis St., Lexington, VA 24450.

An annual publication with scholarly, informative articles about early instruments, composers, and performance practice. Often has articles on early guitar music.

BADURA-SKODA, PAUL and EVA BADURA-SKODA, *Interpreting Mozart on the Keyboard*, trans. Leo Black. New York: St. Martin's Press, 1962.

The main focus of this book is on Mozart interpretation, but the Badura-Skodas also present insights about the nature of successful performance that are useful for any thoughtful performer.

BOOKSPAN, MARTIN, "André-Michel Schub: Thoughts on his Van Cliburn Victory," *Ovation*, October, 1981, p. 21.

Some insights into the inner experience of a pianist deeply immersed in competitive performing.

BUSONI, FERRUCCIO, *The New Busoni: Exercises and Studies for the Piano*, ed. Franzpeter Goebels. Wiesbaden: Breitbach and Haertel, 1968.

Contains some of Busoni's penetrating observations on the art of performing. He was an advocate of mental practice, who felt that one should plan his approach to a piece in his mind. Some of the practice methods here are useful for guitarists.

CASALS, PABLO, *Joys and Sorrows*, as told to Albert E. Kahn. New York: Simon & Schuster, 1970.

The famous cellist offers insights on how to study music. He always sought out the most natural and most effortless ways of playing. His philosophy of music was and still is inspiring. For him music had a high moral and spiritual purpose: to help bring peace and harmony to the world.

COOPER, GROSVENOR, and LEONARD B. MEYER, *The Rhythmic Structure of Music*. Chicago: University of Chicago Press, 1963.

A study of rhythm based on a Gestalt approach that looks at rhythm in terms of groupings or patterns.

DEUTSCH, LEONHARD, *Piano: Guided Sight-Reading*. Chicago: Nelson-Hall, 1959.

An interesting approach to music learning through sight-reading. Deutsch emphasizes that beginners keep up their interest much more if they read quite a bit and do not concern themselves excessively with technique.

GREEN, DOUGLASS, *Form in Tonal Music: An Introduction to Analysis*. New York: Holt, Rinehart and Winston, Inc., 1965.

A good introduction to musical analysis with many examples from the traditional literature.

JAQUES-DALCROZE, EMILE, *Eurhythmics, Art and Education*, trans. Frederick Rothwell, ed. Cynthia Cox. New York: Benjamin Blom, Inc., 1972.

Essays on a method of musical training based on the coordination of music and physical movement.

MENUHIN, YEHUDI, and WILLIAM PRIMROSE, *Violin and Viola*. New York: Schirmer Books, 1976.

An uplifting, poetic approach to violin study. It includes yoga-like relaxation exercises, natural practice methods, ideas for concert preparation, and suggestions on interpretation. Menuhin emphasizes balance in all things musical and personal.

NEWMAN, WILLIAM, *The Pianist's Problems*. New York: Harper & Row, 1974.

A fine handbook, ostensibly for pianists, but chock-full of useful suggestions for any musician. He has ideas about interpretation, stage fright, use of the metronome, repertoire, and many other areas. Highly recommended.

PIERCE, ALEXANDRA, "Characterizing Movement," *Institute for Holistic Education*, Newsletter No. 6, Spring 1980.

Describes a practical approach to help people find appropriate musical expression for the pieces they play by use of imaginative body movements.

———, "Ideation," *Piano Quarterly*, no. 90 (Summer 1975), 34.

This is an explication of the ideas of the pianist Luigi Bonpensiere. The thesis is that piano playing—or guitar playing—is least taxing and most artistic if the player can clearly picture the music in his mind before playing.

———, "Juncture," *In Theory Only*, Journal of the Michigan Music Theory Society, 3, no. 6 (September 1977), 28ff.

In this imaginary exchange of letters between two German music students, Alexandra Pierce explores the neglected world of silence between the notes, phrases, and larger units of music.

SCOTT, CYRIL, *Music: Its Secret Influence Throughout the Ages*. New York: Samuel Weiser, 1958.

A discussion of the hidden influence of music from the point of view of a theosophist-composer.

SHANKAR, RAVI, *My Music, My Life*. New York: Simon and Schuster, 1968.

An inside view of how music is made and taught in India. Shankar gives a beautiful picture of the intimate relationship between teacher and student. He also describes the spiritual approach that is fundamental to Indian music.

SUZUKI, SHINICHI, *Nurtured by Love*. Jericho, N.Y.: Exposition Press, 1969.

An inspirational book by the founder of the Suzuki method of violin teaching. Suzuki's idea is that every child has talent that can be brought out by his natural "mother tongue" approach. He also feels that music, studied properly, is an important character builder for both young and old alike.

SZENDE, OTTO, and MIHALY NEMESSURI, *The Physiology of Violin Playing*. London: Collet's Publishers, 1971.

A scientific study that details body, hand, and finger movements in violin playing. There are interesting parallels that can be drawn between the physiology of violin playing and that of guitar playing.

WARFIELD, GERALD, *Layer Analysis: A Primer of Elementary Tonal Structures.* New York: David McKay, 1976.

A beginning text on a modified form of Schenker analysis. The idea is that music is made up of layers that can be analyzed. The analysis proceeds from the complex musical end product on the top layer down to the simple structures of single tones or interval movements on the bottom layer.

PHILOSOPHICAL BOOKS

BROWER, DAVID R., ed., *Of All Things Most Yielding.* New York: Friends of the Earth/Ballantine Books, no publication or copyright date.

A beautiful presentation of Chinese poetry and color photographs that illustrate the value of living life in accord with nature. The perceptive guitarist will find many hints here about effortless playing.

CAPRA, FRITJOF, *The Tao of Physics.* New York: Bantam Books, 1977.

A fascinating discussion of modern physics and its parallels in Eastern spiritual teachings. For guitarists an important idea in the book is that nature is dynamic externally and yet quiet internally. This is the ideal for musical performance.

EMERSON, RALPH WALDO, *Works*, the Centenary Edition, annotated by E. Emerson. Boston: Houghton-Mifflin, 1904.

Emerson's essays are highly inspirational. After reading an essay such as "Self-Reliance," you feel very fortunate to be alive and human. You feel like doing something useful—like writing a book or learning how to play the guitar.

HALL, MANLY P., *The Secret Teachings of All Ages.* The Philosophical Research Society, 1972.

A large compendium of esoteric information. Includes some fascinating theories about music from Pythagoras and other philosophers.

LAO TZU, *Tao Te Ching*, trans. Gia-Fu Feng and Jane English. New York: Vintage Books, 1972.

This famous work of Chinese philosophy emphasizes living in harmony with nature rather than fighting against it. The implicit message for guitarists is that one should play as naturally as possible in order to be most successful.

MAHARISHI MAHESH YOGI, trans., *Bhagavad Gita.* Baltimore: Penguin Books, Inc., 1969.

This profound work, although it is directed at spiritual development of the individual, has hidden within it many practical principles for the guitarist. The commentary helps put the philosophy in practical terms.

PLATO, *Timaeus*, trans. R.G. Bury. Loeb Classical Library, vol. VII. Cambridge: Harvard University Press, 1961.

This dialogue contains some very intriguing ideas about the nature of music and how it influences our inner selves.

BOOKS ON SELF-DEVELOPMENT

ANDERSON, BOB, *Stretching*. Bolinas, Ca.: Shelter Publications, 1980.

Describes many exercises to keep the whole body flexible. Helpful for performing guitarists.

BLOOMFIELD, HAROLD H., MICHAEL CAIN, and DENNIS JAFFE with ROBERT KORY. *TM: Discovering Inner Energy and Overcoming Stress*. New York: Delacorte Press, 1975.

A discussion of the theory and practice of Transcendental Meditation (TM) as taught by Maharishi Mahesh Yogi. Includes information on how to learn the TM technique. TM can offer the guitarist better memory and concentration. It also helps to calm one's mind and nerves before a performance.

BRY, ADELAIDE, *Visualization: Directing the Movies of Your Mind*. New York: Barnes & Noble, 1978.

A good, practical introduction to the conscious use of the power of the mind. Adelaide Bry describes the technique of visualization and what it can do to help anyone achieve their goals more quickly.

GALLWEY, TIMOTHY, *The Inner Game of Tennis*. New York: Random House, 1974.

This is a practical book, a kind of "Zen and the Art of Tennis" for tennis players who want to master the mental and spiritual side of the game. By substituting "guitar playing" for "tennis," the guitarist will find many good ideas here.

HAMEL, PETER, *Through Music to the Self*. Boulder, Colo.: Shambhala Publications, 1978.

This is a penetrating book that describes the spiritual side of both Western and non-Western music. The author, who is a composer, gives practical musical exercises to help the interested person along the way to self-healing and self-discovery.

HERRIGEL, EUGEN, *Zen in the Art of Archery*. New York: Pantheon Books, 1953.

A concise description of the experience of a German philosopher who learned the art of Zen archery. Shows a high approach to any art: learn the technique thoroughly, but then transcend the technique and let the art flow from you naturally.

HITTLEMAN, RICHARD, *Be Young With Yoga*. New York: Warner Books, 1962.

This is a good introduction to Hatha Yoga, the physical side of yoga. A number of the beginning body postures are included. There are numerous photographs and explanations.

HUXLEY, ALDOUS, *The Art of Seeing*. New York: Harper and Brothers, 1942.

Huxley wrote this book to describe how he was able to overcome his vision problems. One of the principles he used to help himself is what he called "dynamic relaxation." This idea of "activity without strain" is also the basis of good guitar playing and all other psychophysical skills.

JACOBSON, EDMUND, *Progressive Relaxation*. Chicago: University of Chicago Press, 1942.

This is the standard modern work on the progressive relaxation method. It can be very helpful for those who need to "let go" before performing.

LEONARD, GEORGE, *The Silent Pulse*. New York: Bantam Books, 1981.

A fascinating discussion of the idea that each of us has in his innermost being a unique pulse. The thesis is that if you can get in tune with that inner pulse, you will experience great joy and fulfillment. Laced with analogies from modern science.

PATANJALI, *How to Know God: the Yoga Sutras of Patanjali,* trans. Swami Prabhavananda and Christopher Isherwood. New York: New American Library, 1969.

A translation of and commentary on the famous aphorisms of Yoga philosophy. These aphorisms are not just philosophy. They are considered to be practical directives for those who are interested in the ultimate in self-development.

SAMUELS, MIKE, and NANCY SAMUELS, *Seeing with the Mind's Eye*. New York/ Berkeley: Random House/Bookworks, 1975.

A comprehensive treatment of the subject of visualization, including many practical exercises. Guitarists can use visualization to relax before a concert, to generate ideas for compositions, to mentally practice pieces, and so on.

STOCKHAUSEN, KARL-HEINZ, "Spiritual Dimensions," interview by Peter Heyworth, *Music and Musicians*, May 1971, p. 34.

This far-ranging interview gives Stockhausen's unorthodox but profound ideas about music. He feels that its central purpose is a spiritual one: to reveal man's inner nature to himself.

VISHNUDEVANANDA, SWAMI, *The Complete Illustrated Book of Yoga.* New York: Pocket Books, 1972.

A modern presentation of the Yoga approach to self-development with yoga postures (shown in photographs), breathing exercises to calm the mind, suggestions about diet, and a discussion of Yoga philosophy. Some of the ideas here may be interesting to the performing guitarist.

REFERENCE BOOKS

APEL, WILLI, *Harvard Dictionary of Music* (2nd ed.). Cambridge, Mass.: Harvard University Press, 1969.

An excellent one-volume handbook of musical information.

BONE, PHILIP J., *The Guitar and Mandolin.* London: Schott & Co. Ltd., 1972.

A biographical dictionary of famous guitarists and mandolin players. The work is dated and the facts are sometimes scrambled but it is nonetheless a useful reference. It contains many colorful stories and information not easily found elsewhere.

DONINGTON, ROBERT, *The Performer's Guide to Baroque Music.* London: Faber and Faber, 1973.

An excellent short guide to baroque performance practice. An abbreviated version of the following work.

———, *The Interpretation of Early Music,* New Version. London: Faber and Faber, 1974.

An exhaustive study of Renaissance, Baroque, and early Classical performance practice. A must for anyone who wants to capture the styles of earlier music.

GILMORE, GEORGE, and MARK PEREIRA, *Guitar Music Index.* Honolulu: Galliard Press, Ltd., 1976.

A listing of published solo and chamber music for the guitar arranged by composer, title, and chamber music groupings. The listing for each piece includes the name of the publisher and the grade of difficulty.

KARKOSCHKA, ERHARD, *Notation in New Music,* trans. Ruth Koenig. New York: Praeger Publishers, 1972.

This is a good reference for those guitarists who would like to play contemporary music but are puzzled by the notation.

SADIE, STANLEY, ed., *The New Grove Dictionary of Music and Musicians.* London: Macmillan Pub., Ltd., 1980.

A new edition of the venerable Grove's. Contains a number of excellent updated articles on the guitar by Robert Strizich and other scholars.

SCHOLES, PERCY, *The Oxford Companion to Music.* London: Oxford University Press, 1963.

A concise, delightful reference for the musician and music lover. It contains: definitions of musical terms; articles on music theory, history, and performance practice; numerous musical examples; many illustrations; and amusing anecdotes.

MISCELLANEOUS BOOKS

ACKERMAN, EUGENE, *Biophysical Science.* Englewood Cliffs, N.J.: Prentice-Hall, Inc., 1962.

Describes the on-off firing of the neurons in the human nervous system. This on-off action is important for the technique of guitar playing. The implications of this mechanism are covered in *The Natural Classical Guitar* in Chapters 4 and 5 on Dynamic Relaxation and the Play–Relax Technique.

MASLOW, ABRAHAM, *Toward a Psychology of Being.* New York: Van Nostrand Co., 1968.

One of the classic works of humanistic psychology. Maslow was a pioneer in the study of "self-actualized" individuals, that is, those people who are making great use of their potential. Maslow was one of the first modern psychologists to study healthy people instead of sick ones.

Index

Accents, 203
Appoggiatura chords, 207–09, 212–13, 220, 222
Arpeggiation, 222
Arpeggios, 86–87, 95–96, 95 *fig.*, 97, 111
Articulation, 203, 221

Bach, Johann Sebastian, 11, 44, 111, 137, 150, 166, 202, 268
Background material, 198–99
Bar chord position, 73, 74 *fig.*, 75
Baroque guitar, 150
Barrios, Agustin, 163, 166–67
Body relaxation, 25–31, 241–42
Bonpensiere, Luigi, 183–84
Breathing exercises, 48–49, 245, 246
Brouwer, Leo, 8, 81, 176, 241, 246

Cadence, 200
Carcassi, Matteo, 41, 111, 260
Casals, Pablo, 45, 79, 115–16, 193*n*
Children, how they learn, 155–56
Chord fingering, 150
Chords, 94–95, 94 *fig.*
Concentration, natural, 6, 36, 50–51
  physiological approach, 45–49
  psychological approach, 38–45
  stages of, 37–38
Concerts, learning from, 158–59
Counting problems, 187–88, 187–88 *fig.*
Crescendo, 206–07

Damping, 132–34, 133–34 *fig.*, 215
Decrescendo, 206–07
Detaché articulation, 221
Dynamics, 203

Eating habits, 46–47, 242–43
Emerson, Ralph Waldo, 1, 3, 53
Ensemble playing, 256–57
Entrainment, 82–84, 230, 273
Estudio Brillante (Tárrega), 111, 163

Fandanguillo (Turina), 127–28, 127–28 *fig.*, 160
Fast scales, 104–05
Feedback, 218, 251–52
Finger movements, 40–42, 41 *fig.*
Finger tension, 84–85, 85 *fig.*
Fingerboard contact, 141–42
Fingerings, choosing, 210–13, 210–11 *fig.*
Free strokes, 92–97, 92 *fig.*, 94 *fig.*

Giuliani, Mauro, 32, 111, 131–32, 139, 260
Gravity technique, 71–72
Guide fingers, 137, 137 *fig.*
Guitar Music Index, 257, 260

Half-bar, 75
Hand warming techniques, 244–45
Harmony, 44, 200, 204, 205 *fig.*
Hierarchical structure, 200, 200 *fig.*, 204, 204 *fig.*, 224–25
Hinge bars, 138–41, 138–42 *fig.*
Holding the guitar, 60–62, 60 *fig.*
Home base position, 69–70, 70 *fig.*
Huxley, Aldous, 7*n*, 53, 55, 56, 178*n*, 183

Indian master musicians, 156–57
Inner meaning, 44, 181–82, 247–48, 251

Kinesthetic sense, 18–20

La Catedral (Barrios), 163, 166–67, 167 *fig.*
Landowska, Wanda, 15, 35, 115, 136, 233
Lao Tzu, 13*n*, 53, 79
Left hand:
  natural fingering, 148–50, 150 *fig.*
  play-relax technique for, 100–04, 101–04 *fig.*
  positioning of, 67–72, 68–71 *fig.*
  problems with, 72–73
  refining, 136–48, 137–42 *fig.*, 144 *fig.*, 146 *fig.*, 148 *fig.*
  visualization for, 179–81, 180 *fig.*
Legato, 86–87, 112, 128–32, 131–32 *fig.*, 221
Legato chord sequences, 100–03, 101–02 *fig.*

Melody, 42–43
Memorization, 216–17
Menuhin, Yehudi, 47, 81, 100, 145, 172, 267
Method for the Spanish Guitar, 149, 198–99
Metronome, 83–84, 213, 215, 258
Milán, Luis, 42–43, 101, 132–33, 138
Mind-settling techniques, 22–25, 241
Minuet, Op. 2, No. 4 (Sor), using 12-step study method, 195–226, 195–96 *fig.*, 200 *fig.*, 202 *fig.*, 204–05 *fig.*, 201–11 *fig.*, 214 *fig.*
Mistakes, 249–50
Motive, 203
Music, function of, 266–68
Music analysis, 199–209, 200 *fig.*, 202 *fig.*, 204–05 *fig.*

Nail care, 86, 116
  shaping, 117–22, 118–22 *fig.*
  special problems, 124–25
  thumbnail, 122–24, 123 *fig.*
Noncritical awareness, 17–18
Nonguitar music, 198

Pavan No. 3 (Milán), 42–43, 43 *fig.*, 138, 138
  fig.
Pavan No. 6 (Milán), 101, 101 *fig.*, 132–33,
  133 *fig.*
Personal development, 269–76
Phrasing, 203–09, 205 *fig.*, 219–20
Pierce, Alexandra, 182*n*–83*n*, 224*n*–26*n*
Pivot fingers, 138, 138 *fig.*
Planting, 85–87, 87 *fig.*
Practice strategies, 162–73, 165–67 *fig.*
Practicing mentally, 217–18

Recitals, 231
  enjoyment of, 243–51
  learning from, 251–52
  preparation for, 232–37
  relaxation techniques, 241–43
  visualization and dry runs, 237–41
Recordings, learning from, 159
Relaxation, in music, 200–09
Repertoire, 259–62
Rest strokes, 87–90, 88–89 *fig.*, 91 *fig.*, 92,
  96–97
Rhythm, 44, 82–84, 186–88, 203
Right hand:
  natural fingering, 135–36, 135–36 *fig.*
  positioning of, 63–66, 63–66 *fig.*
  problems with, 67
  refining, 116–36, 118–23 *fig.*, 127–28 *fig.*,
    131–36 *fig.*
  speed bursts, 106, 106 *fig.*
  stabilization of, 105–06
Role-playing, 20–22
Rolling chords, 222
Rough spots, polishing, 214–15

Scale fingering, 150
Score, reading mentally, 196–97
Segovia, Andrés, 10, 40, 47, 58, 116, 170,
  191, 219*n*, 243
  concert program sample, 235–36
  as master teacher, 159–62
  tone colors, use of, 126–27

Side stroke, 97–98, 98 *fig.*
Sight reading, 197, 257–59
Silence, meaning of, 224–27, 246–47
Sitting position, 57–60, 59 *fig.*, 62
Slurs, 103, 103 *fig.*, 144–45, 144 *fig.*
Snap stroke, 87–90, 88–89 *fig.*, 97, 105
Sor, Fernando, 1, 10, 32, 68, 73, 75, 97, 111,
  131, 133–34, 137, 140, 148–49, 157,
  164*n*–65, 187, 195
  analysis of *Minuet*, Op. 2, No. 4, 195–226
  complete works, 260–61
Sound purification, 215
Speed bursts, 106–10, 106 *fig.*, 108–10 *fig.*
Staccato, 110–12, 128–32, 131–32 *fig.*, 221
Stacking, 65
Stop and Let Go technique, 26–27
Stretching exercises, 28, 28 *fig.*, 103–04, 104
  fig.
String squeaks, 142–43
Structure, 44, 199–201, 200 *fig.*, 204, 204 *fig.*,
  224–25
Style brisé, 150
Supported stroke, 87, 97, 105, 105 *fig.*
Suzuki, Shinichi, 17*n*, 155*n*, 170, 172*n*, 217,
  268*n*

Taoism, 3, 5*n*–8*n*, 13, 148
Tárrega, Francisco, 38, 98, 102, 111, 147, 157,
  163, 166
Tempo, 203, 215–17
Tempo rubato, 220–21
Tension, in guitarists, 25–26, 241–46, 249
Tension, in music, 200–09
Texture, 201–03
Thumb free stroke, 93–94, 94 *fig.*
Thumb position, 65–66, 66 *fig.*, 70–71, 71 *fig.*
Thumb rest stroke, 90, 91 *fig.*, 92
TM technique, 24–25
Tone color, 125–28, 127–28 *fig.*, 203, 223
Tremolo, 98–100, 98 *fig.*
Turina, Joaquin, 127–28, 160

Velocity, in scales, 186
Vibrato, 145–48, 146 *fig.*, 148 *fig.*, 222
Villa-Lobos, Heitor, 26, 96, 97, 111, 163

Wrist position, 66, 68

Yoga, 3, 5*n*–8*n*, 13, 29*n*–30, 48–49